BASIC
BODYWORK
TIPS & TECHNIQUES

Compiled by R M Clarke from articles published in the
Hot Rod Automotive Performance Series.

ISBN 0 948207 85 X

Published by
Brooklands Books with permission of Petersen Publishing Company
Printed in Hong Kong

ACKNOWLEDGEMENTS

The editors of Hot Rod magazine have for many years produced a number of excellent books in their Hot Rod Automotive Performance Series. Unfortunately these valuable guides are now out of print and as a consequence hard to locate.

It was suggested that if a comprehensive selection of these articles could be combined into a single volume it would be of great value to today's restorers and others that indulge in the hobby.

We are fortunate that the management of the Petersen Publishing Company understand the needs of enthusiasts and have generously consented to us reprinting this informative collection of their copyright stories.

R.M. Clarke

DISTRIBUTED BY

Motorbooks International
Osceola
Wisconsin 24020
USA

Brooklands Books Distribution Ltd
Holmerise, Sevenhills Road
Cobham, Surrey KT11 1ES
England

Brooklands Books Australia
1/81 Darley Street, P.O. Box 199
Mona Vale NSW 2103
Australia

Printed in Hong Kong

CONTENTS

Metalwork Fundamentals

All damaged cars can be repaired; it's just a matter of economics. Because of high labor costs many cars are now considered "totalled" that were previously "repairable." It is amazing to see how mild some body damage is on supposedly totalled cars. Consequently, the current costs of professional body repair can often work to the advantage of the do-it-yourself bodyman. If you have more time than money, you can get some real deals on fixable cars.

A related area that affects the home repairman is the high cost of parts. Since labor is so expensive, many body shops will replace a fender rather than remove the dents. This trend has increased wrecking yard prices for sheetmetal close to factory prices and has created a lucrative market for "stolen to order" body parts. Since body shops often discard repairable fenders, a tour through body shop trash bins could turn up parts you need.

Also, learning to repair panels with the time-honored hammer and dolly methods is a valuable skill.

Even in this era of replacement and filler body shops, there is still a big demand for talented craftsmen who can transform metal with their hands and a few traditional tools. In the growing field of automobile restorations, metalworking craftsmen are highly sought after and handsomely rewarded.

When it comes to making body repairs, there are two methods: the quick way and the thinking man's way. The quick way is to rush into the job just removing the damaged parts without any thought as to how the damage was caused. The thinking man's way starts with a little consideration and inspection of the damage to determine how the dents were caused. When you realize how the damage was caused, it is easier to reverse it.

Know Your Work

It only stands to reason that the more you know about a subject, the better your chances of success in that field. Just as a butcher needs to know about the different cuts of meat before he can start hacking away at a side of beef, so must the body-man know about metal and the design of automobiles before he can start hacking away at the side of a damaged car.

Because of the requirements of forming and use, the sheetmetal used in a car body is of low-carbon steel. If a higher carbon metal were used, the parts might resist certain impacts better, but the panels would be very hard to form at the factory and extremely difficult to repair. Special car bodies have been made from rather exotic steel and other metals through the years, usually as a publicity stunt or part of a research program, but ordinary steel remains the leader in automotive body construction. Strength for mild steel body panels can be achieved with extra reinforcements, strong shape, or a little more thickness in the metal.

Sheetmetal plasticity permits a shape change when enough force is applied. In the beginning, the sheetmetal is a large flat sheet that becomes a fender or a hood or a top panel. When the flat sheet is modified by the press, the change is called plastic deformation. The amount of deformation possible without breaking is relative to the metal's hardness. Plastic deformation is achieved with both tension and compression. Deformation under tension is ductility; deformation under compressive force is malleability. The end result of tension deformation is stretching, and the result of pressure deformation is upsetting. The enthusiast is interested in both aspects of deformation since both stretching and upsetting take place in body panels during modifications and repair work.

When metal is bent, stretched, upset, or changed in shape at a temperature less than red heat, it has been cold worked. That is, plastic deformation has taken place without the use of heat. Of course, how much a piece of metal can be worked cold has a limit, beyond which it will break. As this limit is approached, the metal increases in strength and stiffness. This is called *work hardening*. A good example of work hardening is supplied by bending a flat piece of sheetmetal double without creasing the bend. When the metal is flattened out again, the original bend remains and two new ones are added, one on either side of the first. The metal at the first bend stretched and became work hardened, and so it is stronger than the rest of the metal.

Some work hardness will be found in all body panels, caused by the original press forming. When a panel has been damaged, additional hardness will

Repairing damaged cars can bring a real sense of accomplishment. This Camaro had enough types of sheetmetal damage to serve as a metalworking textbook.

Metalwork Fundamentals

occur and still more hardening will accompany the straightening process.

Elasticity is the ability of the metal to regain its original shape after deflection. Also, when a panel is warped slightly, it may spring back into its original shape when the restraining force is removed. Of course, the harder the steel the greater the elasticity which means elasticity will increase as work hardening increases.

When the metal will not spring back completely to the original shape, it has reached the elastic limit, or the yield point. When a damaged fender is removed from a car, both the fender and the inner splash panel will have a tendency to spring back toward original shape slightly. All sheet steel will retain some spring-back no matter how badly damaged. This is of significance to the body repairman since a badly "waved" panel may return to normal shape when a single, simple buckled spot is removed.

When a body panel is made in a press or die, residual stresses are left in the panel. That is, there will be areas of stress that remain in the panel. Cut through the edge of a hood panel and the two pieces will pull apart slightly; the residual stress

from the original stamping causes this. Such stresses will usually be greater the more complicated the panel shape. Thus, when a panel is repaired it will probably also be restored to a state of minor tension.

Heat is a part of body repair, whether from the torch or from the grinder, and will have three separate effects: scaling, grain structure change, and expansion/contraction. The three effects happen at the same time during a repair operation.

When steel is heated to 430 degrees F., if the steel is clean and bright, the color will be a pale yellow. As the heat is increased, the color will change to straw, brown, purple, light blue, and dark blue, which is reached at around 600 degrees F. The color will then fade to a gray or greenish tone until the first reddish color comes at about 900 degrees F. Various colors of red are then apparent until approximately 1550 degrees F., when the red increases in brightness through orange and yellow to white. Steel melts at around 2600 degrees F.

Scale forms when the heated area is attacked by oxygen; therefore, this scale will form faster on the side away from the torch. When the torch is removed, however, scale will immediately form on the near side. This scale is not a major problem. A definite and progressive change in metal grain structure occurs when steel is heated toward the melting

Here is the same car after the body was massaged back to its original shape. The body was covered with an outstanding custom paint job by Bill Carter of Carter Pro Paint in Chatsworth, California.

point, with a consequent result in hardness and strength. There is not enough carbon in sheetmetal to harden from heating, but it can be annealed. When a piece of metal has been work hardened, it can be returned to the soft stage by rearranging the grain structure. If the metal is heated to the salmon color just above bright red (about 1600 degrees F.) the metal will reach the critical temperature where the grain structure is reformed.

When metal is heated it will expand a given amount; when it cools it will contract. The coefficient of expansion in automotive sheetmetal up to 1500 degrees F. is six-millionths of an inch per degree, which seems infinitesimal. But this is the reason metal will warp when heat is applied. There is a significant difference between heat distortion and stretching. There are four basic classifications to the crown of a particular panel. A "crown" is the curvature of a given panel. There is the low crown (low curvature), high crown (high curvature), combination high and low crown, and reverse crown.

Panels with low crowns have very little curvature, and consequently, very little load-carrying ability. The roof panel is a good example, with slight curves at the edges and a midsection that is nearly flat. At the extreme edges near the drip molding, the top panel will usually curve rapidly with a high crown.

A high crown is often considered a shape that

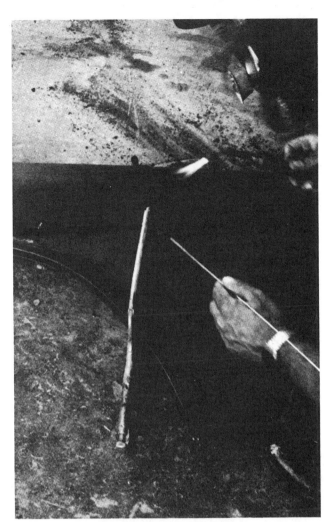

Creative metalmen like customizer Eddie Paul can do much more than repair a fender; they can change the whole look of the car with a torch. This new Mustang quarter panel was sectioned to form a wild fender flare.

curves rapidly in all directions. Such surfaces are quite common on older cars and will usually resist deformation due to damage. Such high crown areas would be the top and front portions of a Model A fender, the body roll at the rear of the top, and so on. The tendency has been away from this type of tight styling during recent times. The modern car is made up of very large low crown panels. Obviously, a high crown area is very strong in itself and will not need reinforcements as will the low crown panel.

The combination of high and low crown panels is very common to the modern car; fenders and door panels, for instance, provide a very strong structure. A door panel is usually much stronger than a roof panel.

The reverse crown shows up in the complicated areas of design, as an inside curve on a hood or fender. A typical example of an inside curve or reverse crown would be the taillight area of cars where the metal is "pooched" out to accept the taillight assembly. These areas have very high-strength concentrations, the reason damage to such an area is usually severe but localized. To the bodyman such damage usually means using some kind of body filler.

Grinding discs can be scalloped like this to make them "floppy" so the edges won't catch in a crevice or seam.

Metalwork Fundamentals

When the metal of a high crown area is struck, the metal can always be expected to push outward from the point of impact. When a low crown area is struck, the metal will tend to pull inward. A combination panel will include both outward and inward forces.

Types of Damage

When a collision occurs, damage will depend on the area affected and the force of the collision. Damage can be separated into five types: displaced areas, simple bends, rolled buckles, upsets, and stretches.

A displaced area is a part of the metal that has been moved but not damaged. If a door panel is smacked sharply, for instance, the entire panel may buckle inward. But the actual damage will be only around the edges of the larger buckle. If the panel is lightly pushed from the back it may snap back into place, and repair is needed only around the small buckles, or edges. If a fender is hit slightly near the headlight, it may cause slight waves down the side of the fender toward the door. There may be a small buckle in the fender somewhere that is holding the

metal down. If the fender is pushed or pulled in a reverse direction from the impact, the displaced metal reverts to orginal shape and only the small buckled places need repair.

Whenever collision occurs, there is usually some form of simple bending involved. In the above case, if the fender is struck hard enough, the small-buckled area may turn into a simple bend, where the metal makes a kind of S-shape as it is forced out of place. As the severity of the simple bend increases it becomes a rolled buckle. In the simple bend, the outside of the bend includes metal-under-tension and the inside of the bend under-compression. This is in a very small area as sheetmetal is so thin, but there is a distortion of the metal involved.

In the rolled buckle, the S-shape of the bend is pronounced, and the metal tucks under itself. Such damage is not unusual to front or rearend collisions and indicates a rather severe impact. For the enthusiast, such a buckle indicates a considerable amount of metalwork, starting with pulling or pushing the panel back into some semblance of shape and then working the buckled area carefully with hand tools.

An upset in metal happens when opposing forces push against an area of metal causing it to yield. Because of this yield, the surface area of the metal will be reduced and the thickness increased. An upset

Here is the fender flare in rough shape. You can still see where the quarter panel was sectioned.

area will tend to gather the surrounding metal and does not, to a large extent, occur in automotive bodies. However, a very small upset can cause the panel to react strangely, sometimes even as though the panel had been stretched. Unless the metal shows signs of having been worked before, chances are the panel has an upset area somewhere on its surface.

Stretching is the result of tension rather than pressure as in upsetting, with stretching typical of the gouge type of damage. When a car bumper rakes down a door panel, it will probably cause a gouge in the panel. This is stretched metal and the repair procedure is usually one of filling the gouge as there is seldom a raised bump anywhere near. A false stretch can result from a nearby upset, but it usually takes an expert to see this.

When making the decision about proper repair procedure, the bodyman must determine the angle of impact; speed of the impact object; size, rigidity, and weight of the impact object; and construction of the damaged panel. Trying to visualize how the metal folded during the impact is the first step to repair, since applying an opposite force will ordinarily pull much of the damage out.

The impact angle is determined by either a direct or glancing blow with a resulting effect on all other areas of the car. A big impact on the front end can cause misalignment at the rear of the body, and so on. If the impact angle is not too great, much of the impact force will be absorbed by the panel. If the angle is high, the impact energy may be diverted, leaving small damage. In some cases, the impact object may be sharp, driving some of the metal before it. This pushes the metal up in front of the object and stretches it behind. A typical sideswipe illustrates this possibility.

Taking the Body Apart for Repairs

It is important to understand that time spent trying to repair or modify a piece of sheetmetal is the same as spending money on the car since time is money. If an untrained metalman spends three hours repairing a 30-minute dent, the cost will likely be too high. Learning to assess the damage is important and not too difficult. A few minutes spent looking at a crumpled fender may save many hours of labor.

One typical consideration would be determining how much of the crumpled front end must be removed for a straightening operation, with the amount of time spent on the total project relative to the amount of body tear-down required. It is often easier to straighten a particular panel if it is removed from the vehicle, perhaps an inner splash

A tremendous amount of metal finishing is necessary to end up with a final product like this. When you realize the amount of work that goes into a set of metal fender flares, it is easy to see why flares cost so much.

Metalwork Fundamentals

Welding generates a lot of potentially damaging heat. To prevent warping, this custom front fender was packed with Moist Bastos.

or collapse of one section to slight misalignment. In all cases where frame damage is suspected, the enthusiast should entrust the vehicle to a frame shop for repair. Such shops are completely equipped with necessary gauges and equipment to check and repair the frame. Repair of the major frame is *not* a backyard project. It is possible to replace small front frame extensions, called frame horns, but nothing larger should be attempted in the home garage. Also, it is possible to save considerable money on a frame repair by removing all sheetmetal that might be in the way. The frame shop will have direct access to the job, so cost savings can be substantial.

Using Hydraulic Body Jacks

Hydraulic body jacks are specialized tools that not everyone owns, but they are readily available at tool rental outlets. These hydraulic body jacks are able to do a wide variety of repairs quickly and easily. If you plan to fix heavily damaged cars, a hydraulic body jack would be a good investment. Whether you buy or rent, a hydraulic body jack can restore buckled metal to near factory fresh shape quickly.

Pulling the wrinkles from a piece of sheetmetal is better than pushing. This is particularly true where the section features low crown construction, such

panel, and sometimes the removal of an adjacent panel makes repair of a specific panel easier and faster.

When body parts are being taken apart, save all the nuts and bolts, as well as small brackets. These parts are seldom included on replacement panels and, as a result, are difficult to obtain individually.

The front sheetmetal can sometimes be removed from the chassis as a unit, by removing bolts down either side of the cowl and one or two bolts holding the radiator core support to the frame. When the electrical wiring and radiator hoses have been disconnected, the front fenders, grille, radiator, and core support can be detached as a single piece. Nothing else on the body is so easily removed. The doors and deck lid are removable at the hinges.

Frame Damage

Any time a vehicle is damaged, it is possible that the frame or frame structure has also been damaged. While some of the damage may be obvious, misalignment can be involved to a great extent without being seen.

Frame damage can run the gamut from twisting

Hydraulic body jacks like this one made by the H.K. Porter company of Somerville, Massachusetts, are great for "pushing" out damaged sections.

as a top or quarter-panel. When tension is applied to a panel, the dented area is pulled back to shape rather than pushed. Pushing or driving a dent tends to concentrate the force in small areas which upsets the metal. This means the upset areas must then be taken out if the final job is to be a success. By pulling the metal straight, there are no upset areas, thus less work. In areas where the primary concern is alignment, such as door posts, pushing with the jack is acceptable if done correctly.

Learning where to attach hydraulic body jack points is a matter of recognizing the proper leverage angles, lift reaction, work hardening of the damaged place, variations of the surface crown, and alignment with the panel crown. Attachment of the jack ends should be done so that the most leverage is applied directly to the bent area. It helps to use a hydraulic body jack with a lot of versatile attachments like the body jacks made by H.K. Porter, Inc., 74 Foley St., Somerville, MA 02143. They make the P-F line of body tools which includes the P-F all angle pull clamp. This versatile clamp allows force to be applied in the most ideal areas.

Lift reaction should be considered when using hydraulic body jacks. When a jack is attached on either side of a dent, there is an action to pull the dent up and a reaction through the jack to force the metal downward at the attachment points. This reaction force will cease when the dent is pulled out, although the jack can still be bumped to increase tension on the metal being straightened. When looking for attachment points for securing a jack in tension-straightening, these points should be strong. The edges of the door or fender would be

Even very tight areas can be spread back to their normal shape with P-F's hydraulic spreader.

good examples.

When a panel has been crumpled, the area most affected will be work hardened due to upset of the metal. When tension is applied to pull the metal back into a rough shape, as much of the area as possible should be worked out with hand tools before the tension is released. The reason is simple enough, since any work done to the metal will tend to stretch it back to the original shape.

Repairing areas of high crown or combination crown design will take more time than simple low crown repair, but the jacks can still be used effectively. However, go slowly at first. In fact, the maxim for any hydraulic jack work, ''Proceed with caution.''

Metalworking Techniques

The initial step after disassembly of destroyed pieces is roughing the metal into shape. This first step will be followed by bumping (hammer and dolly work) and finishing (filling and grinding). Align-

Body jacks are also designed to "pull" out damaged areas. Jacks like the P-F Speed-Master are available with a large selection of accessories to make it possible to pull from almost any angle. P-F's unique BU0285 pull clamp is extremely versatile.

Metalwork Fundamentals

The correct use of a hammer and dolly is one of the most important bodywork skills anyone can learn. A tremendous variety of shapes can be handled due to the many different surfaces on a set of body hammers and dollies.

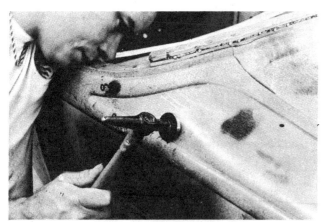

An experienced bodyman knows when to use the hammer on the outside of the dent and when to use it from the backside.

ing is also part of the repair and is usually included with roughing, but it is so full of tricks that we have treated it separately in a chapter called "Panel Alignment."

Sheetmetal repair is like building a house, in that each step builds upon those taken previously, and a mistake made at first will likely be magnified at the finish. Roughing generally means bringing a piece of sheetmetal back into general contour, including supporting members and reinforcements. When a panel is being roughed into shape, it may have force applied by using a hammer and dolly, by pushing with a body jack, or pulling with a body jack. Sometimes a combination of these methods will be required, or all three may be involved.

The importance of initial roughing is emphasized since the newcomer to bodywork will make fewer mistakes in the later stages if the roughing is reasonably successful. The cardinal rule is to always pull if possible, and never push or hammer major damage unless absolutely necessary.

Once the rough shape has been attained and the panel at least looks like part of an automobile, the second and third phases of repair start. This begins

with the hammer and dolly, two hand tools that can easily be misused if the workman is not careful. While the dolly can be used as a hammer, it is primarily used in conjunction with a hammer in both the hammer-on and hammer-off methods.

Hammer-on Technique

When the neophyte begins to learn metalwork, the hammer-on method seems the most difficult. This entails placing the dolly behind the panel and striking it through the metal. It is very difficult at first, but can be mastered with minimal experience. It is advisable to practice hammer and dolly coordination on a discarded piece of metal before attempting an actual repair.

At first, the force of the hammer blow on the dolly is not nearly so important as hitting the dolly at all. It is important to learn a technique wherein the hammer hits with just the right amount of force, time after time. Further, the hammer is allowed to bounce back. That is, the dolly should remain in constant contact with the metal, with the hammer rebounding from the blow. Improper use of the hammer and dolly can be expected at first, with the hammer striking the metal, causing the dolly to bounce away and re-strike the backside of the metal. The dolly will bounce away slightly when the hammer is used

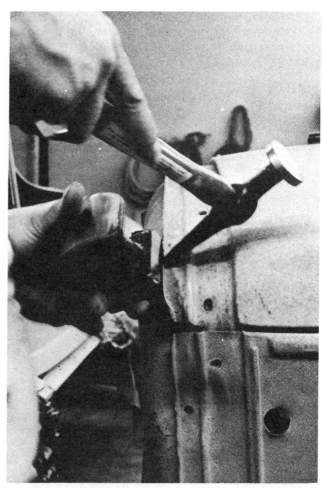

Straightening a wavy lip is one of the easiest tasks you can perform with a hammer and dolly. The dolly serves as an anvil for the hammer.

properly, or snapped with a definite wrist action, but it will not be a pronounced "limp-wrist" bounce.

The hammer-on technique is especially effective for raising a low point in metal as the hammer first tends to flatten the metal being struck. This is followed by the reaction of the dolly as it rebounds slightly from the hammer blow. If the hand holding the dolly increases its pressure, then the tendency of the dolly to raise the low spot also increases.

Hammer-off Technique

In the hammer-off technique the dolly is placed adjacent to the hammer blow, but not directly under it. Learning the hammer-off style is easy after learning the hammer-on technique. The spot struck by the hammer drives the metal down since it is not being supported by the dolly. Movement of the metal transfers the hammer-blow force to the dolly making it rebound the same as with the hammer-on technique. The effect is to drive the low spot up (from dolly force) and the high spot down (from hammer force) with a single hammer blow.

When using the hammer-off technique, the hammer blow should always be on the high metal adjacent to the low spot, never anywhere else. Learning to "see" with the hand is part of metalwork experience, and feeling to locate the low and high parts of the damage becomes a natural reaction. The dolly should be the high crown type, or the portion used should have minimum contact with the metal, and hammer blows should be just enough. Too much hammer effort will cause extra damage. Normally the dolly would be about ¼ inch away from the hammer blow depending upon the metal "springiness."

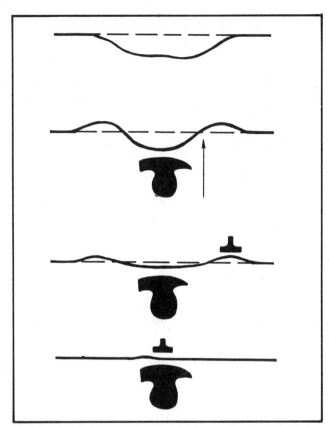

Shrinking a low spot starts with heat, then a blow from behind with a dolly. High spots are worked "off-dolly" as shown, then "on-dolly."

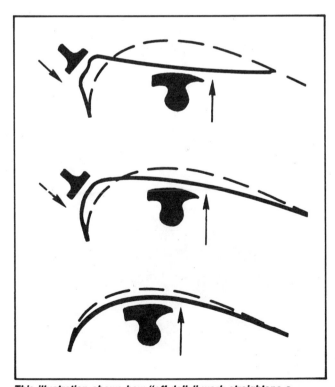

This illustration shows how "off-dolly" work straightens a damaged high crown fender.

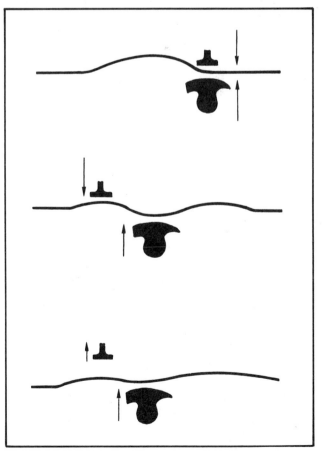

This illustration shows the "hammer-on" versus "hammer-off" dolly techniques.

Metalwork Fundamentals

This pick hammer is going to be used from behind a series of very small dents. The dents were marked with a marking pen for the purpose of this photo. Experienced bodymen know instinctively where to place hammer blows.

Using Pick Hammers

It is very difficult to "hit where you look" when learning to pick up low spots. Since the pick hammer is being driven toward the user and is out of sight behind the panel, the normal reaction is to hit below the desired spot and often off to the left side. Learning to use a pick hammer is a matter of practice, but the way to begin is to bring the hammer into view at first, then move it up to about where the low spot should be. A good guide to keep the hammer working in the same spot is to rest the arm on an available piece of metal which will keep the hammer from wandering during use.

Start with a gentle tap on the metal and see where the blow lands. It may be difficult to locate this spot at first so lay the flattened hand against the metal as a guide. The small bump can usually be felt and the pick adjusted to hit the low spots. Low spots will feel like high spots on the inside of the panel, so the pick head can be rubbed against the metal to locate the spot if the touch is sensitive. Go easy and slow with the pick hammer as too much metal can be hammered up.

Finishing Metalwork

After the hand tools have been used to straighten a damaged section, the metal must be finished before painting. In bodywork, metal finishing means restoration of final surface smoothness after straightening. This means that areas which are still too low or too high can be picked up or lowered, whichever is necessary.

The file and disc sander are two prime tools of metal finishing. The beginner should become thoroughly familiar with the file first since it works slower than the sander and consequently will make only minor mistakes.

Body Files

Body files are usually fitted with flat, 14-inch blades. Holders are available in either wood or metal. Metal ones are usually adjustable.

When a file is used correctly, the many cutting blades will remove minor surface irregularities. When a file is drawn over a freshly straightened surface, the blades will cut on the high or level spots and leave the low spots untouched. So the file becomes a sort of tattle-tale straightedge.

The file should always be moved in the direction of the flattest crown of the panel in order to show up the greatest imperfection in the panel. At the same time the file must be shifted slightly to one side during the stroke for maximum coverage.

After the file has been passed over a straightened

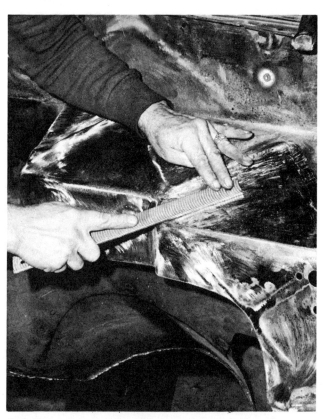

Body files are very useful tools for both preliminary and finishing stages of bodywork. Early in a repair the body file will show where the high and low spots are. In the final stages, the file will smooth the area.

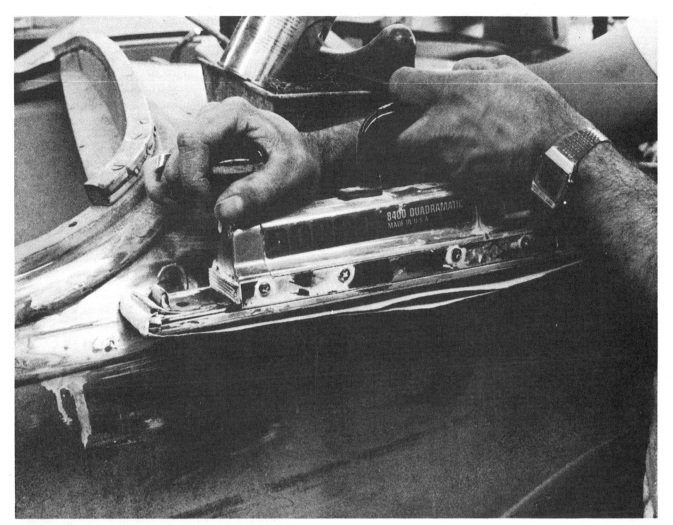

Air files are useful for both preliminary and final finishing. Their sharp edge works well on creases like this. Air files are used mostly for getting large panels smooth and wrinkle-free.

area, any excessively high spots will show up as sharp cuts. Usually very low spots will show up. These spots can be lifted with a pick hammer. Besides the traditional metal files, there are air-powered files that can be used with very coarse grit sand paper to achieve results similar to those reached with metal body files. Since the air files are so powerful, exercise caution when using one.

Disc Sanders

The disc sander is a versatile power tool that can perform a variety of bodywork chores. Most disc sanders are electric, but there are also air powered models. The sanding discs commonly come in 7 and 9-inch diameter sizes.

The grit size of the sanding disc is designated by a number such as #34 or #36 and refers to the size of screen which the grit will pass through. These discs are available in open or closed coat types with the open coat discs commonly used as paint removers. The closed coat discs have a heavier layer of abrasive for heavy-duty use in metal grinding.

Grit size determines how the disc will be used, with the coarse #16 selected for paint removal and coarse cutting. A #24-disc is most commonly used as an all-around grit since it will cut paint and finish off the metal smoothly. However, a #36-grit is better for finishing.

When using the sander rather than a file, the disc is run across the surface at such an angle that the grit swirl marks will bridge across the low spots. This is done by moving the sander back and forth following the flat direction of the panel as with the file. Also, pressure is applied to cause the disc pad to flex slightly. This will produce the best cutting action, but the sander motor will not be so loaded it will slow down. During the side-to-side strokes, the sander is tilted first to one side and then to the other. That is, when going toward the right, the left side of the disc is working; when moving back to the left the sander is twisted slightly and the right side of the disc is working. Moving the sander this way will cause a crisscross pattern which will show the low spots better.

If there has been considerable metalwork, it is advisable to go over the area with a file after the sander has been used. This is a final check for low spots and is particularly suited to the beginner.

After the area is smooth, a #50 or #60-grit disc can be used to buff the metal. While the sander fol-

Metalwork Fundamentals

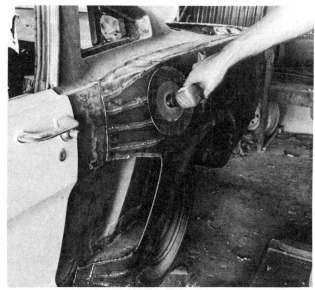

Disc sanders or grinders are among the most useful of all body tools. Their high speeds create a lot of friction when used with coarse sanding discs. This type of energy is necessary to remove welding slag.

A panel can have a false stretch which is easily confused with a true stretch because the false stretch will tend to "oil can" or have a raised hump. A false stretch will always be smooth and unworked and next to an area that has been upset; the raises are being caused by the gathering effect of the upset. A false stretch is usually found around the reinforced edge of doors, hoods, and deck lids where there has been a rolled buckle, and the upset has not been relieved completely. Beating out a stiff buckle which should be straightened under tension is a typical cause of false stretch.

When an area of sheetmetal is shrunk, the high crown or bulge must be upset to bring the bulge

lows the flattest plane of the panel, the buffing is done across the greatest crown, usually up and down. The sander is not tilted on the edge quite so much, so that a much larger part of the pad contacts the metal surface during a stroke. The final buffing cuts down the deeper scratches of coarse discs or a file and is a preliminary to the painting operations.

When using the sander around a reverse crown area, it is advisable to cut the disc in a "star" shape. The round disc edge will have a tendency to dig into the reverse crown, while the floppier corners of a star-shaped disc will follow the crown contour. A disc may have any number of points, depending on how severe the reverse crown is, but as a guide, the more severe the crown, the more points on the disc.

Never use a disc sander without some kind of eye protection. Be careful how the sander is handled, as the disc can cut a nasty wound in a leg or arm.

Metal Shrinking

As far as the bodyman is concerned, shrinking really means the use of heat from an oxygen-acetylene torch to soften metal for a specified upset. A propane tank without oxygen will not give enough heat. When an area is being shrunk, a spot or group of spots is heated and worked with a dolly and hammer, then cooled. While shrinking looks easy, it is a precision job and requires more "feel" than ordinary bodywork.

Stretched metal will have an increase in surface area, either in length, width, or both. In collision damage, the stretched area may be confined to a rather small section, and may show as either a depression or bulge in the panel. If a large section of the panel is stretched, it is usually advisable to replace the entire panel.

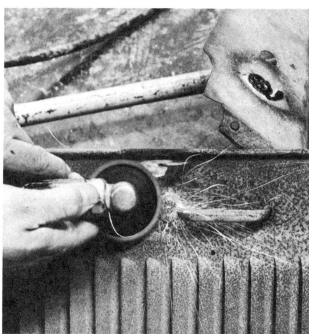

Most grinders are rather big, but you can also get a very compact, right-angle die grinder, which is ideal for getting into areas that would otherwise have to be hand sanded.

back down to its original contour. If a bulge is struck cold, the hammer force is transmitted through the metal toward the edges and little or no effect is usually noted. However, as the bulge is heated the metal at the hot spot will tend to upset readily. When the heat is first applied, the bulge will grow noticeably, but will return to the bulge shape as the metal cools. If the metal is upset while the spot is still hot, the metal will shrink to a state smaller than the bulge. Of course, the hot spot will begin to cool as soon as the torch is removed so hammer and dolly application must be immediate. The hammer does not drive the bulge completely away, leaving a perfectly level surface while the metal is still hot. If this were to happen, the metal would be overshrunk as it cooled.

The rate at which the metal cools will have an effect on the total shrink; therefore it is possible to use a sponge or wet rag as part of the shrinking procedure. If the heated spot is cooled faster than normal, more of the upset can be retained. That is, shrinking can be more effective if the metal is quenched immediately after working with hammer and dolly. The rapid cooling stops the yield of the heated area to contraction-tension, but must be done while the metal is still quite hot. It will take a little experience to learn when and when not to use quenching. If the metal resembles original contour during the hammer and dolly work, chances are that little or no quenching will be necessary. If the area receives too much quenching, buckles will often appear in the surrounding panel and must be worked out with the hammer.

A gouge in a door or quarter panel is typical of the type of shrinking job the metalman will encoun-

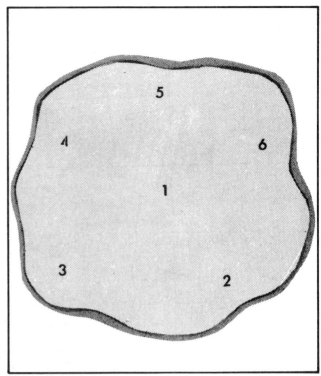

This is the sequence for a heated high spot to be struck with the hammer, using light blows. Work around the edges more than the middle.

ter frequently. Shrinking a gouge is similar to shrinking raised metal, but it is done from the back side.

When shrinking a gouge, the dolly must supply the force to upset the metal from the back side. A small gouge can be bumped out from the back and then shrunk as a raised bulge, but this method is limited to very small damages. The more common gouge requires heating to above 1400 degrees F., or good and red, which will deepen the gouge. The dolly is used as a hammer from the back side, knocking the gouge outward at the deepest point and driving the metal adjacent to the gouge higher than the original contour. The dolly is then held hard against the low point and the hammer used in a hammer-off technique to drive down the surrounding high metal. When the gouge is very close to the original contour, the hammer should then be used directly against the dolly to relieve some of the stress that might cause overshrinking.

A small gouge is usually removed with one or two heatings; a long gouge may require a number of heatings down its length as the hammer and dolly work progresses. Usually, quenching is not needed for a gouge shrink.

Learning to get the proper heat application will be the hardest part of shrinking for the novice, as heat requirements will differ with each type of shrink. The problem is getting just the right amount of heat in·just the right size and spot.

Shrinking is not difficult to master, but it definitely requires patience and practice. After a few gouges have been attempted with success, the beginner will learn to remove much of the gouge with one heat application and rapid use of hammer and dolly.

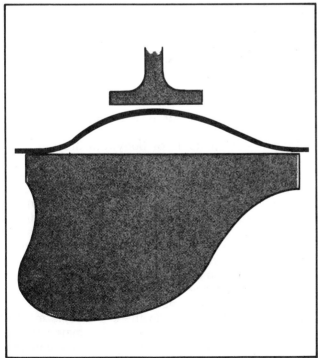

Shrinking with heat is an essential aspect of bodywork. For shrinking a high spot, metal is heated, backed with a dolly, and the hammer applied directly on the high spot.

Bodywork Tools

It takes more than a sledge hammer to pound out dents. To do a really first class job of bodywork, it takes quality tools, many of them unique to auto body repair. These tools range from a simple body hammer to elaborate frame machines. The basic tools are all hand-powered and will fix almost any damage. Since time is money in a body shop, manufacturers came up with a wide array of pneumatic, hydraulic, and electric body tools that are tremendous time savers. The power tools also save a lot of your energy and/or multiply your energy so much that you can do jobs that would be impossible with only muscle power.

As always, your best bet is to start with basic tools and expand your selection as your needs and talents change. If you have more time than money, stick with the hand sanders, but if saving time and energy is important, get some power tools. Always buy quality tools because they will last decades or longer.

Hammers and Dollies

The two basic tools of bodywork are the body hammer and the steel dolly. The hammer is used to pound on the damaged area while the dolly acts as an anvil to back up the blows. The dolly keeps you from pounding the metal too far in the opposite direction. There are easily a dozen different body hammers, but four or five basic ones will handle the majority of dents. The different hammers have different heads, each designed to work best on a certain type of dent. There is some duplication in head styles since some hammers are available in large and small versions. Most body hammers have wooden handles although there are some models with fiberglass handles. If you get hammers with a flat face, a curved face, and a pointed end you should be able to handle most common dents.

You will seldom find a hammer being used without a dolly. Like body hammers, dollies come in a variety of shapes to best fit each dent. Each dolly has several different shaped surfaces to increase its versatility. The best dollies to start with are a universal dolly, an all-purpose dolly, and a heel dolly.

Closely related to dollies are spoons. Spoons are like long, stretched-out dollies or dollies with handles. Spoons can be used to reach areas not accessible to dollies. Since spoons have a greater surface area than dollies, they can be used to distribute the hammer blows over a greater area. Besides being a back-up tool like dollies, spoons can be used like a hammer to slap out dents. Spoons come in about a half dozen different styles. A good first choice for a spoon would be a surfacing spoon or a dinging spoon.

Dent Pullers

Many dents can't be reached from behind for proper hammer and dolly work so a dent puller is necessary in these cases. There are several different types of dent pullers including slide hammers, suction cups, and pull rods. Pry bars are similar in that they are used from only one side of the dent.

Slide hammers are basically a long bar or rod with a handle and a movable weight (weights vary from one to five pounds in most cases). The end opposite the handle has either a hook or a screw to attach to the body. The action of slamming the weight back against the handle forces out the dent. The best slide hammers have interchangeable screw tips and "L" hooks for better access to more types of dents. Unless there is some opening in the body panel or a lip to hook onto, a series of holes must be drilled in the damaged area. The screw end of the dent puller is twisted into the hole and the area is pulled out. The holes are later filled with some body filler.

Pull rods work in the same way as a screw-in slide hammer except that the pull rods are just inserted into the holes rather than screwed in. Pull rods don't remove dents as easily as a slide hammer since pull rods only use the pulling power of your hand. All rod pulls are very similar except that some

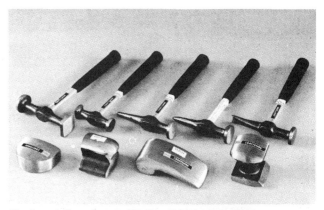

The foundation of any collection of bodywork equipment should be an assortment of hammers and dollies. A nine-piece set like this Craftsman auto body repair set should take care of most dents.

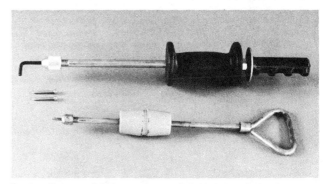

Dent pullers or slide hammers can be used to pull out dents when there is no access to the back side of the panel. The dent pullers come with either screws or "L" hooks for attachment to the panels. The better models have interchangeable end pieces.

have hooked ends and others have "L" shaped ends.

Mild dents that haven't creased or stretched the metal can sometimes be popped out so that the previous damage is hardly noticeable. Suction cups are handy for this type of dent. Suction cups come in various diameters and there are single and double cup models.

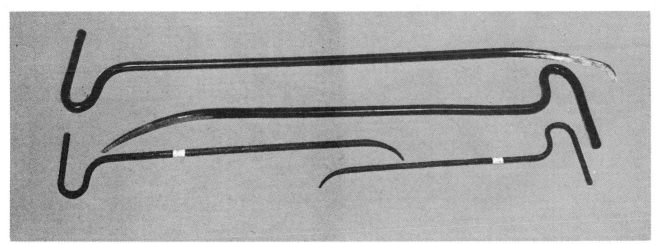

Pry bars can be invaluable in performing body repairs as they allow leverage to be applied to crunched-in panels. Their size is just right for reaching inside crowded access holes.

Bodywork Tools

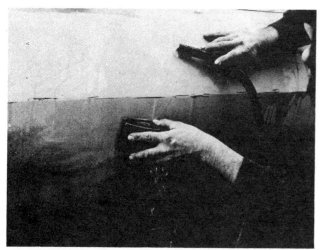

An inexpensive rubber sanding block is one of the best bodyworking tools around when it comes to getting a car straight and smooth enough for paint. Wet sanding makes the paper last longer and the sanding easier.

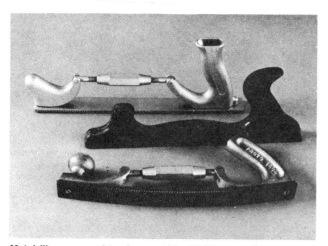

Metal files are used to shave metal off high spots. The holders are available in either wood or metal. The metal file holders can be adjusted for flat or curved surfaces.

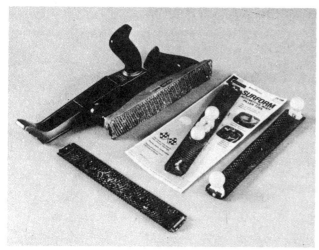

Cheesegrater files are great for shaping plastic body filler. The blades are either flat or half-round. A variety of holders are available, although many bodymen use the files without any holder.

Hand Powered Sanding Tools

When it comes to really fine bodywork, it is tough to beat simple hand tools. A lot of patience, a lot of sandpaper, and a rubber sanding block can produce a flawless finish. Long before there were power tools, craftsmen were turning out beautiful work with hand tools, so there is no reason it can't be done today.

The two basic types of sanding tools are sanding blocks and sanding boards. Sanding blocks are usually about 2¾ inches wide and 5 inches long although there are some that are 9 inches long. The blocks are mostly made out of hard rubber; some blocks are made of plastic. The sanding blocks have a flat and a curved surface. Depending on which side the sandpaper is fastened either flat or curved surfaces can be sanded. A sanding block should be considered mandatory equipment for any bodyman or painter.

Sanding boards are, essentially, long sanding blocks. The boards are the same width as the blocks, but much longer (usually 16 inches although there are shorter models), and they are designed for only one type of surface. Sanding boards are used to keep waves out of long flat surfaces. Most sanding boards are made out of wood, but there are also plastic models. The longer sanding boards have two handles, but the shorter ones usually have only one handle.

Before sanding, some type of file is often used to get the material into rough form. There are two main types of files used in bodywork, the curved tooth metal file and the cheesegrater or Surform file. The metal files are used to lower high spots or to shape lead when lead was used for filling work. The metal files are usually held in adjustable holders which can be adjusted so the file is either flat or curved. There are also wooden file holders, but they aren't as popular as the adjustable holders.

The cheesegrater files have dozens of sharp little teeth that cut through body filler like a cheesegrater, hence the name. The Stanley tool company is the best known maker of cheesegrater files and they call their products Surform files. Cheesegrater files are used almost exclusively on plastic body fill-

Air-powered sanders are real work savers. The most common types are, from left to right, a dual action sander, a jitterbug sander, and an air file. The dual action and the air file are more commonly used than the jitterbug sander.

Air chisels or air hammers are very powerful tools that can cut through panels with ease. This front fender is being cut apart in preparation for some radical customizing.

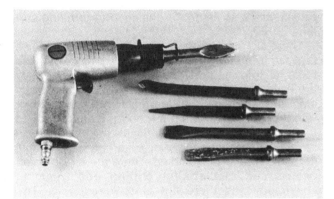

Air chisels can be used with many different bits and chisels to cut panels, break rivets, free frozen bolts, and many other tough tasks. This is a Craftsman air chisel kit.

The straight line sander is nothing but an air-powered sanding board. Straight line sanders are good for working on big expanses of metal. Orbital sanders most closely resemble the standard rubber sanding block. The action of orbital sanders isn't straight back and forth hence the nickname "jitterbug sander." Orbital sanders are used on flat surfaces. The most common and most often used air sander is the dual-action sander (often known as a D-A). Dual-action sanders can be used either as a rotary grinder or an oscillating sander which reduces sanding marks. Dual-action sanders are good for feather-edging the paint around damaged areas. Most quality air sanders have built-in air regulators to control speed.

A very handy air tool for bodymen is the air hammer or air chisel. Air hammers look like a pistol with a spring on the end of the barrel. Air hammers can be used with a wide variety of attachments to cut rivets, punch holes, and cut sheetmetal. The main use of air hammers is to cut away damaged body sections that aren't bolted in place. This is the method to replace a rear quarter panel. There are long and short barrel air hammers. The former have a longer stroke for more powerful blows.

Electric grinders can be used as buffers by changing from the grinding discs to a buffing pad. This Craftsman grinder has two speeds; the slow speed should be used for buffing.

er. The most popular model is the half-round model which is usually used without a holder. There are a variety of holders for cheesegrater files and the files come in many different sizes and shapes. A cheesegrater file should be considered standard equipment for any bodywork.

Air Tools

One of the biggest aids to ever hit the auto body business was the invention of air-powered tools. In the hands of an experienced pro, air sanders, grinders, and chisels can be a super time and labor saver. Air tools should be used with reservations, however, because improperly used they can cause more damage than good. Power tools use their force to create a lot of friction which makes sanding virtually effortless and very quick. This same friction, if left in one place too long, can actually create enough heat to damage the metal or leave difficult to remove gouges and sanding scratches. Air tools can be handy but only when used with discretion.

The most useful air tools are the sanders which come in three basic styles: straight line sander, orbital or jitterbug sander, and dual-action sander.

Air-powered grinders are popular with many bodymen because they are considerably lighter than the bulky electric grinders. The grinding discs are quite stiff, but if the edges are cut, the disc will conform better in concave areas.

Bodywork Tools

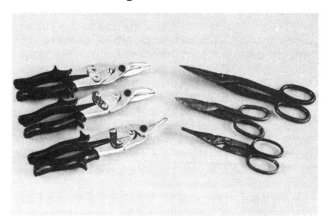

An assortment of metal snips is useful for fabricating patch panels or cutting away damaged areas. The compound leverage snips on the left are used for straight, left, or right cuts. Those on the right are straight cut and duckbill snips.

Vise Grip Pliers come in many different sizes and styles. They are very useful for clamping during welding operations.

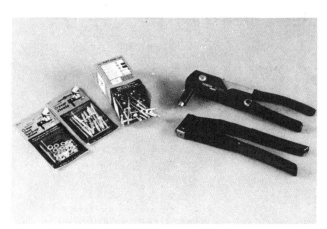

Rivet tools should be included in the average bodyman's tool kit for use when installing patch panels or temporarily holding panels prior to welding.

Air-powered grinders are another very popular type of air tool. The grinders come in a wide range of sizes from palm size to big two-handed models. The small grinders which are usually known as die grinders are great for reaching tight, difficult-access areas. The die grinders come with either a straight chuck or a right angle head. The larger grinders are used to remove all the paint around a dent so the filler will stick. Another use for air-powered grinders is for dressing welds.

Besides air-powered grinders, there are also electric grinders. These grinders are very common in body shops because they can also be used as buffers. For this reason the electric grinders are often known as grinder/buffers, or disc grinders. Some models have two speeds which make them better for buffing work. Electric grinders are usually labeled by the size of the grinding disc and the horsepower of the electric motor. The most common disc sizes are 4½, 7, and 9 inches. Electric grinders are super time savers when it comes to removing paint, rust, or welding slag, but care must be exercised so as not to damage the grinding surface.

There are several other types of air powered tools that are frequently used by bodymen. Most of these tools fall into the convenience group because they are used to perform tasks that could be handled by standard wrenches, but are quicker and easier. Air ratchets are useful when a lot of body panels need to be removed. Impact wrenches are real muscle savers when suspension or other hard-to-remove parts must be disassembled. There are air-powered shears and nibblers for cutting and trimming sheetmetal and there are air-powered drills. The number of air tools is surpassed only by their countless uses.

Hydraulic Power Units

Hydraulic power units or body jacks are special body tools that can turn an ordinary bodyman into a superman. Hydraulic body jacks use the power of 4 to 10-ton hydraulic jacks to push, pull, and spread body damage that would be virtually impossible without the benefit of hydraulic power. There are a tremendous variety of attachments that allow body jacks to undo almost any type of damage. Body jacks are super versatile tools that can

Many specialized tools can be used to make working on cars easier. Many newer cars use Torx fasteners which need either a Torx socket or Torx driver for removal and installation. The tools on the right are door handle tools which make working on interior door handles a snap.

A full face shield, or at least a pair of safety glasses, should always be worn when using tools like disc grinders. Bodywork can be dangerous, so never overlook safety.

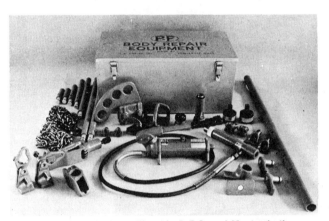

A hydraulic body jack set like this P-F Speed-Master is the type of equipment that can put you into the big leagues. A body jack with the right assortment of accessories can make quick work of otherwise difficult body damage.

handle any damage short of work performed by a full-size frame machine. Body jacks can handle certain types of frame damage, but their biggest asset is the ability to quickly push, pull, or spread damaged areas back into shape for final metal finishing. Body jacks are a necessity for commerical shops and even though they are expensive, many do-it-yourselfers also own body jacks. You can buy a body jack starter set that will do all the basic jobs and add the specialized equipment as the need arises. A home bodyman can justify the cost of a body jack based on the money saved by repairing a badly damaged vehicle at home instead of paying a shop to do the work.

The most important part of a body jack is the hydraulic power unit. This is the heart of the unit and a top quality jack is a must. Just as there is a tremendous price and quality differential among hydraulic automobile lifting jacks, the same difference exists among body jacks. Inferior hydraulic tools can be very dangerous so there is no reason to skimp on quality. Respected body tool companies like P-F Body Tools (H.K. Porter, Inc., 74 Foley St., Somerville, MA 02143) have strict standards to ensure the utmost quality of their tools. In the long

run, if you want to save money, buy a good starter set, not a poorly made "bargain" body jack.

The best body jacks like the P-F Speed-Master, Speed-Midget, and Hydro-Chief also have the best accessories for doing the most thorough work. For example, the P-F all-angle pull clamp is a multi-purpose clamp that can do the work of eight ordinary clamps.

Although pulling a dent out is preferable, there are many instances where pushing is a necessity. There are also many types of damage where access is very difficult. At these times, a tool like the P-F hydraulic spreader is very handy. The hydraulic spreader is a wedge-shaped attachment for the P-F body jack that can fit into a ¾-inch space and then spread to 3¼ inches. The pushing action of body jacks works well in areas like damaged door openings, i.e., fitting a new door into the old opening. The pushing function is also used to repair caved-in roofs.

A hydraulic body jack is equivalent to having several very strong men, yet the body jack is easily contained in a modest-sized toolbox. Besides the tremendous work-saving abilities of body jacks, they enable you to do jobs that previously would have scared you away.

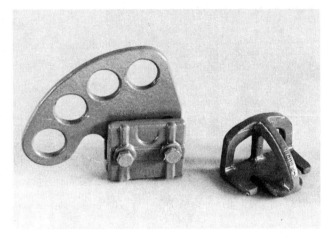

One key to the great efficiency of P-F body jacks is the unique pull clamp and adapter which allows pulls from a wide range of angles.

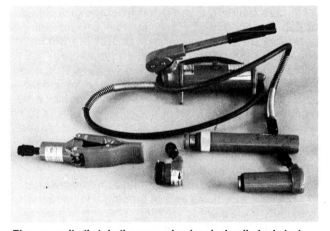

The ram units that do the expansion in a hydraulic body jack come in a variety of sizes so they will fit in almost any area. P-F even makes a hydraulic spreader for very tight situations.

Welding and Brazing

Welding is one of the most useful skills an automotive enthusiast can learn. Whether you are building a street rod from the ground up or fabricating a wild street custom or just doing bodywork on a transportation car, welding will help you do the job better, quicker, and cheaper.

There are many ways to learn welding, and one way is through a school. The best place for a do-it-yourselfer to learn is at a high school or junior college evening class. Most school districts offer adult education classes with several automotive courses like welding, bodywork and painting, and auto mechanics. These classes are usually inexpensive and truly great educational bargains.

A person can also learn to weld at home by reading books and articles and practicing a lot. Practice is the key ingredient to welding. Welding is a precision craft when practiced correctly. Sloppy welding can get the job done, but professional quality welding takes lots of practice.

The two main types of welding the home welder uses are gas welding and arc welding. Gas welding or oxyacetylene welding is used most often for bodywork. Arc welding is used for things like chassis fabrication. Each type of welding has its place in the overall scheme of bodywork.

Gas Welding Equipment

If you are interested primarily in bodywork rather than fabrication, and you can afford only one type of welding equipment, get a gas welding set. Oxyacetylene torches can be used for cutting, brazing, and welding, operations used in bodywork.

There are a variety of torch sets available, but the price range between the top-of-the-line models and the less expensive ones isn't too great. Therefore, we recommend buying the best torch set. The price difference between the best set and a lesser one over the torch's lifespan, usually decades, makes the cost differential almost inconsequential. Torches are generally divided into two categories: two-stage and single-stage.

Two-stage regulators are far better than single-stage outfits because the two-stage units maintain constant pressure to the torch. As the pressure in the oxygen and acetylene tanks on single-stage regulators is reduced, the torch must be readjusted. Single-stage regulators have another disadvantage since they can freeze in cold weather.

Sears offers a good selection of torch sets and other welding supplies that are perfectly suited for bodywork. Their best torch is a two-stage outfit that has a unique new feature: a thumbwheel control knob that saves fuel when not welding. The thumbwheel control allows the welder to switch to a pilot light when the torch isn't used, yet the torch doesn't have to be reset when it is taken off the pilot light setting. The outfit includes two-stage regulators, a welding torch with tips, a cutting torch, 20 feet of hose, a spark lighter, goggles, a wrench, and an instruction manual. An outfit like this Sears Craftsman 9KT5442C is an excellent investment for anyone who is serious about bodywork.

Besides the torch outfit, the other important ingredient for gas welding is the supply of oxygen and acetylene which comes in large cylinders that can either be bought, leased, or rented. Like most business deals, the cost will be about the same no matter which method you choose. There is, however, a dilemma when the choice comes to buying or renting your gas cylinders. A pair of cylinders can cost as much or more than the torch set. Yet, unless you use large quantities of gas like a professional body shop, the minimum cost of a monthly rental or lease

There is a lot of information available on welding from various manufacturers and vocational schools. This information is a valuable reference source for all welders.

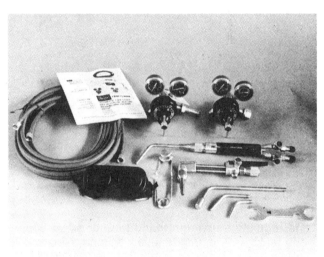

An oxyacetylene torch outfit like this Sears Craftsman two-stage set is the ideal welding equipment for either a home or professional bodyman. The #9KT5442C outfit includes the regulators, hoses, a welding torch with several different tips, a cutting torch, and safety goggles.

Knowledge of welding really expands the scope of possible body repairs. If you ever hope to call yourself a professional bodyman, this ability is mandatory. Here, a rusted door edge is being replaced with new metal. Without welding, the repair would have to be a temporary one using plastic body filler.

agreement can quickly add up to the cost of a set of tanks. If you decide to lease or rent, consult your local welding supply company for details.

Like everything else, the cost of welding tanks is constantly rising so a set of tanks can be an inflation hedge. Our advice, then, is to buy a set of tanks if you can afford the initial investment because welding supply shops will re-purchase your tanks for about half price. Even better, individuals usually are willing to pay about what you paid, especially if the market price has risen.

Oxygen and acetylene tanks come in several different sizes. The sizes are measured by the number of cubic feet of oxygen or acetylene that the cylinders hold. Common sizes for oxygen tanks are 244, 122, and 80 cubic feet. The common sizes for acetylene are 300, 100, and 60 cubic feet. Oxygen tanks

Welding and Brazing

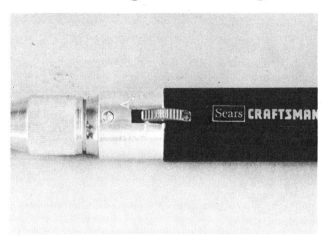

A handy feature of the Craftsman welding torch is this thumbwheel which saves fuel by putting the torch on pilot light when you're not welding. This means that the flame only has to be adjusted once.

Tip cleaners should be used to clean the torch tips. Sears sells this set of 12 cleaners that come in a handy case.

and regulators use right-hand threads while acetylene tanks and regulators use left-hand threads. Also, acetylene tanks have a safety plug (usually located at the top of the cylinder) which is designed to melt at 212 degrees F. in case of fire. The large or medium size tanks are best because the small ones need constant refilling if you do a lot of welding. Nothing is more frustrating than to run out of gas in the middle of a project, especially on a weekend when the welding supply store is closed.

There are many useful welding accessories that you should consider adding to your tool collection. Since gas tanks are heavy and must be stored in an upright position, some type of welding cart is useful. Sears makes a good welding cart, part number 9KT5429N, which has easy to maneuver 10-inch wheels and a sturdy steel frame. The cart has retainer chains to secure the gas tanks and a tray on the back of the cart for carrying the welding rod. Some type of welding cart is virtually a must if you want any versatility with your torch setup.

Good safety welder's goggles are a must as are heavy duty welding gloves; a lot of heat is generated with welding, so don't take chances. An assortment of locking pliers and clamps are handy for positioning work. Tip cleaners will keep the torch tips

free of debris, although the proper size drill bit will also accomplish this task.

Using Gas Torches

A high degree of heat is needed to melt or cut steel, or even metals with a lower melting point. A needle-like flame is needed which will burn consistently with its maximum heat concentrated at the tip. Therefore, acetylene is used as fuel with pure oxygen to "feed" it. When acetylene is combined with oxygen it will burn the hottest of all gases (approximately 6000 degrees F.). Acetylene gas is highly flammable but it is perfectly safe if used with reasonable care. Never apply heat to the cylinder or drop it. Always keep the cylinder upright.

Oxygen isn't harmful but it can puff a tiny spark into a roaring flame. Never oil or grease any part of the equipment, the cylinders, or the valves under any circumstances.

The gas cylinders should be stored and used in the upright position. They can be transported in a horizontal position. When lifting the cylinders to their upright position lift by the protective caps that

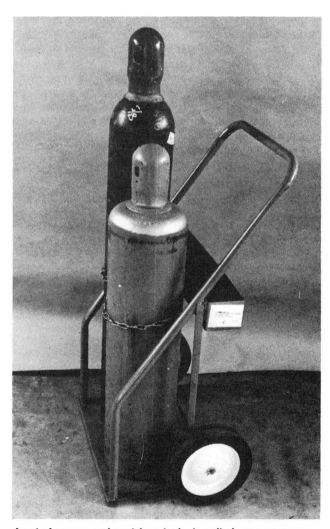

A set of oxygen and acetylene tanks is quite heavy, so some type of cart is necessary if you plan to weld in more than one location. This heavy duty Sears welding truck has 10-inch wheels, a shelf for an extra welding rod, and chains to secure the tanks.

encase the fittings on the top of the cylinders. To use the gases, remove the protective caps, examine the cylinder valve threads and wipe them clean with a *clean* cloth. Next, slightly open ("crack"), then close, both the oxygen and acetylene cylinder valves to make sure they do not stick and also to blow out any dirt or moisture that may have lodged in the valves.

Loosen both regulator adjusting screws until they turn freely, then install the regulators on their appropriate cylinders, tightening firmly but without force. Stand to one side of the oxygen regulator and open the cylinder valve very slowly so the high pressure gauge needle will move up slowly until full pressure is registered. Now the valve should be opened completely. The acetylene cylinder valve should be opened slowly a *maximum* of one complete turn. This is so you can turn it off rapidly in the event of any mishap.

Connect the green (oxygen) hose to the outlet of the oxygen regulator. This hose has a right-hand thread connector. Connect the fuel hose, which is red, to the acetylene regulator outlet. This hose has left-hand thread connections. Next, connect the welding torch to the hoses. Select the welding tip size that is recommended for the job. Now you can install the tip in the torch, snugly, but not too tightly.

Let's assume for the sake of illustration that you wish to weld sheetmetal 1/32-inch thick. Your welding manual states a size "0" tip is required and maximum oxygen and acetylene pressure should be at 3 psi. Now partially open the torch oxygen valve and adjust the oxygen regulator until the pressure rises to 3 psi. Close the torch oxygen valve. After being careful that no flame is about, partially open the torch acetylene valve and adjust the regulator pressure to 3 psi; then close the valve. All pressures in welding and cutting charts are flowing pressures with the torch valves open. If you change tip sizes in the middle of a job and must change pressures, do so with the torch valves open.

To light the torch, open the torch acetylene valve approximately one-half turn and ignite the acetylene with a striker; pointing the flame away from people, pets, the gas cylinders, or any flammable

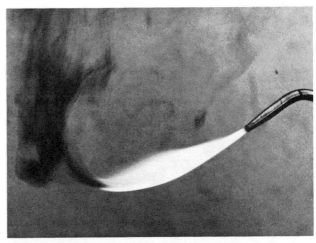

When an acetylene valve is first opened and the flame lit, heavy soot will pour out. Continue opening the valve until the soot stops, then start feeding oxygen into the flame for a proper mix.

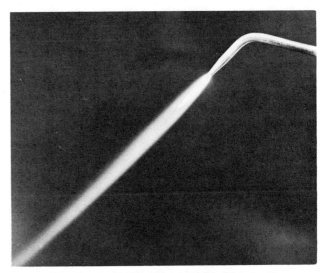

Some oxygen has been added here, but the flame is still acetylene-rich. Note the flame's long central cone.

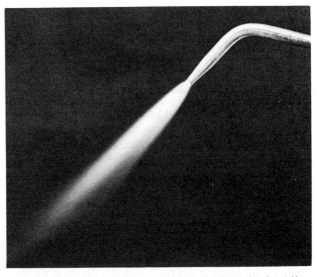

A neutral flame is achieved when the center flame is about ¼ inch to ⅜ inch long. Introduce oxygen until the inner cone just starts to become needle-sharp, then back off until it is the desired size.

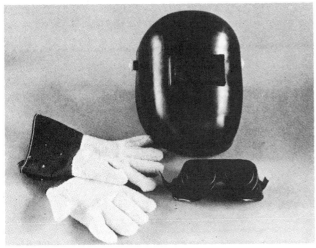

Safety goggles are mandatory for any type of welding. The large welding helmet is for arc welding.

Welding and Brazing

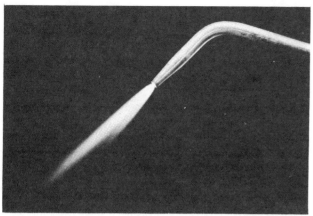

If you bring the inner cone out to a needle-like point and leave it there, you will have an oxidizing flame which will weaken the weld. Note how the outer flame is ragged.

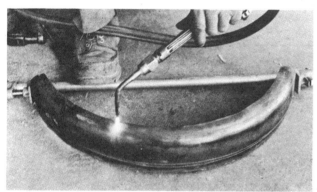

The heat from a torch can be used for work other than welding. Here, heat is being applied to help shrink a metal fender flare. Along with heat, pressure is being applied with a pipe clamp.

materials. Keep opening the torch valve until the flame stops excessive smoking and leaves the end of the tip about ⅛ inch; then reduce slightly to bring the flame back to the tip.

Open the torch oxygen valve now until a bright inner cone appears on the flame. The point at which the feathery edges of the flame disappear and a sharp inner cone is visible is called the "neutral flame." Adjust the torch oxygen valve back and forth until you are sure you have a neutral flame. If too much oxygen is flowing, you'll have an "oxidizing" flame that will burn the metal you're trying to weld, making it brittle and weak. This flame is pale blue without the clearly defined inner cone of the "neutral" flame. Should you attempt to weld with too little oxygen, you will get a flame that is acetylene-rich, which will have a "carburizing" flame, distinguished by its long carburizing feather.

There are two methods one may employ in oxy-acetylene welding: forehand and backhand welding. The forehand method is ordinarily used for welding material under ⅛-inch thickness. This method works by pointing the torch down at an angle, toward the direction that you plan to lay the bead, with the rod preceding the torch. The flame tip preheats the edge of the joint; and the oscillating

motion you use with both rod and torch, moving them in semi-circular paths along the joint, will distribute the heat and molten metal uniformly.

In backhand welding, the torch is moved along in front of the rod in the direction of welding, with the flame pointed back toward the molten puddle and completed weld. The end of the welding rod is placed in the flame between the tip and the weld. The torch needs to be moved slowly along the joint in front of the weld puddle while the rod may be simply rolled from side to side in the puddle. Better fusion between the metals at the root of the weld is normally achieved with this method.

Enough emphasis cannot be placed on the importance of full penetration of the materials being joined and complete fusion along the sides of the joint. Where two pieces are being joined and the joint is quite long, you must consider the expansion of metals in heating, and contraction on cooling. For steel plate being welded, you should tack the pieces lightly at the edge and then tack the pieces along the joint about ¼ inch per foot. This will hold them in alignment but still allow joint closure.

In the long run you're going to have to practice a lot, if you're going to learn how to gas weld. Get some old pieces of scrap metal and practice, practice, practice.

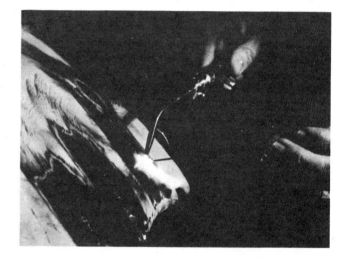

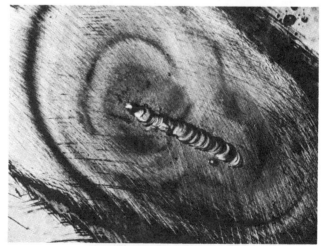

A forehand weld is being applied on this fender. The flame is neutral, with the proper mix of oxygen and acetylene for welding mild steel. The puddles should be uniform.

Brazing and Braze Welding

Learning to braze is easier than welding, but the beginner should learn fusion welding first before attempting brazing. There is a difference between braze welding and brazing although both use nonferrous filler rod that will melt above 800 degrees F. In braze welding the filler rod of brass or bronze fills an open-groove joint or makes a definite bead. In brazing, a closely fitted joint is filled by capillary action of the filler material (as in furnace brazing). Such a connection is really just a thin film of filler metal between the two surfaces, but it can be extremely strong. Furnace brazing is necessary when outstanding strength of precision parts is required.

Around a body shop the term brazing is used to mean braze welding and is used primarily in repairing a joint that was originally spot welded. Brazing of such joints may not be as strong as perfect braze welding or fusion welding, but the joint's strength is usually sufficient. It also requires less heat which means less heat distortion. For this reason most bodymen will steel-weld body panels together, so that the joint is strong even after grinding. Braze welding is done mostly on panels where you can't get at the back side to hammer and dolly it after welding.

Brazing is possible because many nonferrous metals will diffuse and/or penetrate into other metals when temperatures and surface conditions are right. This means the copper base filler material must be melted while the parent metal must be kept at the same temperature. This permits the filler metal to flow over the joint being brazed.

The parent metal must be clean, which can be accomplished by grinding, scraping, or using a wire brush. An easier chemical method is to use a strong flux, but it leaves a residue that is difficult to remove. The bodyman may use a combination of the two, cleaning the joint to be brazed and then using a flux with a low chemical residue.

Flux is both a chemical cleaner and a protective shield for the heated metal surface which allows the molten brazing material to moisten and to diffuse into the parent surfaces. Such a flux can be a powder or a paste, or you can buy flux-coated rods. The coated rods are more expensive than the plain ones but they are much handier to use.

On a good brazed joint, the penetration is called diffusion since the two metals intermix to cause an alloying action at the joint's interface. Such an alloy is sometimes stronger than the parent metal, especially with the newer high-strength brazing rods. The strongest brazed joints are made when the parent metal surfaces are between .003 and .005 inch apart. For the bodyman this means flush.

A good brazed joint should be smooth and bright, with edges that blend smoothly into the parent metal. A pitted or blistery surface or an edge that seems to stand on top of the parent metal means an unsatisfactory job. This doesn't mean the joint won't hold, it just means you need more practice. A very common mistake is to overheat the surface as shown by a fine white powdery material left on both sides of the joint

Brazing is particularly applicable to sheetmetal

An oxygen-rich flame is used here. Such a flame is noted for the sparks it puts out, but the resulting weld is burned, pitted, and weak.

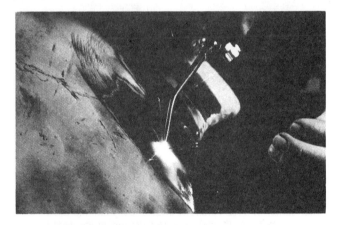

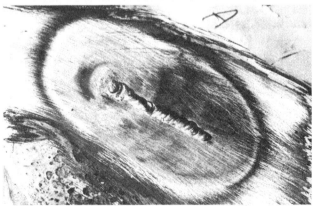

An acetylene-rich flame is used here, which introduces excess carbon into the weld. This is a carburizing flame, which produces a weak weld. This type of flame is preferred when brazing, instead of welding.

Welding and Brazing

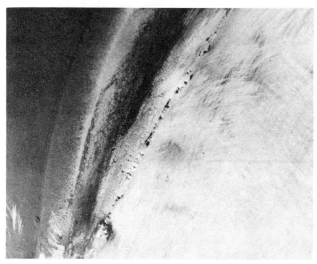

Here is a typical butt-joint of two pieces of sheetmetal which has been hammer welded. A few passes of the grinder and this undistorted seam is almost ready for primer and a few dabs of glaze. A normal overlap seam would have been quicker but would have required lots of filler.

A typical hammer weld operation is this repair of the lower rear corner of a '32 Ford. The original body and the patch piece were cut to fit, and the area surrounding the weld was cleaned of paint. Vise Grip pliers were used to hold things together for welding.

work where you wish to keep excess heat to a minimum, thereby preventing warped panels. But it should not be used for critical suspension parts, not even with a high-strength brazing rod.

Hammer Welding

A very useful type of welding in bodywork is hammer welding. Hammer welding is especially useful in custom work such as chopping tops or in restoration of older cars where pieces from several different cars may have to be joined to make one good body. Hammer welding is basically ordinary gas welding followed by hammer and dolly

work on the welded joint to provide as smooth and distortion-free a seam as possible. Hammer welding is desired when maximum strength and a minimum amount of filler are desired. It also allows the metalman to gain better control over the panel, to shape and mold it the way he wants it with stress in the right place.

Hammer welding is usually employed in three situations: repair of a tear, replacement of a panel, or modification of a panel. In all three the emphasis is upon quality and metal control.

A quarter panel with a tear can be roughed into shape until the torn metal edges can be aligned carefully and then the rip can be closed by hammer-welding. With such a situation the area adjacent to the tear will probably be stretched, but when the metal is welded and hammered, a natural shrinking force is introduced that tends to reduce the stretch. After the initial hammer welding, the area may be treated as a gouge. Keep on shrinking and working the panel until it assumes its original shape.

It is in panel replacement and modification that hammer welding takes on such importance. Unless the panel is pre-shaped to the new contour it is entering (with seams hammer welded), there will be a need for an excessive amount of filler material.

This is not to say that every seam should be hammer welded; far from it. When a panel can be replaced and the joint made by spot welding, riveting, or even ordinary fusion welding—and the joint will not show—fine. But if the seam is in the open and

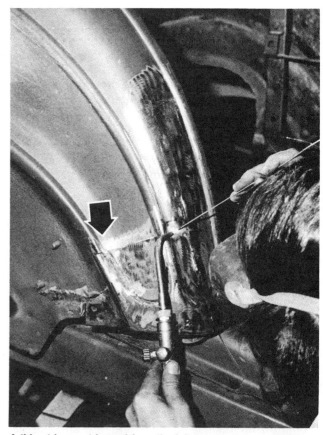

A thin strip was trimmed from the left corner piece so that the center bead would line up on the body, and this was hammer welded in place. The fit of the fenderwell bead (arrow) was accomplished by using the wedge end of a finishing hammer.

affects the panel's strength, hammer welding must be considered.

Take the situation where the bottom edge of an exterior panel has rusted away. Only about 2 inches of the metal is really cancerous, but the replacement strip will be from 3 to 4 inches wide. This strip will usually have very little (or no) crown and will generally include a folded lip of 90 degrees or more. Whether the panel is on a door, cowl, or quarter area doesn't matter. The metalman will be working directly in the middle of a nearly flat surface with heat. That means a high distortion possibility, which requires torch control.

It is absolutely imperative that all hammer welding include the smallest possible weld bead. To accomplish this, the panels to be mated must fit as closely as they can. The replacement panel should be shaped and trimmed first, then held over the area to be replaced and well marked. The bad metal should be cut out with as little distortion as possible. A saber saw or nibbler works well for cutting out the bad sheetmetal.

After the initial rough cut, try the replacement panel on for size. It will generally be off just a whisker because there is usually too much metal remaining on the parent panel. This thin strip may be trimmed off with a good pair of aviation tin snips. The two panel edges should fit flush along the full length with no more than 1/16-inch gap at any part. A gap requires too much filler rod, resulting in a larger bead which isn't desired.

Clamp the pieces together and tack weld the edges. Use very little or no filler rod and make the tack tiny. Speed is important here as well as a very small flame. A correct hammer weld cannot be made if the metal edges lap.

Make sure the edges are level during and after the tack weld. If not, heat the tack in a restricted area and use the hammer and dolly to level the edges. This means a few light taps when the metal is hot.

After the panels are tacked start at one end with the hammer welding process. Be prepared to travel rapidly not so much with the torch as with the hammer and dolly. The railroad dolly is well suited to hammer welding, since it has a number of conven-

Another typical problem that is best solved by hammer welding is replacing a lower, rusted-out area on an early car like this Model A. Here, the rusted section is cut off and the trim line ground straight. Flush fit of the panels to be welded is critical for a good hammer weld.

Vise Grip pliers will keep the panel in place during tack welding; mating surfaces should be hammered up or down to flush exactly during tacking.

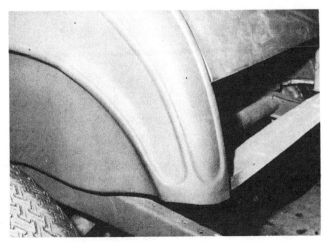
The finished hammer welded repair looks great after a little filling, sanding, and priming.

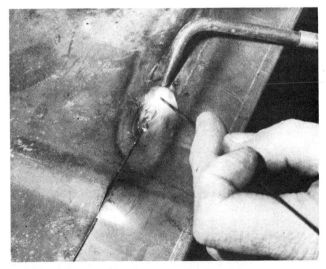
Any time a butt weld is being made, it can distort nearby low crown panels. The torch should have a very small flame; the tip may be laid flatter to direct the flame at the area just welded.

Welding and Brazing

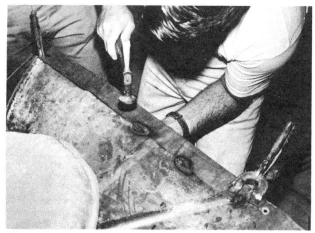

Hammer each tack immediately, as this will tend to shrink the area and eliminate any distortion caused by the heat. It also keeps the edges flush. Don't worry about distortion in the larger panel at this time.

This is how a good fusion weld will look, with a little bead buildup. Such a weld is possible because panels grow together when heated edges melt and form a bond without filler rod drops.

ient crowns and is easy to hold. The hammer face should be nearly flat.

Hammer welding can be done in either of two ways. The simplest method is to weld the entire seam at once then follow with spot heat and the hammer and dolly. A better way is to weld a short 2-inch section, then use the hammer, then weld again. This way the area is still hot from welding and does not need reheating, allowing better control of the metal.

Lay the torch tip more parallel with the plane of travel than with normal fusion welding, thus reducing the heat to the metal. The filler rod can also be held at an opposite low angle to shield the edges. Although the two metal pieces touch, they will tend to grow toward each other even more when heat is applied, allowing the edges to melt and flow together without the necessity of the filler rod. Such flowing may be difficult at first, but can be accomplished easily with experience. An occasional hole will develop which must be filled by a drop from the filler rod.

Immediately upon setting the torch aside, place the dolly against the underside and hold it firmly to the weld. Slap the bead rapidly with the dinging hammer, working back and forth from one end of the seam to the other. This will cause the bead to flatten out and have a shrinking effect on the panel. Continue across the entire joint, alternating between torch and hammer/dolly.

Arc Welding

While an oxyacetylene outfit makes it possible to weld, braze, cut, and heat metal, an AC arc welder does these same things, but in a grander style. An arc welder can build a chassis or engine stand, install a rearend, engine mount, or front axle, or you name it. It's an indispensible item, and used with your acetylene torch, there is little this team can't do.

Arc welders come in a wide array of models. The models range from tiny hobby units to huge commercial welders. The do-it-yourself bodyman should consider an intermediate size arc welder. Typical of the types of arc welders well-suited for the enthusi-

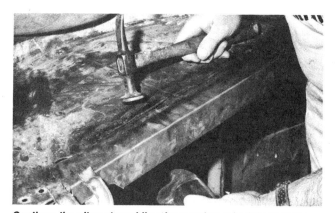

Continue the alternate welding/hammering schedule until the entire joint is closed. Keep the dolly firmly against the underside of the panel to reduce rebound; use hammer smartly.

A pick hammer is used to raise the low spots, but the dolly is kept on top to keep from raising spots too high. This is where experience with the hammer will pay off.

ast are those carried by Sears. The arc welders are rated according to their maximum amperage settings. The higher the amperage the thicker the steel that can be welded. Most arc welders have the capacity to vary their amperage rate. As an example, Sears' best AC arc welder has a range from 30 to 295 amps. The number 9KT20139N arc welder is a dual-range model with a low range for maximum arc stability and a high range for minimum current draw. As with gas torches, the price difference between the top of the line arc welders and the other models isn't very much when you consider the long life span of the welder and the increased versatility of the better units. The arc welders to avoid are the inexpensive little units known as "buzz boxes." These units have such a limited capacity that they aren't good for much automotive work, and they are prone to overheating.

The most poweful home arc welders may require some additional wiring for the average garage since the welders run on 230 volt, 60-Hz. AC power. It is best to wire the system with a 60 amp circuit breaker and direct wiring.

Arc Welding Basics

The keys to successful arc welding are to select the right electrode for the material to be welded and to set the welder at the right heat range for the gauge of metal involved. Practice will teach you how fast to move the electrode, how high to hold it above the work, and which angle is best.

After the welder is connected, connect the

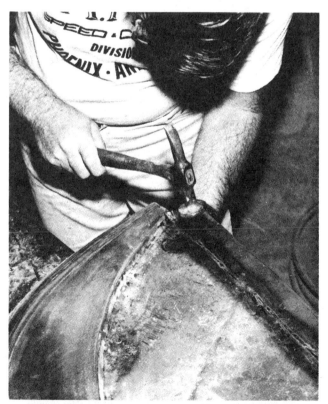

After the new section is hammer welded, the surrounding panel may be worked as necessary since "growth" through heat of welding may cause distortion. In this case, original parts of the weld needed several shrinks to remove "oil-canning."

Although it usually isn't to be found in the average bodyman's tool kit, the shrinking dolly is a handy item. It is grooved to "grip" metal and is used in conjunction with an aluminum hammer.

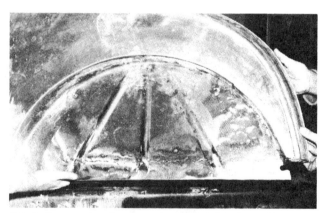

This is the panel as it appears in nearly finished condition. Some tiny low areas remain to be picked up and filed, then the panel will be primed.

ground clamp to the work to be welded. Make sure the connection is good, or you'll waste power and heat up the ground clamp. Use clean dry welding rods (electrodes) and be sure of a positive grip on the electrode by the electrode holder. The thickness of the metal to be welded and the diameter of the electrode determine the amount of heat required for welding. In general, the heavier and thicker a piece of metal is, the larger the electrode and the more heat (amps) it requires. Many welders have guides that indicate what diameter of electrode to use for specific metals. Follow the guidelines, at first, and then use your experience to judge if more or less heat is needed.

If you use too much heat you will burn holes in light metals, or the bead will be flat and porous. Also, the bead will likely "undercut" the work (caused by rapid movement of the rod along its surface, or due to the high heat and insufficient time for the

Welding and Brazing

Arc welders come with a variety of capacities, but only the bigger, heavy-duty units are well-suited for a variety of repair jobs. A perfect welder for the do-it-yourselfer would be a unit like this Sears Craftsman AC dual-range arc welder.

A heavy-duty electrical power source and hookup are necessary for arc welding. This receptical was mounted directly below the fuse box. A 60-amp circuit and direct wiring were employed.

The rate of travel affects the weld as much as the heat setting. Move the arc slowly to ensure proper penetration and enough weld metal deposit. Also, rod movement must be at a consistent speed.

The purpose of the arc is to create an intense heat between the end of the electrode and the surface of the metal to be welded (called the work or base metal). The heat energy generated by the arc is so great that the base metal almost immediately is heated to a liquid state at the point where the arc is directed. This creates a molten pool (puddle) of metal which is always present on the base metal during the welding process.

Making a Bead

The heat that melts the base metal also melts the electrode. As the electrode melts, the metal from it falls through the arc into the molten pool or puddle. This adds additional molten metal, which mixes thoroughly in the puddle, resulting in complete fusion of the two metals. As more metal from the electrode is added and the electrode is moved forward, the material added from the electrode forms a uniform pile of metal known as the "bead."

The first step to arc welding is to strike an arc. This is accomplished by scratching the end of the electrode across the surface to be welded. With a short stroke, scratch the rod end across the base metal close to where you want to weld. You will hear a sputter and see an arc.

As soon as an arc begins burning between the electrode and the base metal, raise the electrode about ⅛ inch above the work. If you don't, it will stick to the work. If it does stick, rock the electrode back and forth until it breaks loose. Keep practicing the art of striking an arc, using different gauges of metal and at different amperages too.

crater to be filled).

Too little heat will result in beads that are too high, as though they lay on top of the work. The bead will also be irregular because of difficulty in holding an arc. With the amperage too low, it is difficult to strike an arc; the electrode will stick to the work and the arc will frequently disappear.

When the right heat is used the bead will lay smoothly over the work without ragged edges. The "puddle" will be at least as deep in the base metal as the rod that lies above it. The sound of the welding operation "crackles," like frying eggs.

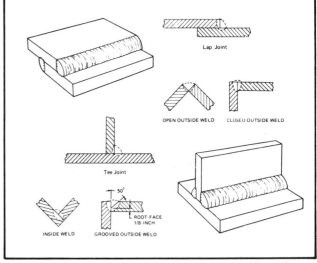

A fillet-weld joint forms a right angle pocket for weld metal deposit. Squaring of edges is usually all the preparation needed. Lap joints are formed by overlapping edges that must touch surface-to-surface on the entire joint for best results. Corner joints are formed by two pieces perpendicular to each other at the edges. On heavy material, the corners must be open or grooved as shown. Tee joints are similar, usually requiring welding on both sides of heavy material.

To lay a bead, first strike an arc and hold it at the starting point for a short time before moving the electrode forward. This ensures good fusion and allows the bead to build up slightly. Bear in mind that the electrode continues to melt off as you move across the work, so you must move the electrode down into the puddle as well as along the path you are following. The electrode should be held at an angle with the end held at a maintained height above the work surface. To ensure proper penetration and evenness, learn to watch the molten pool of metal forming just behind the arc.

The easiest bead to lay is called a stinger bead. It is made by making one continuous pass over the work metal, without any weaving or oscillating movements. If you are right-handed, move from left to right. If left-handed, reverse the movement. With the electrode tipped back toward the direction of travel (about 15 degrees), the arc will throw the molten metal of the puddle away from itself, ensuring good penetration. The average bead, when using a ⅛-inch electrode will be about ⅛ inch high and ¼ inch wide.

Another bead that is commonly used is known as the weave bead. Its purpose is to deposit metal in a wider space than would be possible with the stinger bead. It is accomplished by weaving from one edge of the space to be filled to the other edge and continuing this motion, along with the most satisfactory forward speed of travel. It is a good idea to hesitate momentarily at each edge of the weave so you will provide the same heat at the edges as that in the middle.

Any time two pieces of metal, 3/16 inch or thicker, are butt-welded together the edges should be beveled by grinding. Beveling makes a much better weld, since complete penetration is ensured. Where necessary, a second or third pass over an initial weld can even be made as long as the slag from all previous beads is removed.

An arc welder can be used to weld aluminum, stainless steel, cast iron, and galvanized steel, and for heating, burning holes, brazing, soldering, and so forth, in addition to welding mild steel. While the electrode holder and various types of electrodes will take care of most of these jobs, a convenient accessory is a carbon arc torch. The carbon arc torch is used with an arc welder to braze, solder, heat, bend, and weld aluminum and copper alloys.

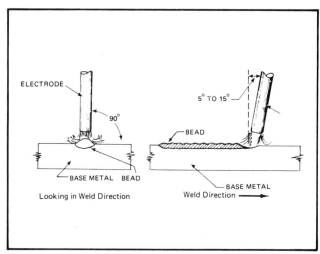

When arc welding, hold electrode perpendicular, but tilt the top or holder end in the direction it is moving (weld direction). Feed your electrode at a uniform rate down to the plate as it melts and forms a bead.

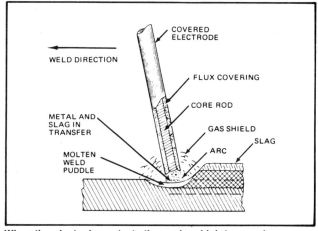

When the electrode contacts the work, a high-temperature arc forms. The heat is controlled by current and space between the rod and the work. The flux coating provides a gas shield against contamination from the air.

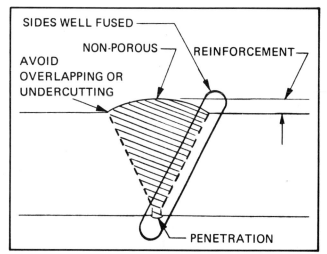

The completed weld should be thoroughly fused to the base metal throughout the groove area. The weld metal should penetrate to the root of the joint with a small amount extending below the surface to ensure a full section weld. At the face of the weld, there is usually a buildup known as "reinforcement."

There is a wide choice of arc welding electrodes on the market for every type of material, including cast iron. Match the electrode to the specific job.

Replacing Panels

Let's face it, nobody really likes dents (except maybe body shop operators). If they did, dents would be offered as optional equipment on new cars. But accidents do happen, giving us the dents the original equipment manufacturers so kindly leave out, and there's really nothing you can do about them except get them fixed.

The economics of dent removal and repair is a complicated matter. Estimating body repair costs takes training and practice. But one fact is very clear: it is often cheaper and easier to replace a body panel completely than to try to hammer and dolly out all the kinks and bends. This is especially true if it is a fairly sizeable body piece, such as a door, fender, or quarter panel. Though replacement sheetmetal, whether purchased from a dealer or an auto salvage yard, can be very expensive, that cost is often less than the labor costs involved in repairing the damaged original. If you decide that replacement is the way to restore an entire or partial panel, this is how to go about it.

Removing Old Panels

Practically every portion of a car's body is available in replacement form from the manufacturer, but exterior panels are normally the only units replaced. Such external pieces include fenders, hoods, rocker panels, and the like.

Before you can replace a damaged panel, you must remove the old one. The method of removal depends largely on how the factory attached the panel in the first place. As a rule, large panels that can be easily distorted by heat are spot welded. Areas that are not easily distorted, or where stress may be concentrated (such as quarter panels), are usually fusion welded in several related seams. Fender panels are usually bolted on and require no welding. If a panel is to be replaced, the general area must be roughed into alignment before the panel is removed.

Panels may be removed in several different ways. If spot welding is involved, each spot weld may be

In some cases there is no question whether to replace or repair. This front fender is definitely beyond saving. It must be replaced.

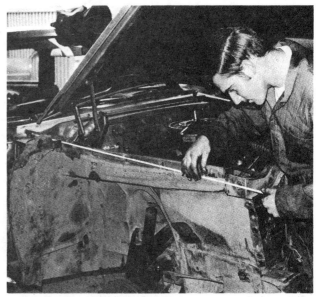

Before installing the new fender, the inner fender panels must be jacked out. Check measurements from the new fender bolt holes on inner panels so they won't be stretched too far.

drilled using a ¼-inch drill bit. Areas near a fusion weld may be cut away with a torch if distortion can be limited and there is no danger of setting the interior on fire. Probably the best all-around tool for removing panels is the air chisel. Air chisels are great time savers in addition to their advantage of producing very little panel distortion when properly used. Other popular tools include the old standby metal snips or cutters, and electric saber saws.

When a fusion weld is to be parted, it is wise to cut below the weld (toward the damaged panel) about 1 inch. This is particularly true if a torch is used. The final trim up to the original weld should be made with a pair of aircraft-type tin snips.

Once a panel has been removed, take time to repair or treat the structure underneath as needed. In the case of replacing a panel to repair rust damage, you must remove any inner rust before reskinning or the rust will return immediately.

Partial Panel Replacement

It is not always necessary to replace an entire panel when only a portion of it is damaged. To replace a partial panel, first mark off the area that must be cut out and carefully inspect the remaining part of the panel for damage or distortion. Measure the exact location of the marked off area and transfer these measurements to the replacement panel (obtained from an auto dismantler, parts car, or factory parts outlet).

Cut the replacement section from the second panel, making the edges as straight as possible. Place this piece against the original panel and scribe a mark around the edge. Cut away the original panel along the scribe lines. Straighten the edges to be matched (body edge and replacement panel edges); then butt weld the new panel into place. Tack weld the section every 3 or 4 inches to avoid heat distortion before finish welding. Finish off as a normal repair.

From here it's a matter of bolting on new pieces and rechecking the fit. While this repair used an NOS factory fender, sheetmetal from a wrecking yard, if straight, works just as well.

When replacing panels, you'll usually need some minor, or sometimes major, adjustment of the bolts that hold the sheetmetal in order to get the gaps between the panels even.

Replacing Panels

This is another example of a good candidate for panel replacement. The rear panel is caved in, and the quarter panel is badly wrinkled.

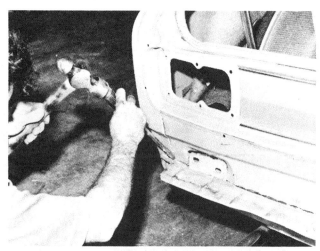

After removing the bumper and trim pieces, a chisel and torch are used to free the tack welded panels from the main body.

After all the tack welds are cut, the entire corner of the body is removed. A torch was used to remove the major portion of the rear quarter panel.

Quarter Panel Replacement

Replacement, rather than repair, of a quarter panel may often be easier, especially for beginning bodymen. Quarter panels are usually riveted along the door post and at the deck opening flange, with fusion welds where it mates to the top. A typical removal would be accomplished by drilling the spot welds and chiseling, torching, or snipping just below the fusion welds. The replacement panel should be trimmed a little long so it can be slid under the original body. Align the new panel with the body and drill holes down the overlap seam, using rivets to hold the panel in place. The replacement panel should be tacked and finish welded and the rivets ground smooth. Finish the repair as normal.

Door Panel Replacement

Other than the front fenders and quarter panels, the doors are replaced more often than any other part of cars. Replacement is usually due to excessive damage or rust that occurs when the door's water drain holes have become plugged. A door can be fully or partially replaced, depending on the damage.

Late-model cars usually have a window opening structure separate from the door panel, which means replacement panels come only to the window. Earlier model cars have panels that carry through to the window opening edges. This means earlier doors will need to be cut and welded somewhere near the top of the door panel, usually just below the window. (Deck lid and hood panels are crimped to the substructure much the same as doors, so replacement is similar.) Again, as with all panel replacement, be careful when welding not to distort the sheetmetal with the heat from the welder.

One consideration when replacing a door, hood, or trunk panel is that often the cost of a good used item is less than the replacement panel plus the cost of repair.

Replacing Top Panels

It is possible for even the beginner to replace a top panel without too much trouble. It is necessary to check the alignment of the roof substructure be-

When cutting a major body panel, have the replacement panel on hand so you'll know where to cut.

Grind off all paint where the new quarter panel will join the main body structure so the pieces can be tack welded together.

The inner fender edge must be drilled every few inches where it rests against the wheelwell. Then it is tack welded into place.

fore replacement, using a tape measure to check it corner to corner, side to side, and front to back. When the substructure has been pushed out and aligned with the doors, remove the front and rear windows. Remove the damaged top, using an air chisel, saber saw, or torch to cut about 1 inch in from the drip rail. After the major panel has been removed, the small remaining strip can be rolled off like a sardine can lid. An alternative method is to drill out all the spot welds.

After the panel is removed, dress down the sharp edges left by the spot welder and try the new panel for fit. It should drop right into place. If it doesn't, the substructure probably isn't aligned correctly. The top panel is then welded into position (use metal screws to hold it in place while the welds are being made) by either spot welding or spot brazing. Finish the repair as normal.

Panel Joints

There are four basic types of joints involved in panel replacement: butt welds, rivet laps, recessed lap joints, and the flange joint. Butt welds (butting two pieces of metal together and welding the seam), and the rivet lap (over-lapping two pieces of metal and using rivets to hold them in place while welding) are the quickest ways to join panels together. More involved are the recessed lap joints, where a recess is placed into the edge of the upper or lower panel so the mating panel will be flush in contour, and the flange joint, where both panels have a 90 degree approximate flange at the mating edge so that they can be joined by rivets or welds.

A recessed lap joint is usually made on the original panel in a high crown area, such as a door. Sheetmetal screws are used in the recess to keep everything aligned while the lap ends are welded; then the screws are removed and the holes filled.

A flange joint is used after the contours of the body and replacement panel are matched perfectly. A clamp is used to hold the flanges together while they are mated together with sheetmetal screws or rivets. The tiny crack that remains on the exterior is filled with body filler or lead.

Which joint you use is usually determined by the location and size of the panel being replaced. Always make sure the welds are secure and properly ground down before finishing your repair; also be careful to avoid heat damaging the new panels.

The upper edge of the quarter panel is likewise welded to the body panel. Then the rear panel is tack welded at intervals and all visible seams filled.

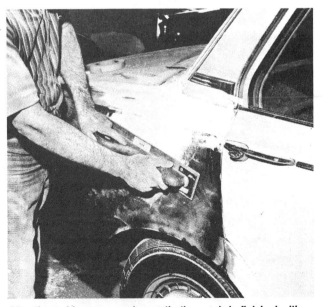

After the welds are ground smooth, the repair is finished with body filler to smooth the joints.

Frame Kinks

Repairing a car body is one thing, but don't forget that everything is based on a trouble-free skeleton.

There are two methods used in the manufacture of today's automobiles to provide a substructure or backbone upon which the car is assembled. The first and oldest method uses a heavy steel frame. The second method uses what is called unit construction where all, or a large majority, of the car is built as a self-structuring assembly with myriad channels and double thicknesses that provide the rigidity required. In either case, the body provides stiffness to the chassis, and vice versa.

And in the event of a severe collision, this backbone or skeleton is often twisted, bent, or otherwise misaligned and must be straightened before the component parts of the body undergo repair.

Truck frames are built for strength; they are designed to carry a maximum load without failure. However, a different design philosophy is followed for automobile frames. A passenger car frame is built to contribute good ride characteristics to the car. Suspension, shock absorbers, tires, and

motor mounts all contribute to overall ride performance. But without a satisfactory frame as a starting point, the ride suffers. In addition, the performance of the body—the noise level, and the degree of body shake and vibration—is a function of the rigidity of the frame.

Over the years, the auto frame has been called upon to carry greater and greater proportions of the total vehicle load. In the early days, car design was based on bridge design and strength was built into the roof

1. In order to insure strength and integrity of repairs, it is necessary to arc weld any ripped or cracked areas in a frame that occur during routine frame straightening process.

2. It is often necessary to heat buckled frames to accomplish a normal repair. Bill Chisholm, of Vanowen Brake & Wheel, North Hollywood, Calif., uses a natural gas torch rather than oxyacetylene, as it gives a cleaner heat and allows a larger area to be heated. Care must be taken not to "Spot Heat" when working on frames as this results in overheating and damage to frame. Proper way is start well out on buckles and move towards the center. In this way a large area is heated to a cherry red, rather than just one small spot.

3. In order to make frames accessible for repairs, it's sometimes necessary to strip the frame of bolt-on parts. An exposed frame is easier to work on during servicing.

4. In this view, a buckled frame horn on Olds Toronado is being heated and pulled on frame rack to straighten it out.

5. Tom Powers and Mike Fortier work at task of positioning the door opening to accept stock door, with hydraulic Porto-Power unit, capable of 10 tons pressure. This is used in conjunction with frame rack, but is for more localized work.

6. Specialty equipment companies have a continuing research program into better ways to repair automobile sheet metal and frames. This complex arrangement from Blackhawk Mfg. Co. includes rails imbedded in concrete. Hydraulic jacks and chains are then used to apply pulling forces.

4

5

Frame Kinks

and pillars much as it was built into the truss members of a bridge. But that has all changed. Increased glass area, reduction in pillar size for styling and visibility considerations, and smaller, lighter roofs have all decreased the load-carrying capabilities of the upper portions of the car. As a result of these changes, a greater burden has been placed on the frame.

Race car builders realize the importance of the frame for achieving predictable, repeatable handling characteristics. In a car such as a NASCAR stocker or a Trans-Am sedan, where space and styling are not primary considerations, bridge-like roll cage structures are incorporated not only for safety but to increase the rigidity of the basic frame design.

Since the frame has such importance, it should be checked anytime

1

2

3

1. With this type of equipment, the worker can pull frame structures and body metal at the same time, cutting down on labor time and customer cost.

2. The hydraulic jack has long been associated with bodywork, is best used to pull rather than push.

3. The home craftsman is not likely to own specialty hydraulic jacks such as the scissor-jaw head shown, but such items can be rented or borrowed. The body man studies the area of impact carefully before using jack.

4. This is the type of equipment the average body shop will have, with various attachments designed for special or unusual jobs.

5. This is the type of pushing jack commonly associated with body and fender repairs; it is here being positioned to push crushed top back into shape. Base of jack is supported on rigid part of flooring.

Description . . . Diamond is a condition where one side of the car has been moved to the rear (or front) causing the frame and/or body to be out of square . . . a figure similar to a parallelogram.

How To Recognize . . . Diamond is caused by a hard impact on a corner or off-center from the front or rear. Visual indications are hood and trunk lid misalignment. Buckles may appear in the quarter panel near the rear wheel housing or at the roof to quarter panel joint. Wrinkles and buckles probably will appear in the passenger compartment and/or

trunk floor. There usually will be some mash and sag combined with the diamond.

How To Locate . . . Diamond damage is determined by cross checking the diagonal dimensions of the frame with a tram gage. Normally, these diagonal measurements are equal to each other . . . the length from the right front to left rear is the same as the length from the left front to the right rear. If these dimensions are different, diamond is present. Diamond can also be measured from the center of a cross-member diagonally across the car to the side rails.

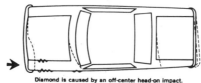

Diamond is caused by an off-center head-on impact.

The damage will extend the full length of the car because one rail has been moved rearward.

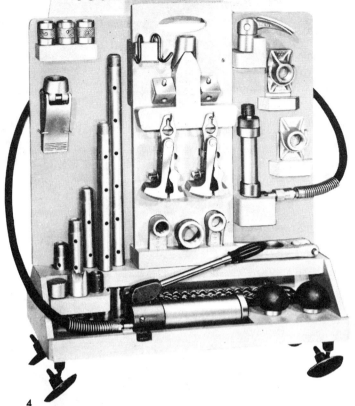

Snap-on
FOUR TON BODY JACK

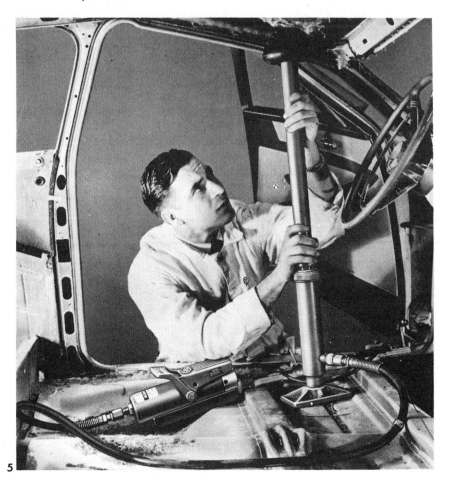

4

5

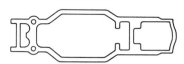

PERIMETER FRAME

This frame is separate from the body and forms a border that surrounds the passenger compartment. It extends forward for power train and suspension support . . . it extends to the rear for trunk and suspension support. Generally, it consists of box or channel-type rails joined by a torque box at the four corners. The torque boxes transfer the primary loads to the frame . . . however, the complete frame relies heavily on the body structure for rigidity.

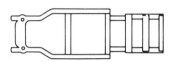

LADDER FRAME

Historically, this type of frame was the forerunner of the various types found on today's vehicles. The ladder frame is similar to the perimeter frame, but the rails do not completely surround the passenger compartment. The rails have less offset and are built on a more direct line between the front and rear wheels. This structure generally has several crossmembers and is reasonably rigid within itself. It forms a strong support on which the body is mounted.

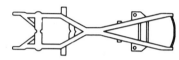

X-TYPE FRAME

Designed as an elongated letter X, this type of frame narrows to a strong junction at the center section. It has considerable front and rear stiffness and a rigid center section. Usually, it has three or more crossmembers to provide torsional stability. However, there are no crossmembers in the center section of the vehicle. This frame forms a rigid structure for the vehicle for mounting the power train, running gear and the body components.

UNITIZED CONSTRUCTION

In this type of construction, every member is related to another so that all sections tend to be load-bearing members. The floor pans, rocker panels, etc. in the lower portion of the body are integrally joined so as to form a basic structure. Heavy reinforcement is used where the engine and suspension are mounted. The front portion generally looks like a separate frame . . . however, the rails are welded to the body structure thereby forming an integral support.

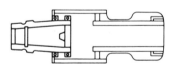

UNITIZED WITH BOLT-ON STUB FRAME

This configuration is found in several models and is particularly noticeable in some front-wheel drive vehicles. A strong, heavy stub frame is utilized to support the engine, accessories, power train and running gear. This frame may have strong, sturdy crossmembers and will extend backward under the floor pan. Back of the cowl, the remaining structure follows the conventional unitized or integral design. The front stub frame is bolted to the unitized body section.

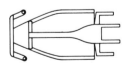

PLATFORM CONSTRUCTION

Somewhat similar to unitized construction, this underbody consists of a reinforced, fairly flat section that forms the entire lower portion of the car. Volkswagon and similar types of cars utilize this construction technique. The lower section which includes the floor pans is a bolt-on assembly which is joined to the body. Therefore, this section depends on the rest of the body for rigidity. It serves as a support member for the engine, running gear and body structure.

Frame Kinks

a vehicle is damaged. This is necessary because of the possibility that the frame or frame structure has also been damaged. While some of the damage may be obvious, misalignment can be involved to a great extent without being seen. In checking for misalignment, diagonal measurements are the quickest method, but in making repairs, referral to original factory information is highly suggested.

1. In the absence of good pulling equipment, the hydraulic jack is used to push frame substructures back into place. When working with jacks measure the amount of progress several times. Do not overdo it.

2. Most body shops are now equipped with this type of lighter-duty beam puller. The beam is attached securely to the vehicle at strong points, then force is applied to pull frame or sheetmetal back into place.

3. In the absence of jacking equipment, the beginner may use this photograph to identify the type of jack head he may need for a particular job and rent or borrow that piece from the local body shop.

4. For straightening frame horns and flanges, Buske Industries makes two wrenches designed to slip onto the flange, utilizing the angled slots, for straightening in many positions.

5. This schematic of a 1970 Ford Mustang is an illustration from the Tru-Way Auto Body & Frame dimension book used by professional frame shops. This is an example of a working chart of the automobile chassis as the repairman sees it, with figures given in inches. These charts are intended to simplify and eliminate error in establishing the location of exact measuring points on the frame.

6. A body-frame straightener such as this rack type is an important piece of machinery in any large body shop. All the major types of damage—diamond, mash, sag, sidesway, and twist—can be repaired on such a straightener.

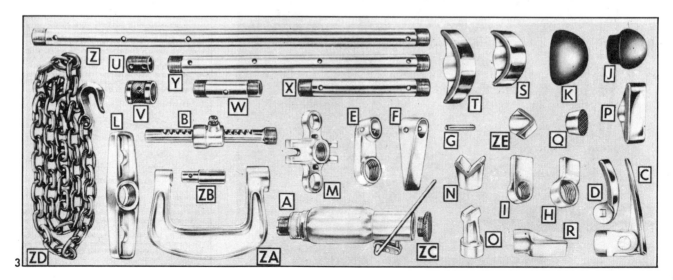

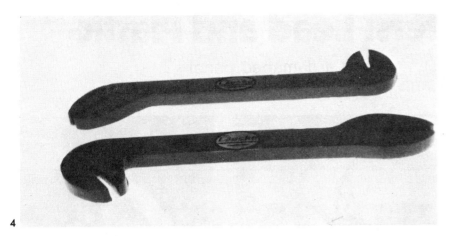

4

Frame checking is usually done at three stages: in assessing how much damage is involved, during the repair, and as a final repair check. The frame can be considered in three parts—front, center and rear—with the front being from the firewall forward, the center the portion covered by the passenger compartment, and the rear what is left.

Frame damage can run the gamut from twisting, to collapse of one section, to slight misalignment. In all cases where frame damage is suspected, the enthusiast should entrust the vehicle to a frame shop for repair. Such shops are completely equipped with necessary gauges and equipment to check and repair the frame. Repair of the major frame is not a backyard project. It is possible to replace small front frame extensions, called frame horns, but nothing larger should be attempted in the home garage.

It is possible to save considerable money on a frame repair by removing all sheetmetal that might be in the way. If the frame shop does not have to spend time just getting to the job, the resulting cost savings will be about eight dollars an hour. And a savings like that is as important to you as a frame is to an automobile. 🖼

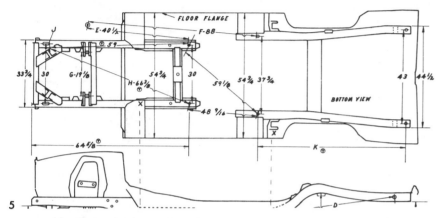

5

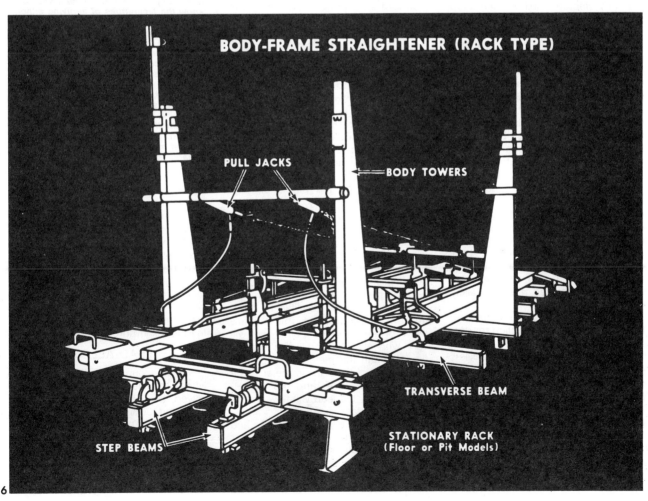

6

The Cheaters: Lead and Plastic

If you can't repair a damaged panel with hammer and dolly, there's another way—fill it!

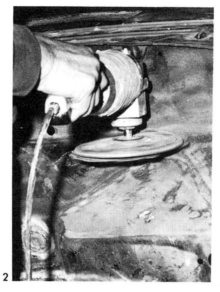

Body fillers, whether plastic or lead, are perhaps the most abused of all repair materials. It is very easy for a beginner to form the unsatisfactory habit of filling a low spot when very little effort would be required to straighten the damage. In many cases, it would be much faster to repair the metal, and save the added cost of the filler. Excessive use of filler breeds poor work traits and, usually, poor workmanship. This has become especially pronounced with the introduction of quality plastic fillers which can be applied by the very unskilled normally with poor results.

Body fillers also tend to be overused by the pseudo customizer who would take shortcuts to disguise the lack of real customizing talent. The employment of plastic or lead is an essential part of body repair and modification, but their use should be limited. When fillers are used, they must be applied with care. Experience comes with use, and as more experience is gained, the less fillers will be used.

Lead solder has been utilized in basic automobile construction for decades, and will undoubtedly continue for many years to come. Plastic fillers are relatively new, and while they do some jobs quite well, they are not to be considered a total replacement for lead. In this respect, the neophyte customizer would do well to concentrate on learning the use of lead first, then go about picking up the few remaining secrets of plastic.

Practically all automobile bodies use lead to some degree during the initial construction, usually at the visible points of panel mating. This would be where the top panel mates with the quarter panels, where the deck-lid skirt panels mate with the quarter panels, on the cowl panels, etc. However, the amount of lead used here is very small, and it's sometimes necessary for the repairman or customizer to melt this lead when replacing or modifying the panel.

Lead is not an unusual substance, but it does have some peculiar properties when correctly alloyed which make it especially well suited for automotive body application. Lead can be heated and easily shaped, it bonds perfectly and permanently to sheetmetal, it is easy to finish very smooth, and it will accept paint like sheetmetal.

Lead will bond to metals because it will tin the surface with its own properties, although tinning is often accomplished with a secondary compound, but the lead itself can be used. This is made possible by heating the sheetmetal to the melting point of the lead (a point that will vary with alloy), using some kind of flux to clean the metal, and applying a thin coat of lead. If the metal is the right temperature and has been cleaned well, the lead will flow across the metal surface like water.

Lead that is alloyed for body and fender repair has its own peculiar melting characteristics, in that it does not melt from a solid to a liquid immediately. Most body leads start to soften about 360°F. and become

1. The use of lead isn't as common as it once was, but it is still used in customizing and restoring. Plastic is the way to go for a commercial body shop, but the metal man should know the techniques of applying either.

2. The subject at hand is a firewall on a '36 Ford undergoing restoration. It had been drilled full of holes for various accessories over the years, and was dinged up in general. First step is to weld up holes, then grind paint, rust, and scale away. A #24 grit disc is used initially.

3. A small rotary wire brush chucked in a drill motor is used to clean all foreign matter from welded seams. Cleanliness before leading is a must.

softer as the temperature is raised. The point at which a particular lead compound will melt is determined by the percentage of tin in the mixture. Furthermore, the body lead alloy will melt below the melting point of pure lead, 620°F., and it may be below the melting point of tin at 455°F. The higher the amount of tin in a compound, the lower the melting point, and this must be understood when lead is being purchased.

LEAD ALLOYS

For all-around shop use, especially where considerable customizing is involved, the 70-30 alloy is best (70% lead and 30% tin). This alloy melts just under 500°F., which gives a wide latitude or plasticity for working in prolonged areas. Lead is available in a wide range of percentages, but anything other than 70-30 or 80-20 is not easy to use. A good example of

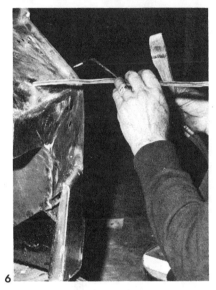

4. A small indentation left when a hole was welded shut is similarly cleaned with a rotary deburring tool.

5. A lead alloy comprised of 70% lead and 30% tin, and available in stick form, is used in car bodywork. Lead will be heated then spread like butter with a wooden paddle, but beeswax (or oil) should be on paddle surface to keep lead from sticking.

6. Note flame adjustment of torch. Tip of flame is allowed to lick over end of lead stick until it softens and begins to crumble. Stick is then pushed onto metal into a low "pile."

this is the solder (lead is really a solder) used for other types of repair work, such as radiators. This particular compound is normally of the 50-50 variety, and the temperature range between where it becomes soft and where it melts is very narrow.

The necessity for lead is usually restricted to filling up low spots if good repair practices have been followed, and even then the area to be filled should be minor. However, this is not necessarily the case with customizing, where lead is usually used to cover a welded seam or as a filler to make a difficult reverse crown. No matter where the lead is used, the steps for application are similar.

There are certain basic steps involved in using body fillers, whether they be lead or plastic. In the case of lead, the area must be cleaned, tinned, filled, shaped and finished. With plastic, tinning is not involved. In the case of the beginner, nearly every one of these steps can lead to unsatisfactory results if these correct procedures are not followed. Remember, if the surface is not cleaned right, the lead may not stick. If the surface isn't tinned right, the lead won't stay in place. It is not easy to apply at first (especially on vertical panels), and shaping can be overdone. The entire job can be botched by careless finishing. Even so, leading is not difficult to master if the beginner is patient and willing to practice.

Paint, welding scale and rust are the foreign agents that are normally on any surface to be leaded. It is necessary to clean a larger area than will be covered with lead, since the filler must blend perfectly into the surrounding metal. An open-coat disc on the power sander will remove the initial paint, while a cup-shaped wire brush on the same sander will make short work of any weld scale or rust in the cavities. If this type of wire brush is not available, a smaller brush in an electric drill, or even a hand brush, can be used. The small abrasions left in the metal from the disc sander make an ideal surface for the lead to adhere to.

Acids have been used as cleaning agents, but they are more trouble than they're worth. Muriatic acid can remove weld scale and rust; paint stripper will take off paint, but these chemicals do seep down in hidden cracks and will come out and haunt you later after the finish paint is on.

After the surface has been cleaned of all foreign materials—that is, the surface is all bright and shiny (this is difficult if a welded seam is to be leaded, but it's essential)—the entire area must be thoroughly tinned. Lead will have difficulty sticking to the metal unless it has been properly tinned.

TINNING FLUX

Some kind of tinning flux is necessary, as the flux is a chemical cleaner of the steel. Since this is usually a two-step operation in bodywork, the flux will leave a burned residue after tinning and must be wiped away before lead is added. Tinning flux comes in a variety of types, but the kind normally associated with other forms of soldering is not acceptable in bodywork. Auto supply stores carry a wide range of tinning agents, in-

The Cheaters

cluding the pure-liquid type and the popular compounds, composed of flux and powdered lead. The compound has the advantage of applying the tinning lead at the same time the cleaner is being applied.

When tinning with the compounds, some method must be devised to get the compound onto the heated surface. This can be nothing more than a wadded rag, but the best is a piece of tightly wound steel wool gripped in pliers. The steel wool is pushed around in the tinning powder then applied directly to the heated panel.

When a liquid flux is used, the area to be tinned is first lightly heated then the flux brushed on. *Remember: heat applied during leading must be very closely controlled since it can distort panels, particularly those of the low-crown variety.* After the area is brushed with tinning liquid, heat the metal with brief passes of the torch until it is hot enough to melt the lead pressed against the surface. When pressing the lead bar, just a small mound will melt; then as the metal becomes too cold, the bar crumbles. A slight twisting motion of the bar will help get the correct amount. Repeat this brief heat and solder treatment to about one-third the area to be covered with lead.

At all times, the heat is applied in very brief brushing strokes, then removed. This controls the heat of the panel and the lead at a fairly constant level, somewhere between initial lead softening and actual melting. Of course, during tinning, the lead is actually melted.

To spread the lead over the surface and thereby gain the full tinning advantage, heat an area around a lead mound or two. As the lead changes appearance from the solid, grainy look to a shiny look (careful here because the change is rapid), wipe it across the panel with a wadded clean rag. Make all the wipes in the same direction, and make sure the entire area is tinned. There will be a series of overlapping wipe strokes, and when slightly cooled the tinned area will appear dull in contrast with the freshly sanded steel. While the lead is being wiped over the surface to get a good tin, the flux residue is being wiped away. It's obvious that tinning is an alternate heat-and-wipe situation. Compounds are best wiped with a rag after application, also.

Be careful when using heat and the rag on a tinned area. If too much pressure is applied to the rag, the tinning film can be completely wiped away. If too much heat is used over a tinned surface, the film can burn

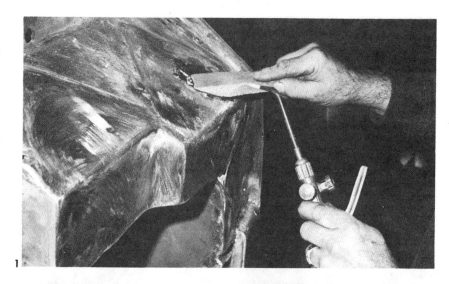

1. While lead remains in near-molten state, paddle is used to push lead around. Flame is repeatedly applied to keep lead nearly molten.

2. Vertical areas are difficult to do since lead melts and falls away, but practice will make such jobs easier. Lead is allowed to build up higher than surrounding surface; since second coat cannot be applied.

3. The #24-grit disc may be used for grinding lead, but a finer abrasive grit is better for the beginner as lead tends to cut rapidly away and it's easy to grind too deep and ruin the job. Grinding is primarily to clean surface crust off lead, knock down the high spots, until surface is shiny wherever lead was used.

away. If a surface will not take a complete tinning, that is, if there are some small spots of bare metal that continue to show, it means the metal is not completely clean. Don't leave small, uncleaned and untinned spots and hope to bridge over with lead, such as craters in a welded seam. Get the metal as clean as you possibly can!

CONTROLLED HEAT

Up to this point, it is possible the

lead procedure could have been accomplished with a welding torch, or a blow torch, or even a cutting torch. Practically any kind of heating flame could have been used, provided the heat was used sparingly. But from now on the heat must be controlled more carefully, so properly adjusting the torch is of utmost importance.

Unlike all phases of welding, leading only requires a soft flame, a flame that is spread over a wide area. Generally, a medium-size tip is selected, one that might be used for welding slightly heavier steel gauge then sheetmetal. The acetylene is turned on as with welding and the torch is lit. Next the oxygen valve is opened slightly. The idea is to get a long, fuzzy flame, which is usually made up of a long, irregular blue cone with touches of yellow at the extreme tip. Even if the flame is toward the yellow side, it will still work.

When applying this flame to the metal, keep the tip well back and use just the end of the flame. Let it "lick" at the work. This will get the temperature up near where you want it and keep it there without undue heat concentration in a single, small area. Use the flame on the lead similar to the way it is used with brazing; flick the

flame tip onto the metal, pass it across the lead, then flick it away. Now repeat this process until the desired results are achieved.

It is important to learn good torch control before the application of lead can even be considered, since merely keeping the unfinished lead on the panel will seem almost impossible at first. The secret is in keeping the lead at that particular temperature between first softening and melting.

The beginner is advised to work on horizontal, flat panels at first, until some experience has been gained in learning to recognize when lead is beginning to soften and how to control the torch flame. The beginner trying to lead a vertical panel, such as a door, will find most of the material on the ground. At the same time, using a relatively flat practice panel, such as a hood, will encourage good heating habits. Remember again, too much heat and the panel will distort.

APPLYING LEAD

Lead can be applied in one of two basic methods: from the bar or from a mush pot. The former is the most common for smaller areas, the latter is better for large areas or for beginners who have trouble keeping the

bar at the right application temperature. The mush pot is nothing more than a melting container in which lead bar(s) have been melted. The torch is kept directed toward the pot when not being played over the metal surface to keep the lead plastic, but not at the runny, melted state. The lead is then scooped out of the pot on a leading paddle and applied to the metal surface, like stucco on a building wall. The metal surface must be kept at the right temperature, too, but since the large mass of lead is well heated, it can be spread with the paddle (a kind of wooden trowel) over a relatively large area. A mush pot can be anything, even an old hubcap. However, such a large amount of lead would mean either poor metalwork, or a very large welded seam. The latter is common to many customizing projects, such as top chopping and body sectioning. In these cases, it is best to hammer weld the seam, but if this isn't possible, the leading practice must be accepted. Even so, the lead is applied over a relatively narrow band.

More common is the application of the lead directly from the solid-bar state. If the panel is horizontal, this isn't too difficult since the melted

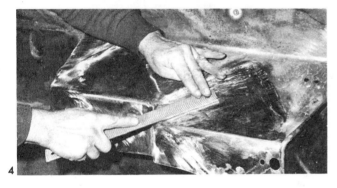

4. Final step in leading is to use a fine-toothed body file to bring the leaded areas down to height of adjoining original metal. If low spots or cavities show up from cross-filing, more lead cannot be added, as it will ruin previous work. Solution is to leave necessary filling to heavy priming and lots of block sanding.

5. The advent of plastic fillers that do not need heat to harden, have made it easy for sheer novices to become "body men." Plastic should never be applied over metal more than ¼-inch deep. This cross section piece was obviously "fixed" by a hair-brain.

6. Plastic fillers rely on a catalyst for hardening. There are many types available today, but in all cases go strictly by the manufacturers' instructions when mixing in the hardener. If not, you may have to wait a month for the stuff to set up, or just a few seconds. Thirty minutes is ideal hardening time, for it allows you to carefully apply the stuff, then take a breather before filing begins.

The Cheaters

lead will run onto the metal and puddle. Anywhere else, however, the puddle will continue to run onto the ground. When applying lead in this manner, heat the panel until the right temperature is reached, then the flame is played over the tip of the lead bar, usually about one inch of the tip. As the bar tip softens it is pressed onto the panel and the bar will break off right where it is too cold to stick. This can be accentuated by twisting the bar slightly as it is being pressed onto the panel. This procedure is repeated over the panel until enough lead has been applied. It is better to get too much than too little but more lead can be added as needed. Until experience is gained, keep pressure on the lead stick and make it crumple onto the panel.

The appearance of the lead is the key of successful working. When the solid bar begins to get shiny on one of the exposed edges, the temperature is about right for the plastic state. If the torch flame is kept on the lead, the shiny appearance will spread throughout the bar, which usually means the temperature is too high. When this happens, the lead will suddenly become liquid and run off the panel. Keeping pressure on the bar as it is heated will cause the bar to fold into the metal when it is hot enough, yet well before it becomes liquid. As a rule, apply the rough-lead buildup in the center of the working area.

Lead paddles are rather peculiar things in that any specific paddle probably will not feel exactly ''right'' when new, but even the beginner may find that an older, used paddle feels perfect the first time. Generally, new paddles seem large, sometimes unwieldy. There are good arguments for all sizes of paddles, but one about 4 inches long, excluding the curved

1. Never mix more plastic filler than you're going to use at a given time. The stuff left over will harden just as fast as that applied to the car. Although cardboard may be used as a mixing surface, as in previous photo, sheetmetal or glass is better, since foreign matter must not get mixed into plastic. After catalyst is added, the goo is thoroughly mixed.

2. This quarter panel had really taken a beating. Because the owner couldn't afford new sheetmetal, body man Lennie Morris repaired the damaged quarter panel.

3. Attempt at reaching the lower portion of the panel by crimping the trunk floorpan failed.

4. Attacking from the outside, Morris pokes holes through the quarter panel. A Morgan knocker is then inserted to pull the bow out of the metal.

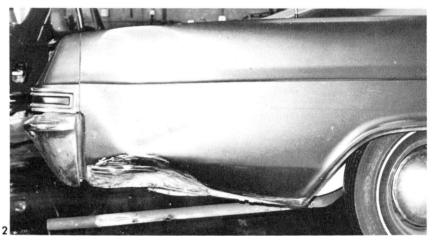

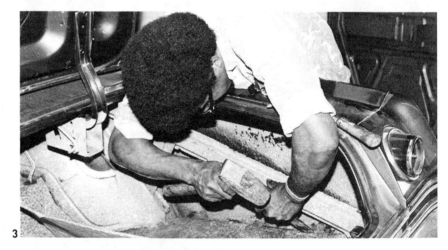

handle, is good for beginners. Paddles are made of quality hardwood, with a variety of face shapes ranging from flat to very high crowns. At least one flat and one half-round design should be in every toolbox.

The hardwood paddle can be burned by the flame, as most well-used paddles invariably are. This is bound to happen with so much alternation between flame and paddle on the lead surface, but burning will be reduced to a minimum as more experience with flame control is gained. Also, lead will tend to stick to the plain paddle. To counteract this tendency, the paddle face must be treated with a thin film of oil or beeswax. An ideal paddle lubricator can be made by cutting the side from a polish tin, then folding an oil soaked rag therein. Very lightly heat the paddle face and rub it on the rag, repeating as found necessary during the paddle process. Some body men feel beeswax has a better lubricating quality than oil. The minute the lead seems to drag or stick to the paddle, it should be lubricated as soon as possible.

PADDLING LEAD

Getting the lead onto the panel initially will seem extremely simple compared to paddling the lead out, simply because there is a certain amount of manual dexterity required in coordinating the flame and paddle. Still, paddling lead is not unlike plastering a wall. Imagine yourself standing at a wall. The plaster trowel is usually held in the right hand, and the mortar board in the left. As a glob of plaster is stuck to the wall, it is immediately troweled out, otherwise the glob would fall. This alternating between left and right hands becomes a smooth movement with practice.

The same goes for paddling lead. The paddle is held in the prime working hand (left or right, as the case may be) and the torch in the opposite hand. The beginner will have a tendency to overheat the area at first, which may cause the lead alloy to separate into lumps of lead and tin. If this happens, more lead must be applied. The direct reaction to this overheat is an underheat, where the beginner then tries to work lead that is too cold to be spread.

Getting the lead and the surrounding metal up to the right temperature is done by holding the flame well away from the panel, with the tip of the soft flame just licking the surface. Move the flame over the area to be worked, which includes the metal and the lead, never stopping in any one spot. The idea is to heat everything uniformly, but it does not mean heating an area bigger than can be worked with a few paddle strokes.

Watch the sharp edges of the lead during this heating; mash down on the lead buildup often, as a test. The minute one little edge of lead starts to brighten, the entire area of lead being heated is close to the plastic working state. Move the torch rapidly from this point on, flicking back to the lead only momentarily to keep the heat up.

The beginner will keep the lead in place by mashing down on it at first, which will show how soft and workable it really is. The torch plays across the lead and the paddle is used to push the lead around where it is needed. Rather than scrape the lead across the panel, it should be pulled. That is, do not lower the leading edge of the paddle and scrape, but raise the leading edge and pull the softened lead along. If the lead starts to get too hot, it will get brighter, so skip a couple of passes with the torch. If the lead is getting too cold, it will be harder to spread, or won't spread at all. Paddling lead across a metal surface is like buttering bread. If the butter is too warm, it flows too thin; if it is too cold, it doesn't spread at all.

Be careful not to keep heat on a lead area too long, as heat will cause

5. Morgan knocker has a screw tip at one end which threads into the punched holes. The knocker uses the inertia of a 3 to 5-lb. sliding weight (arrow) to remove dents.

6. Starting at the lower left corner, Morris works progressively across and up the dented area. Opposite end of knocker is L-shaped to allow it to be used to straighten flat areas such as the lower lip of the quarter panel.

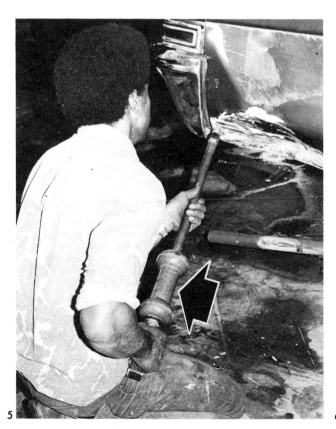

5

6

The Cheaters

the lead's grain structure to become coarse. Heating an area several times and repaddling it may cause this structure change, which leaves pit holes in the finished job.

At the same time, do not get the surrounding metal too hot, as this will raise the temperature in the lead and cause it to run off. Too high a temperature will also encourage metal distortion. If some distortion is apparent the leaded area can be quenched with water after the paddling is finished but before the lead has become too cold. Throw water on the leaded surface with a rag or sponge, then as soon as the lead is cooled, rub the sponge or rag over the surface. Don't attempt this water quenching while the lead is still very hot (after paddling is the correct time, with no additional heat applied) as it will ruin the lead job. If the lead is too cold, the distortion will not be pulled out.

The beginner will find that not having enough lead to work will be his major trouble once the paddling technique is mastered. It is difficult to go back and add lead, since the temperature must be brought up carefully. The new lead must be applied and worked without overheating the already paddled lead film, and the two areas of lead must be heated enough to flow together at the mating point. If there is too much lead for a particular spot, it can be removed with the paddle while it is still in its plastic state. Ideally, the lead surface should be reasonably smooth and only slightly higher than the surrounding metal.

When lead is being used to create a specific surface, as in customizing, the amount used should be as little as possible. In past years, lead was often used as a substitute for good

metal shaping, a chore now often taken by plastic fillers. The term ''lead-sled'' came to mean any poorly done custom car. Thanks to better trained customizers, plastic filler or lead is used sparingly when it comes to major modifications.

FILING FILLERS

Both lead and plastic fillers file and grind away faster than the surrounding metal, so care must be taken not to cut the filler too much, nor to make gouges and scratches in the filler's surface. The beginner is cautioned to use the file for final finish work on either lead or plastic, as it will cut slower than a disc sander, and the long surface of the file will level the filler with the area of the surrounding metal.

The file will cut deep gouges if allowed to run uncontrolled over the lead. If the file is not held firmly, it may skip up on one edge, which will make a very bad cut, a cut that may not file out. It is possible to learn a lighter filing touch for filler by pulling the file rather than pushing it.

Another common mistake beginners fall heir to is cutting away too much of the filler, whether lead or plastic. There is almost always a crown to the surface being filed. If the file or sander is run across the filler only, until the edges are feathered, chances are the filler will be flatter than the crown. The correct procedure is to start on the edges and work to the middle, running the file lengthwise to the crown. This keeps the file cutting the minimum amount of filler to reach the level of the surrounding metal, gradually forming the correct crown in the filled area. The filler in the middle of the repaired depression is the last to be filed.

When the area is finished with the

file, all the edges should blend smoothly into the metal. If there is a tiny, low spot at the edge that does not smooth out, it may be picked up slightly or filled with putty later. A large, unfilled area indicates the lead was not run into the surrounding metal far enough, or the metal has distorted. Additional lead is the usual remedy if the panel cannot be picked up.

After the initial filing, the area should be block-sanded with #80 grit production paper. This paper is coarse enough to cut the file marks from the filler without loading up. It is only intended to finish off the filler and not to shape it, although such paper can be hand-held to finish off difficult areas, like reverse crowns. The disc sander should be used on a filler only by a professional. Of course, the beginner is not going to know the disadvantages of improper sander use unless he tries it, but the trial should be only on a practice panel. Generally, the sander cuts so rapidly that the beginner finds the filled area cut too low and flat. There is a certain health hazard associated with using a disc sander on lead also, in that the sander causes a fine lead dust that can be absorbed into the skin and/or breathed into the lungs. This can cause lead poisoning if kept up over a long period of time.

In summary, lead is an invaluable aid to the body man and customizer,

1. Morgan knocker was only partially successful. This panel had been banged before and the metal has work hardened.

2. Morris uses an air chisel to break the spot welds between the inner and outer portions of the quarter panel. Lip was rewelded after it was straightened. Pop rivets will work if you don't have access to welding equipment.

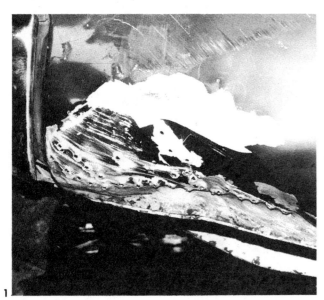

3

4

5

3. The lower edge of the panel is backed up with a bodywork dolly as Morris works the metal with a body hammer. Keep the dolly firmly against the underside of the panel to prevent rebound.
The panel was worked in this manner up to the crease line.

4. After grinding down to bare metal, the first layer of filler is applied.
Use a wide blade putty knife or a plastic squeegee. Apply plastic with a firm sliding motion to ensure bond and force out air bubbles.

5. Cheese grater is used to eliminate high and low spots before the filler gets hard. Use a light touch. Plastic is just right to work when it peels through the grater openings in long strings.

but it must be used properly. Never use lead where the spot can better be repaired or shaped; only use lead if it is an economical and fast method of repair or modification.

PLASTIC FILLERS

Plastic and fiberglass repair procedures are often mistaken for one and the same thing, but they are not. The so-called plastic filler is basically a substitute for lead, while the fiberglass repair is primarily for fiberglass surfaces, but may be used on sheetmetal. In this respect, the latter is almost always used only as a repair of a rust-rotted area that could only be repaired by panel replacement or patching. This type of fiberglass repair is fully discussed in the chapter on fiberglass.

A tremendous amount of energy has been expended during the past two decades in plastic filler research, in an effort to create a true no-heat filler that will work as well as lead. While a perfect plastic filler has yet to be found, the product of today is vastly improved over that of a few short years ago. Today, plastic can be relied upon to give a good, hard finish that will not shrink or crack with age, yet will adhere to the metal even under the most extreme temperature conditions.

There are many companies making plastic fillers, since the composition lends itself to small, local production as well as major company manufacture. Prices for such fillers range from very low to quite high, and about the only guideline for the beginner is to use the filler that the majority of local body men use. A plastic filler usually takes about 30 minutes to harden, which means that where time is an important cost factor, the use of lead may be faster. It takes less skill to apply a plastic filler, but the dust created from grinding some plastics can injure the lungs. By and large, the plastic filler has a definite place in auto body repair and customizing techniques.

Because the metal cannot be worked after a plastic filler has been used, it is imperative that all high spots be driven down before the application of plastics. The area to be filled must be cleaned of rust, paint and welding scale, as with lead. Grind the metal with a $\neq$24 opencoat disc to give a rough metal surface for good plastic "bite," then wipe away any oil or waxes that might prevent a good bond. Clean an area larger than that to be repaired with surrounding paint feather-edged before the repair is started. This will allow the filler be spread into the surrounding metal to ensure the necessary buildup. Do not spread the filler over any paint, as it will probably peel later on. To cut down on the labor involved, do not fill more than is absolutely necessary.

Plastic fillers of this nature include a resin base and a catalyst. Unmixed, the two agents remain pliable over a long period of time, but once the catalyst is added to the resin, it will harden in a matter of minutes. It is possible to control the hardening time somewhat by the amount of catalyst (hardener) added, but the best course is to follow mixing instructions on the containers.

The most common type of plastic filler kit includes a specific amount of

The Cheaters

resin (usually contained in quart cans) and a small tube of liquid hardener. Normally, no more than two small drops of hardener are required for a golf-ball size hunk of resin. Any type of plastic filler must be thoroughly mixed. Since the mixture should be kept free of any contaminants, a piece of safety glass is the best mixing "board" available. It is easy to clean and store. Cardboard will work in a pinch.

Never mix more plastic than immediately needed, even if the fill will require several coats. The filler on the panel and that on the mixing board will harden at the same rate, so the unused portion is useless once it has been mixed.

Plastics can be applied with a wide putty knife, a rubber squeegee, or practically any kind of flexible straight edge. The rubber squeegee is perhaps the easiest to use, since it will tend to follow body contours and leave a smoother finish than the others.

As soon as the plastic is completely mixed, it should be applied to the work area. Apply the mixture onto the area with a downward-sideways motion to force out any air bubbles. These bubbles must not be left in the work, as they will shrink or burst later after the paint is applied. At the same time, this pressure will cause the plastic to gain maximum bond with the roughened metal.

If the area to be filled is more than ¼-inch deep, successive filling is necessary, with each coat allowed to dry before the next is applied. Such a deep fill might be a gouge, in which case the deepest part of the fill would receive the plastic first. No plastic would be feathered to the edges, instead this would be kept for the last coat.

If too much hardener is used, or if the material stands too long before it is applied, it will tend to roll up and pull loose from the metal. Don't both-

1. A second layer of filler was added after the first had hardened completely. Filler should never be applied more than ¼-inch deep.

2. Lower edge of panel is filled and high and low spots leveled out. Top portion of panel has been pulled back into shape and ground down to bare metal. Next, plastic will be applied.

3. After plastic filler has hardened, it is filed as described in text. If severe low spots show up, more filler can be added—unlike lead. When the surface has been built up properly, minor low spots or chips in plastic are wiped with glazing putty. Then an open-coat grinding disc backed with soft rubber backup pad, is used to featheredge filler to metal.

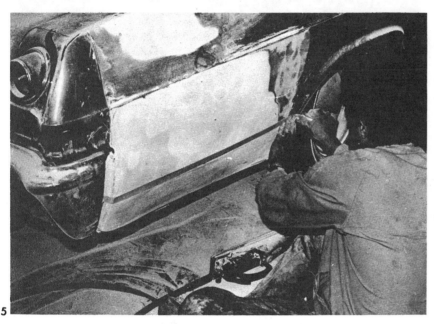

a very light touch, shaping carefully until the filler is almost down to the desired height. Let the plastic harden for a while longer, then finish it off with a long, flat block and #180 grit sandpaper. Coarser paper will tend to leave scratches. The long sandpaper "file" will smooth the filled spot into the surrounding area just as the lead file does. Air files, pneumatic tools having a long, narrow platen taking coarse sandpaper up to about 4-ins. by 16 ins., should be kept out of the hands of the novice. They cut too fast, at up to 3500 strokes per minute, and will eliminate a carefully formed crown of filler in short order. Used judiciously, though, and with experience, they have made the use of plastic fillers populars due to the speed (thus, time-saving) at which they operate. Finally, finish the area for painting with a regular rubber sanding block and #220 grit sandpaper or garnet paper.

If the plastic is allowed to become too hard, it must be worked out just as lead with a regular metal file and/ or a disc sander. The beginner will find the file as necessary here as with lead since the filler can be cut down too low. If the sander is used, a respirator or some kind of nose protection should be used to protect the lungs against the plastic dust.

Plastic fillers should not be used as a substitute for poor body repair or sloppy customizing, no matter how easy they are to apply. Just as the lead-sled name was often attached to custom cars of old, the "putty-car" is common today. Using too much plastic filler is just asking for trouble. Plastic should never be used where the body is liable to flex or where strength is required, just as lead should never be used to bridge a gap that should have been welded. Nor is plastic acceptable as an edge. If an area must be filled out to an exposed edge or lip, lead should be used at the edge, then the plastic added. The lead won't be as strong as sheetmetal, but it won't chip like plastic.

In areas where there are extreme temperature fluctuations during short periods of time, plastic fillers have been known to give problems. If this is the case, local body men will have found which plastics should be utilized.

Apply a primer-surfacer that is recommended over plastic, as some paint compounds have a bad effect on fillers. The auto parts store specializing in paints will know what compounds will work. Should problems occur after the paint is applied, it will be only because of poor filler application (surface not clean, etc.) or because the paint is reacting to the filler.

4. Upper portion of fender has been ground down, as compared to lower part which has yet to be featheredged.

5. Final step before preparing for paint is running tape where original fender had a contour line, to be sure the line is straight. Disc grinder is used to "sharpen" up the edge of the stock crease line.

er going further; mix a new batch and start again.

Finishing plastic can be either very easy or extremely difficult, depending upon how long it is allowed to set before the finishing process is started. It is not uncommon to see a gouge obviously filled by the car's owner with plastic. Usually the owner has applied the filler rather roughly and apparently waited until the plastic has become very hard before attempting to file or sand it smooth. By then, it required a very sharp file, a disc sander, and lots of elbow grease. He had none of these.

A regular body file is not used to work plastic. The type of file used is referred to as a cheese grater, the kind of file often found in wood working. Blades for these files are available in a variety of sizes, as with normal lead files, for unusual contours. Special holders are also available, although the blade can be used without a holder.

Plastic fillers set up hard because of chemical interaction, thus they do not "dry" in the normal sense of the word. However, they are affected by high temperatures, so they will harden faster on a very hot day. To speed this hardening, lamps used for paint drying can be directed on the mixture. At any rate, it is best to begin working the material while it is still "soft." This can be determined by touching the surface lightly with the grater. When it is just right to work, the plastic will peel through the grater openings in long strings.

Work the area with the grater and

Tin Bending Tips

Picks, dollies, hammers and jacks. Here's how to use the tools of the bodyman's kit.

One of the important parts of learning how to do bodywork is the experience of working on many different types of dents, bumps and gashes. A good body man can do a job fast and well, simply because there isn't any type of collision damage that he hasn't seen at least once before. And if he's really experienced, he's not only seen it on *one* make of car, but probably on *every* make that's on the road today.

To photograph work in progress on several different kinds of collision damage, we went to Santa Monica College, where we talked to Eddie Kile, the body shop instructor. Eddie had lent us a hand on the Pound-Out Parade chapter in our last edition and we know that if there is one person in the bodywork business who knows

where it's at, Eddie fits the bill—he's been in the body repair business for so many years that he automatically examines your car for signs of previous damage.

Because he was in the business long before all of the quick-fix plastics came on the market, Eddie Kile knows that a good body repair man is one who can work metal, not just

HOW-TO: Malibu Rear Door

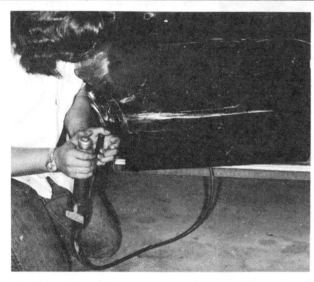

1. The nasty gash in the side of this Malibu rear door was accompanied by a healthy dent in the panel and is typical of the damage that occurs if you cut a pole too sharply.

2. After using the Porto-Power with a wedgie inside the door to restore panel configuration as much as possible, a hammer and block of wood are used to knock out the smaller gashes.

3. A series of holes are drilled in the gash and a knocker is used to pull out the metal. Small damage to a panel can often be corrected by this step alone.

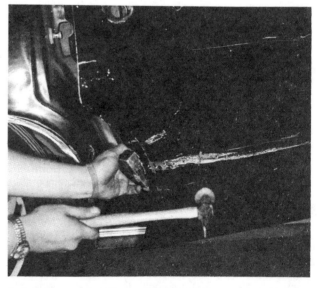

4. A hammer and dolly are used to bring the door edge back to shape. This step is important in lining up the door so that it'll close correctly.

slap some filler into the hole and smooth it out with a board. "We use filler, meaning lead or plastic, only when the metal itself cannot be repaired," Eddie said, "but because of auto styling and the types of damage that occur today, pure metal working is becoming harder and harder to do without at least a bit of filler."

The following series of photos show Eddie's students at work on several different types of common collision damage, which run the gamut from those types you can work on in the backyard to those that require equipment only a professional body man would have access to.

5. Judiciously applied, the spoon and hammer will contour the door panel, taking out most of the high spots. Go easy to avoid knocking metal in too far.

6. A flexible disc sander and #16 grit paper takes the finish down to the bare metal fast. Although many body men don't wear them, goggles are recommended for safety.

7. Finish is removed from low spots and crevices with a wire brush. Wear goggles here also, as a sliver of metal can end a bodyworking career.

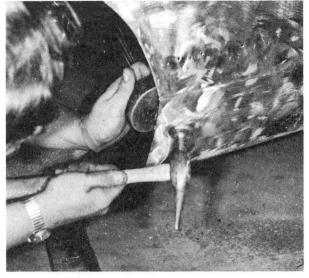

8. A final working of the door edge with hammer and dolly assures a perfect fit and reduces the possibility that the untrained eye will be able to detect that damage.

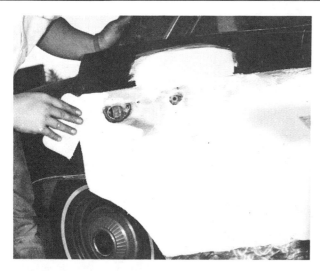

9. Body plastic is mixed and applied evenly above the lower crown line. You could do the entire panel at once, but shaping the crown line is more difficult that way.

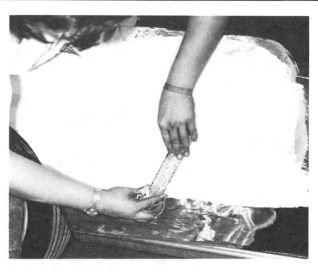

10. The cheese grater must be used at just the right moment. If the plastic is too wet, it drags and if too dry, it can't be filed. In this case, sand it down, and reapply.

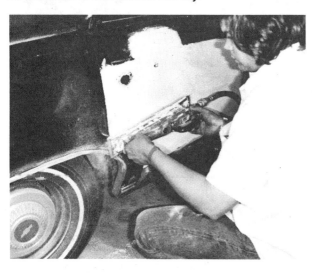

11. A final sanding with the straight line sander will remove the cheese grater marks and show up any low spots that require another filling and featheredge prior to priming.

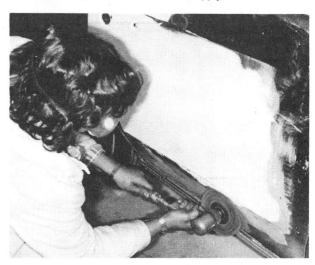

12. The small disc sander cuts the plastic along the crown line. Then apply plastic below the crown, file and sand. Use of filler here is unavoidable.

13. The leading edge of the rear quarter panel must be straightened. A knocker used with a hammer pulls the metal back out where it can be roughly shaped.

14. With the door handle back in place and a coat of primer on the metal, the crown line of the door is checked to match the quarter panel crown line repair.

1. Crumpled rear fender on Chevy II is a tossup—to straighten or to replace? We're going to pull it back and do a bit of metal working, so off comes the bumper and trim.

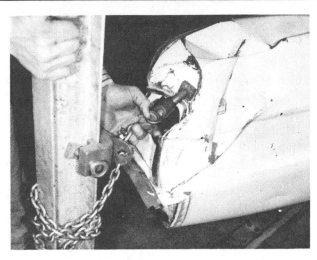

2. The Blackhawk pulldozer is fastened to the damaged area after the spotlight has been removed. Using the pulldozer is sure a lot better than using the push jack inside.

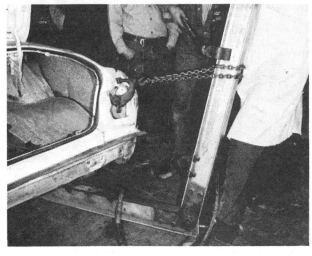

3. Instructor Eddie Kile supervises the pace of panel restoration as his class watches. The trick here is to not go too far, or not far enough—but just as far as necessary.

4. The placement of the pulldozer attachment unit is changed as the fender begins to assume its original shape. It's impossible to pull it out from one location.

5. As the pulldozer is operated, the fender is hammered from inside to smooth out wrinkles and keep damaged area from tearing further which would just mean more work.

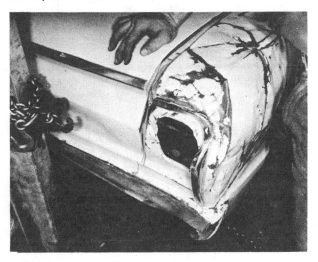

6. Damaged area has been restored to gross configuration by pulldozer, and now it's up to the body man and hand tools to do the rest. Job doesn't look so formidable now.

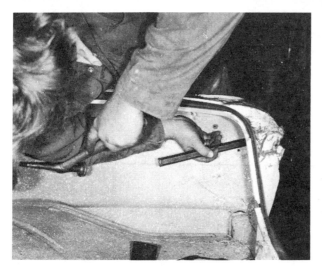

7. Hammer and punch used from inside applies local pressure to the edge of the stoplight opening. Some minor tearing of opening edge metal will be unavoidable.

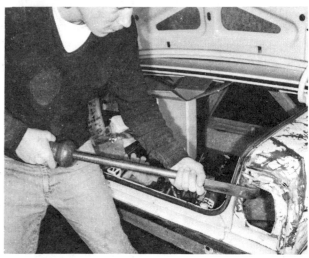

8. A large knocker and claw pulls the fender in toward the trunk. This is fastest way to move the entire unit at once. Again, go slowly for obvious reasons.

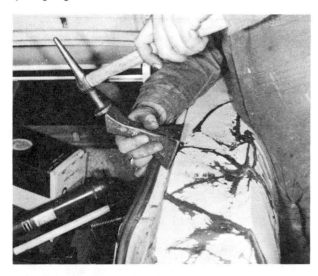

9. Fender line is reestablished with a hammer and dolly so that when the deck lid is closed, the gap between the panels will be very nearly uniform.

10. The tear in the metal along the panel line is welded with torch and steel rod. Adjoining edges of rip must be dollied into alignment before welding begins.

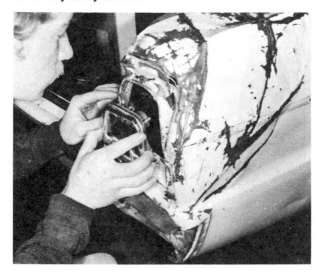

11. Stoplight unit is tried periodically to check on its fit and the progress of the repair. Several trial fits will probably be necessary before this job is finally completed.

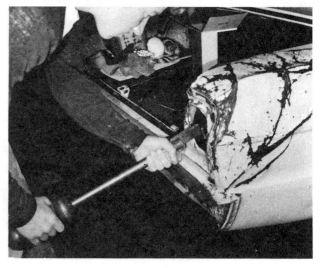

12. Fender still has to move slightly toward the left, so the knocker and claw are used again. Go cautiously so that you will to avoid tearing the welds open.

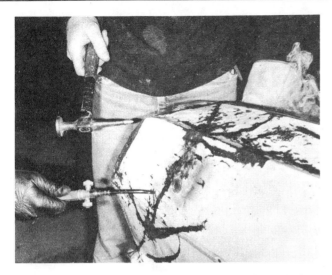

13. The metal bulge along the crease lines is removed by heat shrinking the fender. To get rid of the bulge, heated spots are hammered smartly while they still glow red.

14. A new trim moulding is used as a guide to fender repair progress. The stoplight fits correctly at this point, as does trim. It's looking good, but a lot of work remains.

15. The entire area is ground to bare metal with high spots removed as much as practical. Where the grinder shows up severe low spots, they are tapped up, then grinding resumed.

16. Remaining high spots are heat shrunk into place as fender assumes a considerably different appearance than at the beginning of the job. Fender can be saved after all.

17. Low spots are ground with wire brush to remove all of the old finish and to clean out any scale from torch or other foreign matter that might be on the surface.

18. This is one of those jobs where the use of plastics is almost unavoidable for a fast, smooth finish. When Pat Nolind finishes, this fender will be ready for painting.

HOW-TO: Comet Engine Compartment

1. Comet front end was struck at 135° angle, completely ruining this front fender and grille. All this will be removed and replaced with new metal.

2. Comet is unit-body construction and measuring the two diagonals of the engine compartment reveals that impact moved front of compartment ¾-inch to the right.

3. Blackhawk pulldozer has 3-ton capacity and is connected to radiator shield panel at one end and to frame at the other, giving it something to pull against.

4. Note that pulldozer is secured to radiator shield panel in two places before pressure is applied. This prevents attachment bolt from being pulled through lighter metal.

5. Additional pressure is applied by angling a Porto-Power unit with its ram pushing from the lower left frame member to the upper right corner of engine compartment.

6. With both units in operation, compartment begins to move into line. Porto-Power and pulldozer are more arms for body man. New sheetmetal can now be fitted.

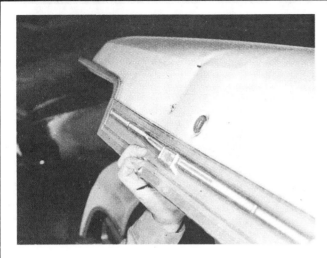

1. Deck lid damage is typical hazard of stop-go driving in heavy traffic. Trim removal is always the first step in gaining access to damaged area.

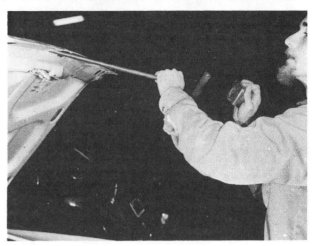

2. Difficulty in repair is compounded by double panel. Picking bar is inserted through holes in inside panel and struck with dolly to help spring outside panel back to shape.

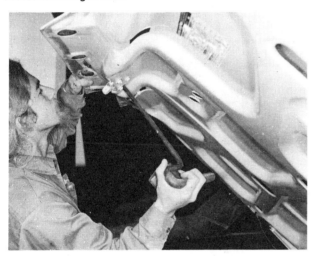

3. If sufficient leverage to move deck lid panel can't be obtained from one angle, try another. Bar is used wherever it can be inserted and pressure applied.

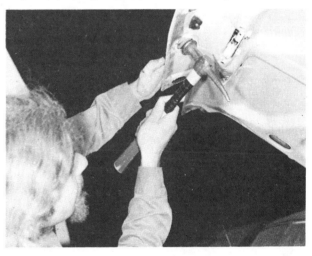

4. Deck lid line is straightened with hammer for perfect fit once trim is replaced. Inner panel access holes make it possible for a pry to be inserted.

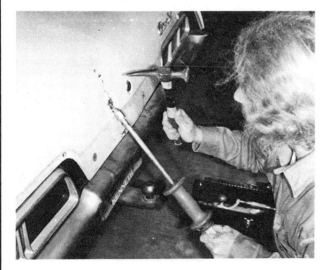

5. Knocker and hammer are used to pull out remainder of crease in outer panel. As outward pull is exerted on knocker, pick hammer "unlocks" stresses in metal.

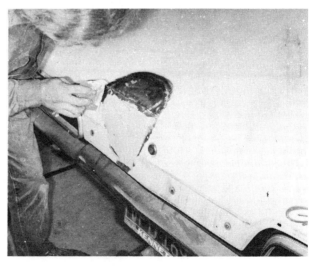

6. Repair area is ground to bare metal and plastic applied. Once sanded and primed, the trim is replaced and the car is ready for the customer.

HOW-TO: Mustang Quarter Panel

1. Mustang rear quarter panel damage is common but complicated by the lower sculpture panel line at point of impact. Interior trim panel is removed as the first step.

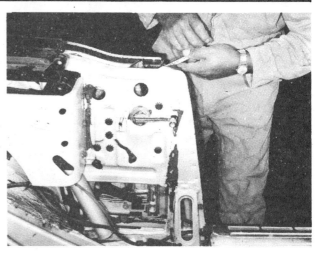

2. Window and mechanism must all come out before repair can be effected. This is slow and tricky procedure, and location; relationship of parts must be remembered.

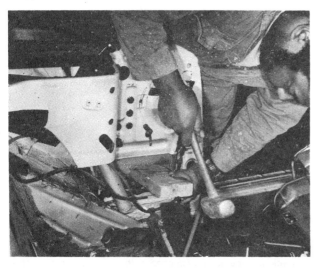

3. Once window mechanism is out, some of the panel contour can be restored with a hammer and block of wood. This should be done before bringing jack into play.

4. But for most of the damage, the 4-ton Porto-Power unit with wedgie attachment is necessary. In some cases inner panel would have to be cut to get jack in.

5. Once the attachment is set in place, watch outside of panel as Porto-Power is operated. As panel portion regains original shape somewhat, move wedgie to another area.

6. It is virtually guaranteed that some parts of panel will spring back too high. Equalize with a body hammer to keep repair process progressing evenly.

7. Here's another tricky step—restoring the sculpture line by working the metal with a hammer. Remember, lots of light hits are better than a few hard ones.

8. Heat shrinking the bulge behind the panel sculpture helps to bring the sculpture line back to normal. Spots are heated cherry red, then rapped with hammer while still hot.

9. Grinding is the next step and care is required to avoid cutting through the metal as the disc is tilted. If disc edge is trimmed to sawtooth edge, it'll lessen digging tendency.

10. The upper sculpture line is also worked with the grinder. Once these two areas are completed, the rest of the repair area is sanded down to the bare metal.

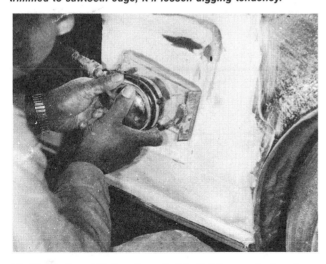

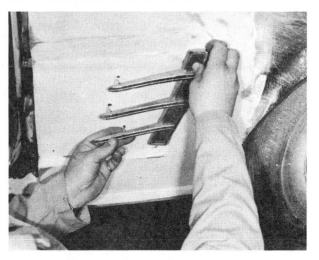

11. Plastic is applied and sanded to finish a perfect restoration of the sculpture lines. Finishing crevices isn't necessary because the trim will hide any crevices that remain.

12. Before priming, the trim is temporarily refitted to the panel as a double check on sculpture line and panel contour and any adjustments that were made during repair work.

HOW-TO: Chevrolet Hood

1. Hood and grille were damaged in two places. Bumper, grille and trim are not salvageable so will all come off and be replaced with Chevy agency parts.

2. Porto-Power unit is placed between hood hinge and grip wrench. Any hydraulic ram like this pushes at both ends and has to be placed with care or you'll bend something.

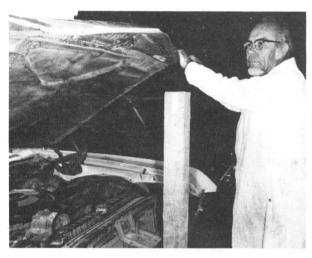

3. After using the Porto-Power, Eddie Kile brings the hood down on a 2x4 with a sharp blow to help spring damaged area out as much as possible, repeating if necessary.

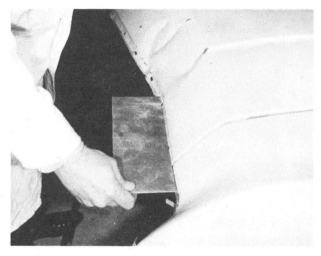

4. Eddie uses a piece of aluminum to check panel edge line for correct fit. Eyeballing it isn't good enough here, as gaps are often deceiving.

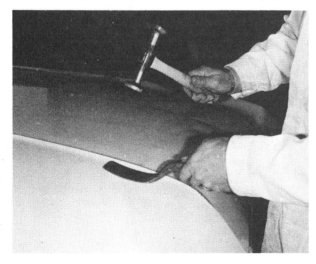

5. Spoon and hammer are also of help in spring-hammering the damaged area back into place. Spoon is lightly but repeatedly tapped as it's moved over the area.

6. New trim is now fitted to hood line to check progress and to determine further steps to be taken in repair. Eyeballing, or rubbing with palm may turn up more damage.

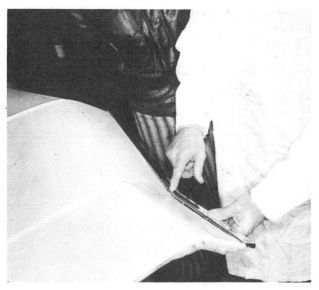

7. Edge line is almost restored on this side. Working a hood like this one without the new trim as a guide is almost impossible, since you can't eyeball a crooked line.

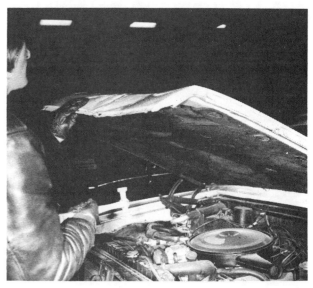

8. Hood is held and hammer used from underside. Double panel construction of hood makes this a slow and tedious stage. Sometimes a pry can be inserted between panels.

9. Reversing the direction of the hammer blows helps to keep the repair uniform instead of turning the creases into a large bulge; go back and forth over area.

10. Grinder and #16 grit paper are used to cut the high spots and to remove the finish to the bare metal. Keep disc nearly flat to panel so metal won't be cut clear through.

11. Low spots can be cleaned with a wire brush though this will take a lot of elbow grease to get them absolutely clean. There is a better way to do this.

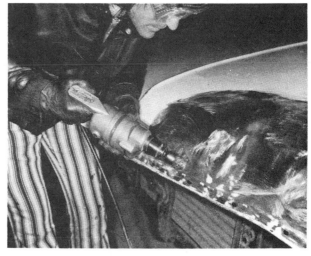

12. Using a power drill and wire brush is much faster. Once this is finished, plastic is applied and sanded to restore panel configuration completely.

HOW-TO: Dodge Front End

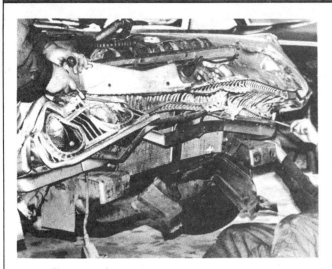

1. This Dodge suffered a square hit on the front end, and while it would be normal to replace sheetmetal with junkyard parts, none were available for this model.

2. Radiator was knocked into fan, so it too must be replaced. All the parts damaged beyond repair had to be purchased new; expensive but necessary.

3. A problem always encountered with damage this severe is getting at the nuts and bolts to remove the pieces. Sometimes a torch is needed, though pry worked here.

4. Left fender could have been repaired, but the time it would take would necessitate a cost greater than a replacement fender, so it will be junked out.

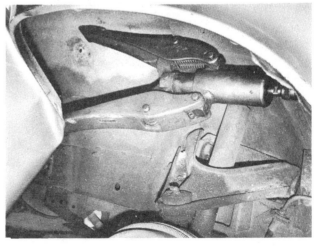

5. Though both fenders will be replaced, they are left in place temporarily. With damaged grille and related pieces off, jacks will be used to pull the fenders out.

6. As fenders are jacked out to approximate shape, they'll bring adjoining panels and related bracing with them which will simplify attachment of new fenders.

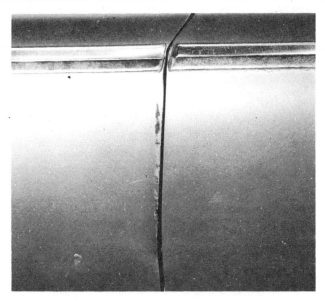

7. Fenders were hit hard enough that the gap between the doors was closed. Jacking old fenders back to the proper position restores gap so new fenders will align.

8. Everything that will be replaced has by now been removed. Frame horns were knocked out of alignment so next step will be jacking them back into alignment.

9. Next, inner fender panels are jacked out with a bulldozer jack. Measurements from new fender bolt holes are checked on panels so they won't be stretched too far.

10. Because old fenders had been roughly aligned before removal, new fender bolts on in pretty good alignment and needs only minor adjustment to get the gap even.

11. Hood gap is also checked between cowl, to see if hood had been shifted in accident, and between fender as reassurance that fender is located where it should be.

12. From here, it's a matter of bolting on new pieces, then paint preparation. Obviously, sheetmetal from a wrecking yard would have eased the job considerably.

HOW-TO: Ford Quarter Panel

1. Two-inch depression in rear quarter panel of '70 LTD is deceptive. Regular body shop would fill with plastic. We're going to work sheetmetal first to near perfect contours.

2. Safety light on side of fender is easy to remove by going through trunk. On this car, rear fender panel is also inside wall of trunk. Loose objects in trunk can dent fender.

3. The worst of the dent can be removed with a hard rubber hammer. This brings panel closer to its original shape; be sure you don't make the dent worse.

4. Rubber hammer is exchanged for the flat surface of a picking hammer. Smaller and harder head will flatten wrinkles when backed up with a flat dolly.

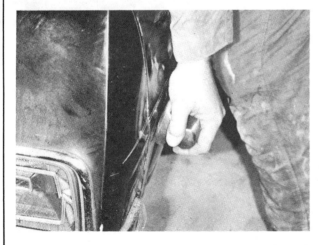

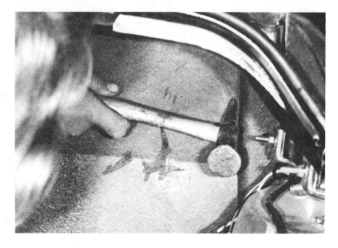

5. This operation is done with a dolly pressed firmly against the exterior of the panel, exactly opposite the area struck with the hammer. Light raps will help shrink metal.

6. Sharp end of picking hammer is used in tight spots that are close to panel corners and hard to reach with flat side. Use care with pointed end, don't use flat dolly here.

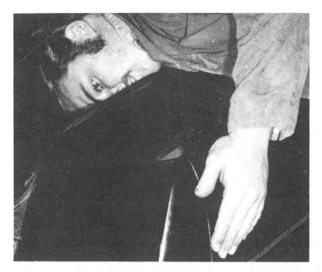

7. Hand is used instead of dolly for this hammering operation, because sense of touch avoids creation of high spots that will have to be ground out later.

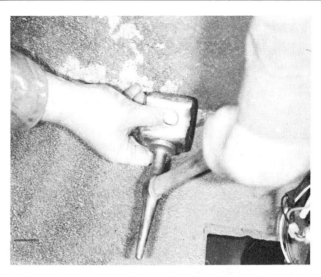

8. Panel is fairly smooth, but it's still a bit low. Work entire area slowly and evenly with hammer and dolly to bring damaged area back to original shape.

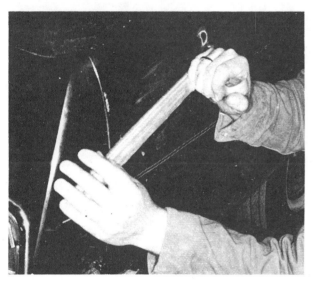

9. Body file is pressed into service to remove high spots (and paint). This part of the job requires plenty of muscle and a good eye. Different files will help here.

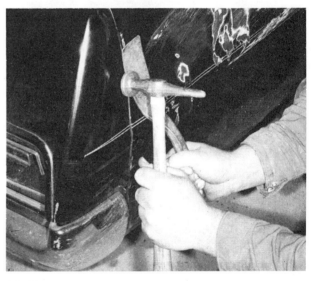

10. Match the end of the panel with the fender cap with a spoon and hammer. Always ease into hammering steps gradually to avoid overworking the metal.

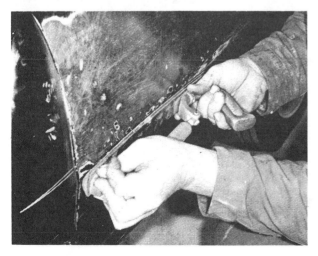

11. Most fender panels have a sculpture line which must be redefined when the fender is dented. Here, a contour file is used above and below the line. Don't file peak thin.

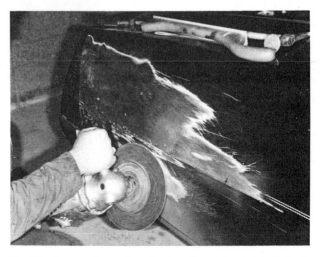

12. After hammering and contouring is nearly complete, body grinder is used to remove all paint in the area. Expose bare metal to prepare for plastic, or filler will not stay.

13. Low spots will appear quickly because they will contain old paint. Clean them out thoroughly with rotary brush, or filler will fall out eventually. Surface must be clean.

14. Because the metal was worked very close to perfection, only a very thin coat of plastic filler is needed. Plastic should be used in thin layers in finish coats.

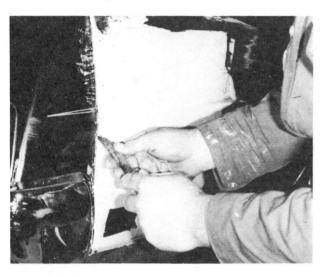

15. Remove excess filler from between the two adjacent panels with a sharp instrument. Do it while the filler is still wet, as it is much easier. Plastic will set in 3-10 minutes.

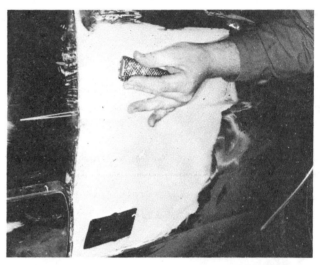

16. Use a cheese grater rather than a file when working thin applications of plastic filler. Begin work just after filler begins to set to remove excess. Use hands to check shape.

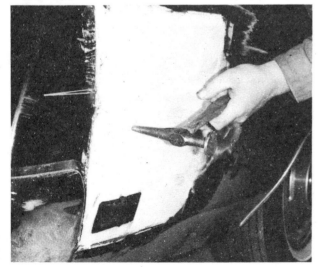

17. Use of the grater may expose some high spots. These may be hammered lightly tinto place, but use care when hammering on filler or you may crack it. Note hole for safety light.

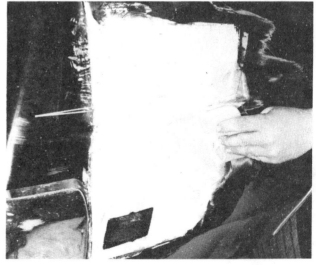

18. Final application of plastic is also thin. Cheese grater will be used once more, then repair spot is ready for final sanding and priming. "Green stuff" may be used to fill pits.

1. Rusted out seat wells in this '60 El Camino pose a common problem for drivers living in snow-bound or salt-air sections of the country. Salt attacks sheetmetal with vengeance.

2. Short of replacing the entire floorpan, there's no way to halt effects of rusting. But years of life can be added by brazing in a new sheetmetal patch. Remove all damaged metal.

3. After measuring and cutting to the size of the patch area, sheetmetal should be trial-fitted to ensure that brazing is done to unrusted metal. Use heavy gauge metal for patch.

4. Further trial fitting and trimming will provide a tight, close fit that will conform well to the seat area. Note this floor was completely rotted out. Driver must have had wet feet.

5. Tack new floor every 4 to 6 inches with brazing rod and torch. Additional hands might help in pressing new piece down for tight contact with pan.

6. Once tack spots are made on all four sides and corners, entire seam is brazed. Seat can then be positioned and new bolt holes can be drilled for seat and seat belts.

Rust Repair

Rust—it's that flaky orange stuff you see on so many vehicles. It's a great color for autumn leaves and good exterior paint color, but when it appears on a vehicle's sheetmetal, rust is trouble. Rust destroys more vehicles each year than accidents. It never sleeps or takes a holiday. Though winter is the season when the worst vehicle corrosion occurs (especially in areas of heavy rain and snow, and where salt is used to de-ice the roads), a vehicle can rust anywhere, any time. Domestic and foreign vehicle manufacturers have increased the use of "anti-rust" galvanized steel, undercoatings, and zinc-rich primers in recent years, but any vehicle built is going to start rusting the first time it gets wet.

What can be done about rust? Quite a lot, but how much depends entirely on the severity of the problem. Within the broad spectrum of rust types are several different categories, a sort of the good, the bad, and the ugly of corrosion.

The good (only comparatively) is what is commonly called *surface* rust. Surface rust is the first stage of exterior sheetmetal corrosion; it is the light flaking you see on a pickup bed wall, around wheelwells, on wheels and accessories, or around places where the paint has been chipped or scratched. Surface rust is the easiest to repair.

The bad category of rust is *hidden* rust. Hidden rust often goes undetected for months or even years, camouflaged by bodywork or paint. It starts out like surface rust, as a light flaking, but because it is inside the door panels or covered with paint or accessories, you can't find it or stop it from spreading. There's little you can do about hidden rust short of tearing apart the door panels, inner fender liners, or tailgates every few months. Under poorly prepared exterior sheetmetal, hidden rust shows up as bubbles or blisters in the paint. When you do find hidden rust you should fix it immediately.

The ugly category is the so-called *major* rust that

can turn a door or fender into sheetmetal lace. Once a car body starts to look more like Swiss cheese than an automobile, it's time for major surgery. The more advanced major rust is, in terms of total surface area, the more difficult and expensive the repair will be. With major body rust, it is often cheaper to replace a whole door or fender than to patch the existing sheetmetal.

There are three basic steps to busting any kind of rust. Remove the rust, repair the metal, and re-cover the repair. But before you can start putting the cuffs on corrosion, it's a good idea to figure out why the rust appeared or you may be starting the rust and repair cycle all over again. The most obvious reason a vehicle rusts is that it gets wet and doesn't dry out. But getting wet is not the problem— staying wet is. Moisture traps include the following areas:

Inner doors—Most vehicle doors have built-in drain holes. If the lower edge of your car's door has rusted out, chances are good that the drain hole has become plugged. Unplug it while making the repair or the rust will come right back. Fenders—Moisture and mud often get trapped between fender and fenderwell, keeping the metal wet and promoting early rusting. While making the repair, be sure to seal cracks or openings in this area.
Under bumpers or other bolt-ons— Any place where accessories have been attached to bare metal, such as mirrors, hitches, or light brackets, are potential moisture trapping areas. After repairing rust in these areas, be sure to prime, paint, and protect the surfaces being mated.

Removing Rust

Once you've figured out the severity of the rust, the repair can begin. The first step is to remove the rust. This is the most important

Rust—it doesn't take a genius to spot it in this advanced state. Major rust like this can be repaired, though it is often cheaper to replace the whole panel.

One method of removing all rust is to have the metal dipped in a chemical stripping tank. Due to the complete disassembly required, dipping the vehicle is usually reserved for complete restoration jobs or for from-scratch street rod buildups.

step because if you don't remove all the rust, it will come right back. There are several ways to remove rust; all have their advantages and disadvantages.

One of the easiest methods is to remove the rust chemically. There are a wide variety of chemical rust removers, from naval jellies to sprays. When using chemical rust removers, the best advice is to use moderation. Follow the instructions of the specific product exactly, and avoid getting the chemicals in your eyes or on your skin. Some of these chemicals are very strong and can damage good sheetmetal if not carefully controlled. Be sure to remove all traces of the chemicals before priming or repainting the vehicle. Paint and primer won't adhere well to chemically coated metal, and that can cause more problems, including additional rusting. Chemical stripping is relatively expensive and is most suitable for small jobs. The exception is a professional chemical dipping, available in most major cities, which is often more economical for removing rust from an entire frame or body during a complete restoration or rebuild.

Another method of rust removal is sanding. Just as a little steel wool and elbow grease will clean up a rusty chromed wheel, some sandpaper and a lot of elbow grease will get rid of all but the worst rust. Sanding is safe and leaves a good, well-prepped surface for painting. For repairs of large areas you should invest in a few basic air tools, such as a dual-action or orbital sander. Many companies offer quality air tools that pay for themselves many times over in saved labor in just one job. When sanding, whether by hand or with power tools, take the rust-ed area down to bare metal to ensure that all traces

Rust Repair

Chemical rust removers, such as naval jelly, are much easier than dipping for small areas of rust.

of rust are removed. The disadvantages of sanding are that it's time consuming, strenuous, and only usable on rusted areas that have a solid metal base. Areas that have rusted completely through are not suitable for this method of rust removal.

Another method that works very well on major rust is sandblasting. Not only does it eliminate the rust by beating it away with high-powered blasts of abrasive sand particles, but sandblasting also reveals weak spots in the metal as well as lightly etching the surface for a good adhesion of primer and paint. While sandblasting equipment is available for sale or rent from many sources, a check of the Yellow Pages will usually locate a commercial sandblaster who can get rid of your rust very cheaply. The disadvantage of sandblasting is that you run the risk of stressing the remaining metal while removing the rust. If attempting to do your own blasting, be sure to check with an expert for advice on picking the right grit sand and the right air pressure for your specific repair.

The final method of rust removal is the most severe, cutting out the affected metal. This method allows you to discard whole body panels or just a section, using a hacksaw or air chisel. This method should be used only for completely rusted out areas, because the rest of the repair procedure is time consuming and expensive.

Repairing the Metal

Once the rust is removed, it is necessary to repair the remaining metal. Areas that were only lightly rusted should be sanded smooth or filled with spot putty or body filler, as needed. When sanding or removing paint to reveal bare metal, the metal should be carefully conditioned with a chemical surface prep to prevent re-rusting and provide a good, etched surface for the primer to bond to.

Rusted areas that have been cut out will need to be patched. This involves cutting sections of sheetmetal (22-gauge is recommended to match most vehicle bodies) to fit the area removed and welding these patches into place. The patches should be clamped into position and carefully tack welded (alternating areas of tacking so as to avoid any heat warping of the body panel) before they are finish welded. The welds should be ground smooth and the surface finished with body filler and spot putty before priming and painting.

Recovering Repaired Areas

The final step in busting rust is to keep it from coming back. Repaired exterior sheetmetal should be properly primed and then painted immediately, if possible, on the day of the repair. Primer will not totally seal an exposed area; moisture can get underneath it and start attacking the metal again. A good paint coat is the best sealant against the elements and can protect your vehicle from renewed rusting. Underbody areas should be sealed with silicone sealant, undercoating, or body tar, all of which are available at automotive paint supply outlets. Never leave bare metal exposed for any length of time.

Once the repair is covered, you should use a few preventative measures to keep rust from coming back. Get your vehicle professionally undercoated if it isn't already. Thoroughly wash your car after driving in mud or over salted roads, rinsing the vehicle's underside well. Let the vehicle dry completely before putting it into a heated (humid) garage. In winter, don't park a snowy or icy vehicle in a heated garage. The snow or ice will melt, but not dry up, and the rust cycle will start again. Keep the exterior waxed year round, and touch up nicks and scrapes as they happen before rust gets a foothold.

Automobiles aren't meant to last forever, but with a little luck and an aggressive anti-rust attitude, you can keep your precious metal for a long, long time.

An ounce of prevention goes a long way where rust is concerned. A well-waxed and often-washed vehicle is less likely to suffer from the harmful oxidation caused by chemical, salt, or dirt deposits.

Common Rust Removal and Repair

1. This is a good example of surface rust on a primed pickup bed. Surface rust is easy to repair if caught in time. Left unchecked, it will rust right through the metal very shortly.

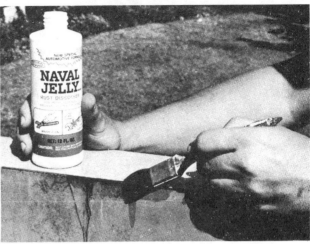

2. When using chemical rust removers such as naval jelly, always follow the directions on the label and protect your eyes and skin from the fumes or direct contact. Naval jelly is brushed on, and the rust washed off.

3. Another method of rust removal that works well on minor rust spots is sanding. When hand sanding, make sure you sand all the way to bare metal to remove all traces of rust.

4. Air tools, such as this orbital sander, take the trouble out of lengthy hand sanding. Again, make sure you remove all traces of rust. Any rust that is not eliminated will seed the rust cycle from underneath.

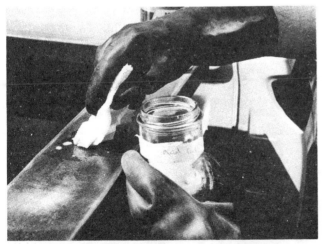

5. After sanding, wipe the metal down with a degreaser to remove residue and rust flakes. Then use a chemical surface prep solution to etch the metal for a good primer bond.

6. Spray the bare metal immediately after sanding and prepping with a heavy coat of primer. Apply the finish coat of paint as soon as possible, as primer alone will not seal out rust-causing moisture.

7. Sandblasting is an excellent method of rust removal. Commercial sandblasters can be located by checking the telephone directory, or you can rent a small sandblasting machine and do the job at home.

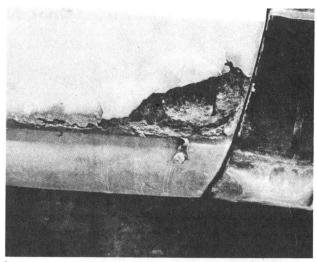

8. Major rustouts commonly occur where water becomes trapped, as it was inside this door. Rustouts like this should be cut out and patched.

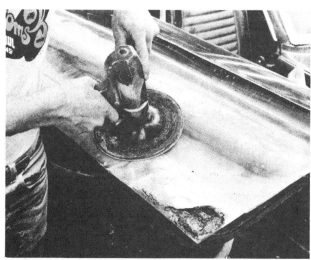

9. For ease of repair, the door was taken off the car and placed on a workbench. The first step in the repair was to grind off all paint surrounding the rusted area to determine how far the rust had spread.

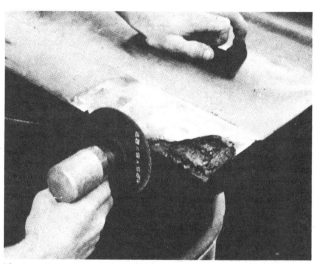

10. A body grinder was used to break the lower seam of the door. This step was made much easier due to the extensive metal decay.

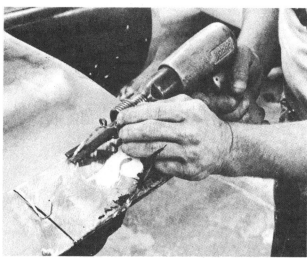

11. Once the door's outer skin was separated at the bottom edge, the entire rusted area was cut out with the help of an air chisel. Note the body filler indicating previous stopgap repairs.

12. This door had more rust and a few small holes under the outer skin. The rust was ground out and the holes brazed.

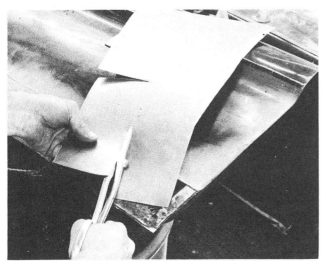

13. Next, a patch was carefully measured and cut from a piece of 22-gauge sheetmetal.

14. After the holes under the outer skin were brazed with a welding rod, the area was flattened with a hammer and dolly and the excess welding material ground smooth.

15. The patch panel was slowly and carefully tack-welded into place, with efforts taken to minimize warpage. The welds were worked over with a hammer and dolly to make the door smooth and flat. Then they were ground smooth with a disc sander.

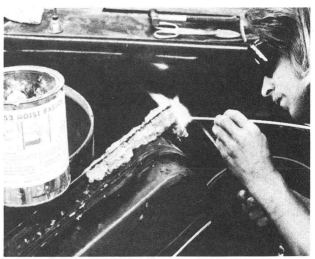

16. The bottom seam of the door was gas-welded shut. Both sides of the seam were packed with Moist Bastos to prevent heat warpage. The excess welding material left on the door seam was ground off.

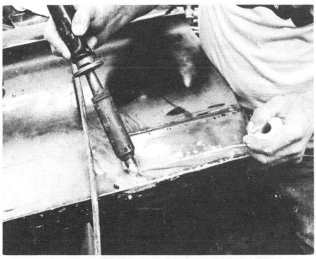

17. A heavy-duty soldering iron and acid-core solder were used to fill the tiny imperfections left after the welds were ground down. Then the whole area was covered with body filler and finished in the normal fashion.

18. The completed repair brought an old, rusty door back to life. The same techniques can be used to repair rust on almost any part of a vehicle.

Panel Alignment

Many times a car can be in an accident and superficially not be damaged. That is, the fender may not be buckled, yet something just isn't right. What usually isn't right is the fit of the panels. For example, a fender can be moved back against the front of the door edge so that the door can't be opened. The force of a collision can bend hinges and braces without actually denting the body. This kind of damage means that the pieces no longer fit properly—a frustrating kind of damage. Fortunately, the alignment of panels is relatively simple as long as you know how to tackle the problem without making the alignment worse.

Checking the Problem

There are two kinds of alignment involved in automotive bodywork: alignment of the basic substructure and alignment of the various panels, both stationary and opening. When repairs are

made, if the reinforcement structure is not exactly perfect, the external panels will not align. The keys to repairing panel alignment problems are to accurately determine where the damage is and to locate the correct position of the panel. Thoroughly measuring and checking the problem before any work is done is a must.

It is possible for a panel to be completely out of alignment without a visible sign of damage. Consequently, you must look for hidden damage. A slight unnatural kink somewhere in the frame may lead to an entire unaligned front or rear body section. The best way to check for this misalignment is with a measuring tape.

Measurements are used for comparison since cars are basically symmetrical. These comparisons are usually diagonal, and are known as X-checks. The checks include four general body sections: the front section, from the front door forward; the center section, which includes the small area from the front door to the rear door; the rear section, from the rear door to the trunk; and the trunk, or deck section of the vehicle. Measurements are taken in the same places for all types of vehicles.

The same kind of diagonal measurement can be used for X-checking all aspects of the car: from frame to body substructure to individual panel openings. Once a starting point has been established, and all other sections have been checked for alignment, then each section can also be checked against the other. This type of checking is just an extended version of the individual section checking, since a specific point is selected on opposite sides. All measurements must coincide with their opposite measurements and will normally align if the individual sections are all right. When measurements are taken between sections, it is wise to double-check your work by taking measurements from several different reference points.

Alignment of the vehicle extremities, the front and rear ends, is usually a matter of making the hood and deck lid fit. Before these panels can be tried for a fitting, the openings must be aligned as closely as possible. The deck area is harder to align than the front end because the quarter panels are welded to the mating panels. When there is major rear end damage it is necessary first to straighten the frame. Once the frame is straight, it is possible to push or pull the crumpled metal back into place until the trunk flooring again aligns with the frame.

Working from frame/flooring reference points, the inner body structures are straightened until the deck lid opening checks out perfectly according to the X-reference. If the deck lid has not been damaged, it should then fit the opening. If the lid must be straightened, it can now be repaired to fit the opening. Finally, when the panels surrounding the opening are straightened, the damaged rear end can be reshaped, but a considerable amount of measuring will be required.

Even if the door wasn't hit directly, it is still a good idea to check all openings after an accident. Tolerances should be within ⅛ inch.

Diagonal checks can be made on all openings: doors, trunk, and hood. Be sure you know where the problem is before attempting to solve it. Double check your measurements.

Diagonal measurements, also known as X-checks, are necessary to determine if part of a damaged vehicle is out of alignment. This Camaro was hit hard in the side, so metalman Eddie Paul made many comparison checks during the straightening process.

The gap between the hood and fenders should be checked with a measuring tape. Check all around the hood's perimeter.

Front End and Hood Alignment

The big advantage to aligning front sheetmetal is that the entire front end assembly is bolted on. The fenders are attached with several bolts into the cowl structure and the radiator-core support bolts to the frame. If these bolts are removed, all the sheetmetal ahead of the cowl, except the hood, can be lifted off. Cars with unit body construction do not disassemble in this manner, since the front fenders

Panel Alignment

Sometimes hoods and trunk lids can be muscled back into alignment. Only pull a little at a time and then carefully compare measurements.

Whenever the front end of a car is hit hard like this, you can be pretty sure there will be alignment adjustments needed. Any time the front end is hit, the frame and suspension should be checked by a competent frame shop before trying to align the body panels.

and inner fender panels form part of the frame/body unit. However, some cars use unit construction for the main body with a subframe bolting to the firewall. This is common to Chrysler Corporation products and some GM products like Camaros and Firebirds.

Since front end pieces are so easy to remove and replace, it is possible that replacement with used parts will be the most economical. In any case, when a front end is being worked on, it must be returned to perfect alignment or the hood will never fit properly.

There often is room for a very slight change in hood opening size since the grillework and inner panel bolt holes are elongated, but this is minor and should not be considered a substitute for proper repair. As a rule, if the core supported panels and the grille assembly do not fit well, realignment is in order. As with most other parts of the body, the flooring or frame provides the basis for most X-checking measurements in the front sheetmetal section.

Any damage to a hood that is repairable will require constant checking, both of itself and against the fender/grille opening. The hood can be checked for correct dimensions with the same X-check procedure or diagonal measurements, but twist or contour damage can only be checked

against the fenders. At the same time, a new or replacement hood may need minor tweaking to fit either a repaired or undamaged front end.

Hoods are normally held in place by spring loaded hinges. The hinges hold the hood in an open position but can also be designed to pull the rear of the hood downward when the hood is closed. Small rubber buttons along the fenders, cowl, and grille rest form vibration dampeners between the hood and surrounding panels. There is a considerable amount of built-in adjustment in the hinges but only one or two are generally needed during the fitting process.

It is often necessary to shift the fenders to get the right hood opening. If a particular fender is too high, too low, too far aft, or too far forward, all the attaching bolts should be loosened and the fender shifted by use of a long lever such as a 2x4. In the case of fore/aft movement, a hydraulic jack will do the trick.

The proper use of shims and washers can solve many front end alignment problems. The rubber stoppers on many cars are adjustable by screwing them further in or out. If you are unsure about any changes, scribe the original location before loosening any bolts. This way you will at least be able to return to your starting point.

This repaired Mustang illustrates a common source of alignment problems. Original, new, and used parts, plus some repaired sections, now make up the front end. Careful assembly and alignment is necessary to obtain a proper fit from such a variety of parts.

An assortment of wood blocks can be quite handy in solving minor alignment problems. The left side of this trunk lid was a little high, so the block was placed on the right side and pressure exerted on the left corner.

Deck Lid and Rear Panel Repair

As with doors and hoods, deck lids should fit closely and securely. The problem of providing and maintaining deck lid alignment is intensified by the fact that there are only three points of minor adjustment—the two hinges and the latch.

The deck lid is aligned when it fits the body all the way around. Usually the lid is in alignment if the gap between the lid and body/fender panels is the same circumferentially; but this doesn't mean the lid is sealing. The seal can be checked by putting chalk on the body flange edge and then closing the lid. The chalk will be transferred to the weather strip at the points of contact. If the lid is not sealing along most of the bottom edge, it can be sealed either by drawing tighter with the latch or by loosening the hinge bolts and sliding it forward or lowering it slightly.

If the deck lid seems to be twisted on the hinges, the lid can probably be twisted by hand to fit. Open the lid and place something like a rubber mallet between the body and the lid on the side that is sealing correctly. Push downward on the opposite side, but do not use excessive force. After a few test "heaves" check the lid for a fit, then repeat if necessary.

Along the quarter panels/fenders, chances are that the body flange will be too high. If so, tap with a mallet on or very near the flange to bring it into alignment. If this area is too low, use the hydraulic jack. Making the lower edge of the lid fit is a matter of either hammering the lower body panel out or bending the lid. If the lid is not sealing tightly at the latch, adjust the latch. If the center part still does not seal, place two equal pieces of 2x4 (or two rubber mallets) at either side and push forward along the lid center. If one corner is high, place the mallet under the opposite corner and push down on the offending corner. If both corners are high, place the mallet under the middle and apply equal pressure to both corners.

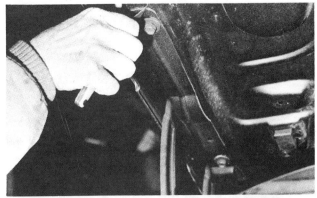

Whenever a hood or trunk lid is removed or adjusted, make a scribe mark around the hinge flange as a reference; make small movements and check, then retighten the bolts.

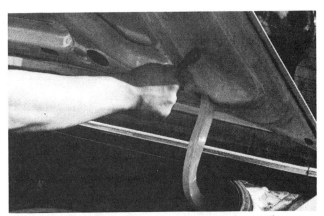

When adjusting hinges, it is only necessary to loosen the bolts slightly. You want to pull the panel into position rather than have it fall or come off the hinges. Remember, these panels are heavy and can easily pinch fingers.

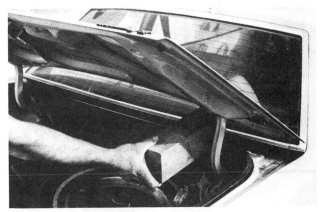

A block of wood can be used at the front edge of a trunk lid to raise or lower it depending on whether you lift on the back edge of the lid or push down on it.

If both corners of a deck lid are sealing poorly, it may be necessary to place a block in the center of the trunk and press evenly on both corners. On larger trunk lids it helps to have one person on each corner.

Door Repair and Alignment

Perhaps the most perplexing panels to keep in alignment are the doors, since they can become misaligned through use, age, and damage. A door will be out of alignment when the contours do not match the surrounding panels and when the door itself is not exactly centered in the door opening.

Panel Alignment

When trying to make a trunk or hood seal properly, be sure the rubber cushions are intact, in good shape, and properly adjusted if the cushion is on threaded stock. Also check the condition of the weather stripping.

To check how a door is sealing, place a strip of paper in it and close. If the paper slips out of the closed door anywhere in the opening, that point isn't sealing.

The ever-popular 2x4 piece of wood can be used on door hinges, but try the hinge adjustments before using force.

A long piece of wood will work as a lever to lift a sagging door. It also works to have a helper lift up on the door handle while you adjust the hinge bolts.

If there has been extensive damage to a door or door frame, chances are the opening itself will have sustained some damage and must be carefully X-checked. At the same time, distortion of the door opening can be caused by frame misalignment, body twist, and other seemingly unrelated factors. If damage is involved, the opening must be X-checked to make sure it is ready for door alignment.

The surface contour of the door in all directions must match that of the surrounding panels. When checking for misalignment, the opening gap around the door perimeter should be uniform. There may be a slightly larger gap on one side, but this should remain uniform along its length.

While making the visual alignment check, look at the scuff plate to see if the door is dragging (sagging). Open and close the door slowly and note whether the door raises or lowers as it latches. If there is an up or down movement, the door is out of alignment vertically and is being centered by the dovetail.

There are two specific controls that keep a door in position when closed: the striker plate and the dovetail. The striker plate is the latch and the dovetail limits up-and-down movement of the closed door. The dovetail's function may be integrated with the latch mechanism, but sometimes it is included separately to keep the door from jiggling up and down on the hinges.

Striker plates can be adjusted over a relatively wide range, but before any adjustments are made the striker should be replaced if worn. A little wear is no problem, but excessive wear, which is visually apparent, or sloppiness in parts (such as a rotary latch) dictates replacement. If the door won't close or fits too loosely, the striker needs adjustment.

Spacers may be required to make strikers fit properly. If spacers are required, first add some caulking compound to the striker where the lock extension engages. Close the door to make an impression in the compound, then measure this compound thickness. If the distance from the striker teeth to the rear edge of the clay depression is less than 11/32 inch, spacers and different length attaching screws will be needed, as follows:

Dimension	No. of spacers	Spacer thickness	Striker screws
11/32-9/32 in.	1	1/16 in.	original
9/32-7/32 in.	1	⅛ in.	⅛ in.
7/32-5/32 in.	1 each	1/16 & ⅛ in.	⅛ in.
5/32-3/32 in.	2 (⅛ in.)	¼ in.	¼ in.

The dovetail does not correct door sag, but it will allow slight movement of the door up or down for adjustment. The dovetail on older cars will probably be very worn and should be replaced.

There is considerable adjustment available at the hinges, but no hinge work should be attempted without making sure this is where the problem lies. This is especially important on older cars that do not have hinge adjustment in the fore/aft plane. Such hinges must be spread or closed. If the door sags, the usual remedy is to spread the lower hinge slightly, which moves the door bottom closer to the pillar. Sometimes, the upper hinge must also be closed to correct sag.

A hinge can be spread by placing some kind of interference between the leaves. Most bodymen rely on a hammer or screwdriver handle. First the handle is placed between the opened hinge leaves, then the door is partially closed. When the handle is tight in the hinge, the door is forced toward the car. Sometimes it will close if the interference is slight. Make all force spreading adjustments in small increments to keep from spreading the hinge too far. After each force session, check the door for proper fit. Proceed slowly!

If the top hinge must be closed, the hinge has to be removed. If the door has been damaged and the hinge bent, the distortion will be apparent. Repair is a matter of squeezing the hinge leaves together in a large vise.

If the car has adjustable hinges, as most modern cars do, close alignment is possible with very little labor. Remove the striker and dovetail assembly so they do not interfere with the way the door actually hangs in the opening. The major difference among makes of cars is whether the hinge adjustment is made at the door or at the pillar. All types of adjustable hinges are adjusted by loosening the bolts and forcing the door to a new position. Loosen the bolts a little bit at a time only.

If the door alignment cannot be corrected by adjustments to the hinges or the striker plate assembly, the trouble lies in either door body opening or door contour. If the door contour is not correct, it could require special tools in severe cases or nothing more than a knee and two hands. If the door is not contoured (bowed) enough, the top and bottom must be bent inward while the middle is kept stationary. Any time you apply force to a door, do it slowly and carefully.

Door contour work can be especially difficult on very old cars that used wood as the major substructure (early Chevys are a prime example). If the substructure is wood, all rotten sections should be replaced and all joints glued and fitted with wood dowels or new screws.

Making body parts fit properly is one of those time consuming tasks, but it is the kind of attention to detail that separates the really good bodymen from the rest of the crowd.

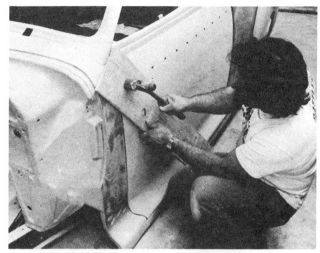
Using a block of wood and a big hammer to make minute alignment adjustments to a door isn't for the faint of heart. Take care to use a large enough piece of wood to disperse the blow. Centering the blow will cause a dent.

Most older cars rely on shims between the body and the frame to solve alignment problems. If the body is correctly shimmed, the doors will fit properly.

Whenever you encounter a damaged bumper, you should check the bumper braces for alignment if you expect the new bumper to fit correctly.

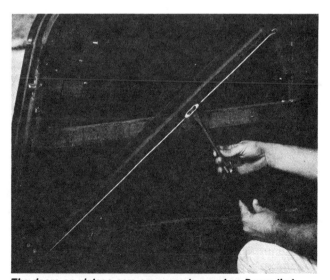
The doors on vintage cars are prone to sagging. Doors that use wood in their frames can be helped by the installation of a tension strap with a turnbuckle as shown here.

Fiberglass Fundamentals

Fiberglass is a material that's well known, popular, and almost universally accepted as the major alternative to steel in the construction and customizing of cars, trucks, and related vehicles. Yet it remains one of the most little understood substances in the entire body and paint industry. While there are many body shops around the country that specialize in fiberglass repairs, they make up only a very small percentage of all professional body shops. Chances of finding qualified, experienced fiberglass repairmen at a regular shop are not good. There is virtually no similarity between metal and fiberglass when it comes to repairs. Given the shortage of fiberglass repairmen and the ever increasing number of 'glass-bodied Corvettes, street rods, kit cars, and special interest vehicles, it's no surprise that more and more car owners are turning to doing their own fiberglass repairs.

Fortunately, even though fiberglass tends to be used most commonly on exotic-type cars, there is really nothing exotic about working with fiberglass. But before you can work with it successfully, it helps to know a little about the chemistry behind fiberglass-reinforced plastic. Unlike sheetmetal, fiberglass, with its plastic "skin," does not stretch or compress; it rips, tears, and melts when heated. Even the simplest fiberglass repair involves a complicated chemical bonding of fibers and resins. Although a metal repair can be pounded smooth and filled, a similar plastic repair must be patched from the outer and undersides, sanded, filled, sanded, and filled again as many as three times. And because the chemicals in the resins used must cure between steps, a typical fiberglass repair will take twice as long as a metal repair.

Fiberglass is a combination of three elements: glass fiber, polyester resins, and catalysts. By itself, resin is easily formed but has little strength. This is the job of the glass fiber reinforcements, which are available as either interwoven or matted blankets.

The resins themselves come in a number of forms, including phenolics, acrylics, epoxies, ureas, and polyesters. Polyesters are used because they are inexpensive and easy to control. Resin works well with glass fibers because, though it is manufactured in heavy liquid form, it cures or hardens as a solid. However, the hardening process requires heat in the range of 200 degrees F. That's where the catalyst or activators come in. The catalyst "kicks" the resin into an exothermic (outside heat) reaction. The amount of catalyst added to a batch of resin will control the drying or curing time of the fiberglass. When using catalysts, remember that shop temperature will also affect curing, with the time speeded up on a hot day and slowed down on a cold day.

Of the two types of fiberglass material, the woven cloth is the strongest. It is used for the base material of many fiberglass pieces such as kit car bodies, street rod fenders and sports car flares, and spoilers. Mat, on the other hand, is designed to give thickness and strength to a laminate. The glass fibers in the mat are laid so they run in one direction. The next sheet is then laid with the fibers going in the opposite direction; thus a kind of plywood effect is obtained, ensuring strength.

When working with fiberglass, remember that it can irritate the skin. This irritation can be avoided by using a protective cream on the hands or by wearing rubber gloves. Also, wear long sleeved shirts, button your shirt collar and use a respirator if necessary. Fiberglass dust kicked up by a disc grinder may irritate the nostrils.

Resins should be used in well ventilated areas, since toxic fumes are involved. These same resins accumulate on tools, shoes, clothing, practically everything. Everything should be cleaned with lacquer thinner, which is an excellent cleaning agent, while the resin is still soft.

Fiberglass on Fiberglass

The use of fiberglass in the automotive industry increases every year. There are three general kinds of fiberglass parts being used: matched metal molds, spray lay-ups, and hand lay-ups. With matched metal molds, chopped fiber and polyester resins are mixed, the catalyst is added, and the combination is placed in a male/female mold. Heat and pressure are applied and the finished product is ready in a few minutes. This method of making parts is fast and inexpensive, although not always strong.

With spray lay-up, chopped fiberglass roving is blown into a female mold along with catalyzed resin. The mixture is then rolled by hand and allowed to cure at ambient temperatures. This type of lay-up is popular with smaller manufacturers, although the builder must control the percentages of fiberglass and resin to control strength.

Hand lay-up is generally saved for one-off fiberglass pieces. Fiberglass mat, cloth, or roving (or a combination of these) is laid in the female mold and saturated with resin. The entire surface is then rolled to ensure proper mixture and balance throughout and to remove air bubbles. Pieces formed this way are usually very strong and thick, but the process is costly.

Repair of any of these types of fiberglass parts is pretty much the same: remove the damaged material, bevel all edges, grind off any paint and the protective gel coat to reach the raw fiberglass underneath. This should be done on both sides of a repair. Then cut a piece of mat and apply to the inner surface with the resin mix. Cover the mat with a piece of resin-saturated cloth pressed firmly in place. After the repair is allowed to cure, grind the surface smooth and either re-mat or fill the remain-

Fiberglass is an ideal material for custom work because it is lightweight and very easy to work with when creating new shapes and forms. This full custom Corvette was created by mixing and matching existing aftermarket fiberglass parts.

Fiberglass Fundamentals

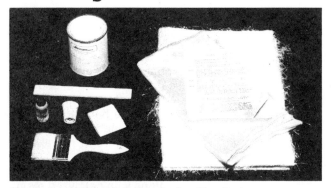

The fundamentals of fiberglass begin with a basic understanding of the chemical processes and some basic supplies, including 'glass mat or cloth, resins, catalysts, and safety equipment such as rubber gloves and respirator.

ing low spots with plastic body filler. Finish the filler as you would a metal repair. Remember that this process must be repeated on each side of the repair. Some repairmen claim you can repair small cracks with pure resin and filler, but for a permanent and strong repair you should always use mat or cloth for reinforcement. The process takes more time, but the repair will last many times longer when done right.

Besides using fiberglass to repair fiberglass, the material works very well as a medium for bonding fiberglass parts together. Adding fiberglass flares, spoilers, scoops, and the like, is a relatively simple process of attaching, bonding, filling, reinforcing, and finishing (see accompanying flare how-to). A fiberglass on fiberglass repair or addition can be as strong as, or stronger than, the original piece.

Tools and supplies you'll need for most fiberglass repairs or add-ons include a disc grinder, cheese-grater file, screwdrivers, small rubber body putty squeegee, small roller, sandpaper, goggles, respirator, and gloves to protect yourself, as well as some

Fiberglass isn't just used for Corvettes and plastic-bodied street rods. There are many fiberglass accessories including flares, spoilers, and whale-tails that are easily riveted onto steel-bodied cars and trucks.

acetone to clean resin from you and your tools. You'll also need fiberglass mat or cloth along with resin and catalyst, all of which should be available at major paint and body supply outlets.

Fiberglass on Metal

We said at the beginning that there is very little similarity between fiberglass and sheetmetal. It should be no surprise then that the two materials don't really mix very well. The problem relates to their basic makeup. Fiberglass does not bend or stretch the way metal does. It has a rigidity that causes it to flex and expand and contract at a different rate than metal. While it is entirely possible to attach fiberglass flares, scoops, and other pieces to metal vehicles, even the best workmanship will eventually crack and deteriorate due to this unequal flexing and expansion/contraction.

The key to attaching fiberglass to metal, when the two are to be molded together rather than just riveted on (leaving a visible seam), is to prepare the metal to bare surface for maximum bonding and to attach the fiberglass part as securely as possible. This means, for example, in the case of a fiberglass hood scoop, to run rivets or screws as close as possible (every 1-2 inches) to limit flexing. Then carefully apply mat or cloth, using epoxy resin instead of polyester, as the latter will not adhere well to metal. Finish the molding with plastic body filler, being careful to avoid heavy filler buildup which is more susceptible to chipping and cracking.

Finishing and Painting

Finishing and painting fiberglass is not much different than finishing and painting metal. After you feel that the surface of the car or repair is virtually free of all imperfections and you have spot puttied in any pinholes or flaws in the plastic filler, you can proceed to priming. Most professional fiberglass repair shops recommend using a lacquer primer-surfacer. Before applying the primer, go over the 'glass with 80-grit, 100-grit and then 220-wet and 320-wet sandpaper. Apply several coats of primer, hand sanding the area with 320-wet paper between coats. Before painting with the color coats, go over the body or repaired area one more time. Fiberglass is susceptible to pinholing, caused by bubbles in the fiberglass popping through the paint. Again, fill any pinholes in the primer with putty, re-sand, prime, and check the body again. When you are satisfied, let the body dry out. Unlike metal, primed fiberglass needs to cure (at least two weeks is recommended). It's not only the primer that is drying, but all the chemicals underneath.

After curing, the fiberglass can be painted. Lacquer, not enamel, is again recommended because it is easier to spot in and dries faster during painting (eliminating the problem of dust and dirt getting into the paint finish). For a top-quality job, spray four or five coats of lacquer, color sand, and then spray an additional five to 10 coats. After the lacquer has been rubbed out you should have a vehicle that truly qualifies as a plastic fantastic.

Molding Fiberglass to Metal

1. Ready-made fender flares are available for many makes of vehicles. Some can be riveted right on while others require opening up of the stock wheelwells with an air chisel, as shown on this Datsun Z-car installation.

2. The fender opening is trimmed until a close fit between the sheetmetal and the flare is achieved. The front fenders on this particular application bolt right on.

3. The quarter panel is ground bare, and the flare and body are coated with a bonding epoxy. While one person holds the flare firmly against the car, a second person drills and rivets it to the inner fenderwell sheetmetal.

4. To provide a smooth transition from the body to the flare, a thin swipe of body filler is applied into the seam.

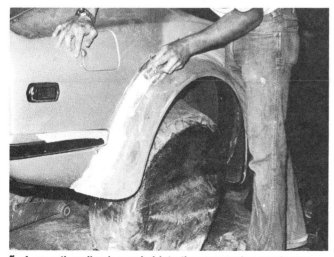

5. A smooth radius is sanded into the seam using sandpaper wrapped around a short length of heater hose.

6. The flare is finished by block-sanding and priming. After painting the flares to match the car, the job is done. Besides looking super, the flares accommodate larger-than-stock wheels and tires.

Fiberglass Repair

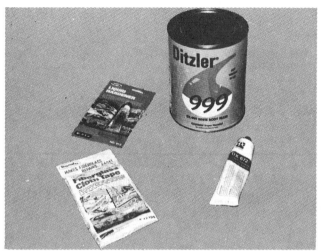

1. There are many ways to make a fiberglass repair—most of them wrong. A good repair starts with proper materials. For a proper fiberglass repair, you will need fiberglass mat or cloth, resin, catalyst or hardener, and plastic body filler.

2. We followed the repair of a '59 Corvette at D&D Corvette and Fiberglass Repair, San Bernardino, California. The Vette, like many, was suffering from cracks caused by a previous, poorly done repair. The first step was to remove the old panel.

3. After locating the bonding strip on the inside of the fender, a cutting disc was used to cut through the bad panel, leaving the bonding strip underneath intact.

4. A hammer and chisel were used to pry the panel away from the strip and then from the rest of the car in one piece.

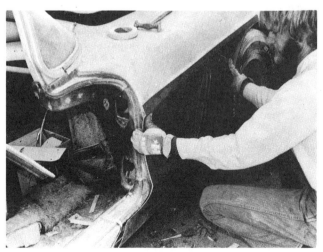

5. The new panel was test-fitted into position. A lot of grinding was necessary to make it fit properly and blend into the contour of the fender.

6. One of the tricks used by D&D is to blow the fiberglass debris away from the working area with a fan. It is also a good idea to always wear gloves, a respirator, and goggles when working with fiberglass.

7. Using a 36-grit sanding disc, all traces of the old binding adhesive were removed. The disc is coarse enough to remove the excess material without damaging the fiberglass. It leaves a textured surface on which the new bonding material can adhere.

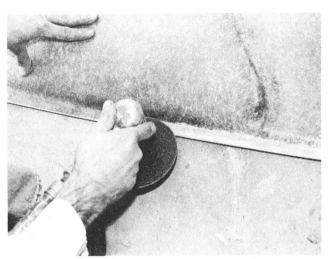

8. The areas of the new panel that would bond to the car were then roughed up using the 36-grit disc.

9. The panel was then screwed into place with special tapping screws made to work with fiberglass. They have a portion of the beginning threads removed so they won't damage the glass.

10. With the screws in place, a visual check was made of the fit. Note that the door was reinstalled to make sure the body line would flow properly from the door to the panel.

11. Eckler's Bonding Adhesive has the consistency of day-old oatmeal. It was mixed with cream hardener until the mixture took on a light red color.

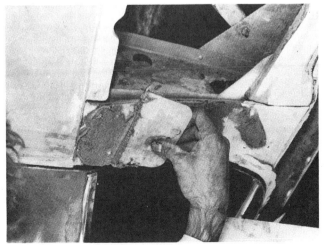

12. Then the thoroughly mixed adhesive was generously applied to the points where the new panel would connect to the body.

13. With the panel loosely positioned, the screws were reinstalled and left in place until the adhesive had thoroughly dried. Once the screws were removed, the resulting holes in the panel were filled with resin and smoothed out.

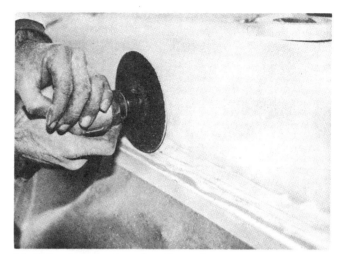

14. Using the 36-grit sanding disc, a "V"-shaped groove was cut along the point where the two panels butt together.

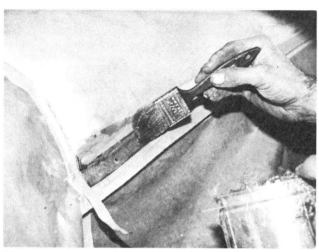

15. Masking tape was laid on both sides of the groove, marking the limits of the area to be resined. Using a paint brush, the resin/hardener mixture was brushed into the groove.

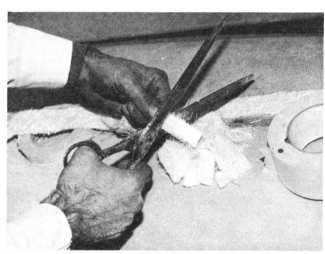

16. Fiberglass mat was first cut into ½ and 1-inch-wide strips, and then further cut down into small rectangles.

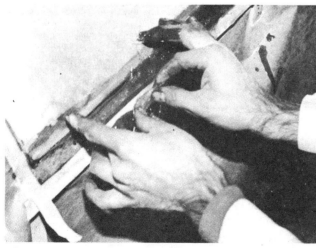

17. The rectangles were soaked in resin and placed in the groove. After the narrower rectangles were laid into position, the wider rectangles were added for a layered effect that filled the groove completely.

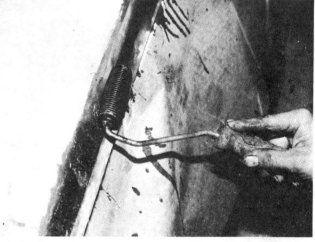

18. A roller was used to remove any air bubbles trapped in the layers of resin-soaked fiberglass mat.

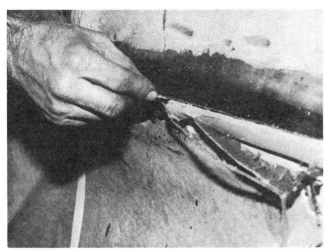

19. Once thoroughly dried, the excess mat and resin were cut away with a razor blade.

20. The disc grinder was used to smooth the panel joint so it was flush with the rest of the car. In areas where a bonding strip was not used as a backing panel, a temporary strip was used to support the panel from behind.

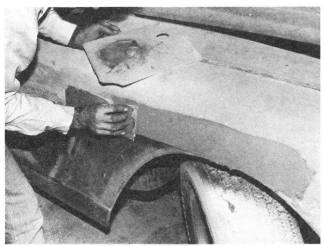

21. A thin coat of plastic body filler was then spread over the panel joint. Nowhere on the repair should filler be more than 1/16-inch thick.

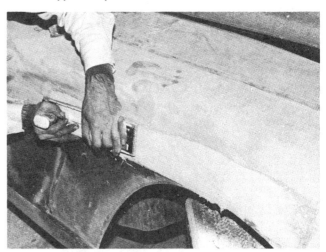

22. The filler was then sanded smooth with 40-grit paper, forming the final contour of the finished fender.

23. After sanding, gelcoat mixed with hardener was sprayed over the entire fender to fill any pinholes or nicks. D&D recommends the use of six heavy coats of gelcoat to ensure the fender is well sealed against flaws and future cracks.

24. The finished fender looks as good as new, and probably is stronger. As is, it is ready for priming and final painting.

Molding Fiberglass to Fiberglass

1. Installing fiberglass fender flares on a fiberglass body is relatively easy. Start by mounting the flare in the desired position, using the locating tabs as a guide.

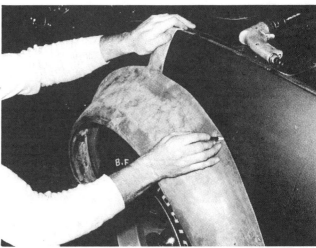

2. Secure the flare to the car with sheetmetal screws, using the holes provided. Use a grease pencil to mark a line on the body along the edge of the flare. Then remove the flare.

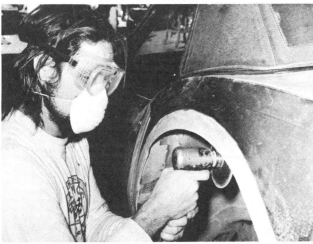

3. With a saber saw or small grinder, cut a new opening about an inch lower than the marked line, closer where you approach the doorpost. Grind the back of the flare and both sides of the body around the wheelwell.

4. Reinstall the flare with the screws, and cut off the locating tabs. Be sure the flare fits the body well before adding extra screws at 5-inch intervals.

5. Mix a small batch of adhesive and catalyst, using about 20 drops of catalyst to a golf ball-sized glob of mounting adhesive.

6. Back out the screws and pack the adhesive between the flare and the body. Then tighten the flare firmly against the body and squeegee the excess adhesive off the seam.

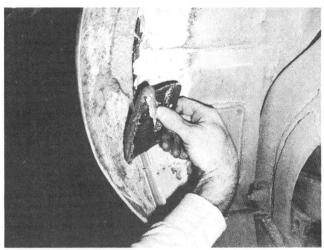

7. Fill the gap between the flare and the car body with adhesive. Pack it in solid and work out all air bubbles. Allow the adhesive to cure until fairly hard (about two hours).

8. Work the resin/catalyst mix into small mat patches. Do not soak the patch. Tear the mat apart to produce fuzzy edges for better overlapping. Cut the 'glass cloth slightly wider.

9. Mat patches should overlap the adhesive used to fill the space between the flare and body. Work out all air bubbles before applying wider cloth patches over the matted area.

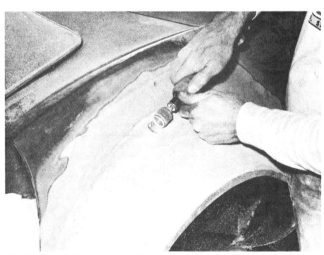

10. Next, grind out screw dimples and sand the entire surface with 80-grit paper to remove the surface gloss. Fill the dimples with adhesive and grind flush when semi-hard.

11. Slightly thin the plastic body filler with resin after adding the catalyst. Squeegee a thin coat over the seam area, filling all surface flaws. Allow this to cure.

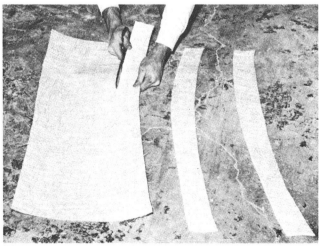

12. Then cut 3-inch-wide curved strips of mat and tear them into 6-inch lengths. Curved patches will fill the fender without wrinkling. No cloth is used here.

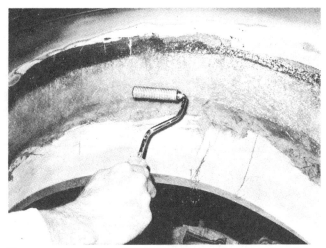

13. Using an old paint brush, work wet patches down into the seam area. Then use a roller to press out excess resin and force mat down against body and flare.

14. Use 24-grit paper with a very flexible backing pad to grind down the area to the desired finished radius. Then feather the patches into the surrounding body.

15. Use a plastic squeegee to apply a fairly heavy coat of body filler to fill any low spots. Wipe the filler on in long, smooth passes.

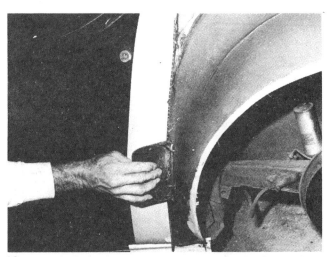

16. Using a piece of cardboard in the door opening keeps the edge straight. Work the body filler in against the lower edge, shaping carefully at the lower tip of the flare.

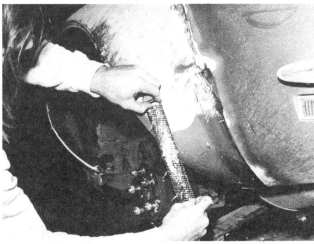

17. Once the filler has set up, work the entire area with a cheesegrater file, removing and shaping the body filler while it's still soft.

18. After sanding the filler with 40-grit paper, refill any low spots. Before priming, the flare should be sanded progressively with 80-grit, 100-grit, 220-wet, and 320-wet paper to obtain a glass-smooth finish.

Using Fiberglass with Wood

1. Fiberglass is more versatile than many people think. Here fiberglass mini-truck fenders are extended by mating them to wooden spacers. After cutting the spacers, use a grinding disc to rough up the edge of the flare.

2. The fiberglass resin is then applied generously to both the wooden spacer and the fender edge. Once coated, join the two immediately and position carefully.

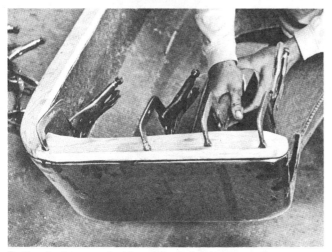

3. Use C-clamps or locking pliers to hold each section securely in place.

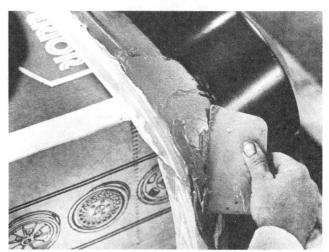

4. Fenders extended more than 1 inch should receive a strengthening layer of fiberglass cloth. Such conservation jobs can utilize body filler to enforce and smooth the bond.

5. The fenders are then finished on a workbench or 55-gallon drum. A combination of Surform file and sanding blocks are used to finish the wood, filler, and fiberglass.

6. The widened fender looks as though it came from the mold that way. The fender now covers the extra wide wheels and tire completely while retaining stock fenderwell flaring.

Vintage Bodywork

A visit to a local old car swap meet is the only proof needed to realize that the price of old car body parts has gone right through the ceiling. The really good parts and solid, unfinished cars are in the "if you have to ask, you can't afford it" bracket. The affordable cars and parts are the kind that even people who have been in the hobby less than 10 years categorize as "I threw away better stuff than that just a few years ago." Any crumpled, rusted old piece of sheetmetal is likely to turn up at a swap meet for sale.

Two things can be deduced from the current state of affairs at old car swap meets: the whole hobby has gone stark raving nuts, or the supply of quality vintage tin is rapidly disappearing. The situation is probably a little of the former and a lot of the latter. People no longer have the luxury of discarding dented fenders and bolting on a set of new or cherry used ones (although there are an ever increasing amount of quality reproduction steel body

parts and patch panels); so previously ignored vintage tin is now being salvaged.

It is not uncommon for several totalled old cars to be pieced back together into one good car. This is particularly true of the more desirable open cars. It seems like there are more steel '32 Ford roadsters around today than in 1932. The trend to salvage almost any old car is mixed with the trend toward flawless bodywork. Old cars are no longer jalopies used to putt around town in. Old cars of any type are valuable possessions and many once common cars are being restored to a level previously reserved for the great classics.

The desire for flawless cars and the shortage of good raw material means that the bodymen of this country are doing a great business in fixing up old cars. Hobbyist restorers are having to learn more and better skills to keep up with the state of the hobby. A person who can turn out near-perfect vintage bodywork is a person who can enjoy an in-

Really great vintage sheetmetal is getting harder and harder to find. Even seemingly good bodies can need extensive massaging once the paint is removed. Sanding this '32 Ford roadster door revealed many low spots. Also, notice how rust has started to eat away at the lower edge of the cowl.

Many restorers and street rodders like to remove all traces of old paint and rust by having their cars chemically cleaned. This process will remove all old body filler so you will know exactly what repairs are in order.

triguing occupation and a healthy income.

The key to vintage bodywork is old time craftsmanship just like the care that was used to build the cars in the first place. Shortcuts and quick fixes aren't desired in vintage bodywork. Patience, and attention to detail are important traits that can bring handsome rewards.

When working on old cars, try to keep everything the way it is supposed to be. When enthusiasts crawl over and under a car, they look for bad metal in the deck lid (flat spots that run across the lid are very common), high and low spots in the metal panels directly above and below the deck lid, short vertical waves in the quarter panels above the rear fenders (also very common), and flat spots in the hood and irregular fender edges.

Typical of the special problems encountered in old cars are the problems with deck lids. Deck lids are relatively low crowned panels that normally have a curve in both directions. When flat spots appear, they usually appear as bands about 4 inches wide, from one side to another.

The quick and dirty way to repair a "banded" deck lid is with large amounts of plastic filler, but this isn't the best way. The metal should be worked. Raising all the low bands can be accomplished by either picking and prying or by cutting the inner panel away and working with a hammer and dolly. The latter is preferable. When the inner panel is cut out, use tin snips or a panel cutter. Do not use the torch. This panel removal technique can also be used with doors.

With the inner panel removed, work up the low spots. Since the metal will tend to work harden during this process, the panel will hold shape better after working. Always check the progress with an adjustable body file. Since the flattened spots will have displaced the panel elsewhere, the edges of the bands will tend to be high. After a panel is perfect, the inner panel is spot-brazed back in place being careful not to use enough heat to cause external panel distortion.

The body panels directly above the deck lid on older cars are not as large as the deck lid, but often

The lower sections of old cars are especially prone to rustout. The only sure way to cure the problem is to cut out the damaged area and replace it with a new panel.

An ever increasing array of reproduction patch panels are available for rust repairs. The supply of patch panels is particularly good for early Ford products.

Vintage Bodywork

Welding tends to warp sheetmetal, unless the patch is hammer welded using a dolly behind the panel. This patch panel was hammer welded for most of its length, but lower heat brazing was used at the ends, because there is no way to get a dolly behind these areas.

The deck lids of old cars can be full of flat spots. The deck lid should be worked up as much as possible with a hammer and dolly. A thin coat of filler can be applied and worked with a sanding board or air file to finish the deck lid.

To gain access to deck lids and doors, it is sometimes necessary to cut out the inner support structures, straighten the panel, and then weld the support section back in place.

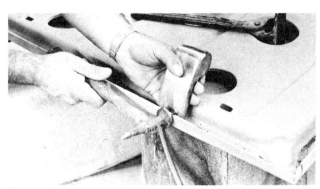

Many bodymen overlook the flange lip of deck lids. These lips get wavy over the years and should be straightened with a hammer and dolly.

cause as much trouble. The upper panel normally requires work to smooth out low spots. Again, these spots can be filled with plastic, but since the panel is easily reached it is better to work out the dents in the traditional manner. The lower panel is not so easy. This particular piece of sheetmetal is usually hemmed over a rather substantial brace.

The lower panel is one place where plastic filler is almost unavoidable. There is seldom room to get a dolly or even a pick of some kind inside the bracing. The alternative is to weld up any cracks (they usually start at the upper and lower edges where this panel is riveted via a flange to the quarter panels), grind and lead if necessary, and straighten the flanged lip along the deck lid opening. To get a perfectly smooth contour often requires the use of plastic filler. When working such a large area which has a very low crown in both directions, it is an advantage to rely primarily on large sanding files.

One area of the deck lid that is often overlooked is the flange lip itself. This should be cleaned thoroughly with a rotary wire brush, both inside and beneath. Clean out all the old paint, rubber, and cement, and then weld up the minute cracks that are sure to be present. Do not prime the lip heavily; instead use a thin coat of primer/surfacer and a thin coat of color to reduce its tendency to chip.

Quarter panels are the dead giveaway as an index to quality of bodywork on older cars. While rust is possible at the bottom edge, vertical waves are common in the area around the fender opening. These imperfections may have been caused by a rear end collision at some time, but many undamaged bodies also have them.

Fixing Fenders

Banged up fenders with cracked and split seams are one of the most common problems with vintage sheetmetal, probably because the design of old cars made the fenders vulnerable. Also, the fenders weren't supported as well as modern ones are. Vibrations also play a big part in the

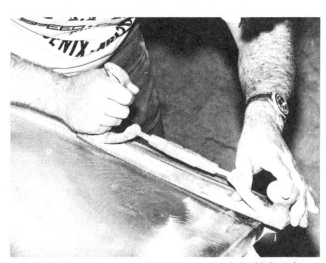

Adjustable body files are widely used to check for high and low spots when repairing vintage sheetmetal. Use the file carefully so you don't take away too much metal.

The attention paid to vintage bodywork today far exceeds the care given to the cars when they were new. Here is a Model A roadster being worked on at Customs by Eddie Paul. The entire underside and inner body areas were painted with Ditzler acrylic enamel with hardener. All of these hidden areas should be painted before the exterior of the body.

It is best to remove fenders from the body, either for repairs or painting. Very often there is a noticeable ridge of old paint buildup from previous paint jobs where the fenders were left intact. Removing the fenders also makes it easier to install new fender welting after the paint job.

downfall of old fenders.

A good way to diagnose wavy fenders is with either a plumb level or a plumb bob. Position either of these vertical plumb devices at stations down the fender edge and make chalks on the pavement below. Connect these marks with a line to determine how straight the fender edge really is.

Fender edge repair on older cars is best done with a hammer and dolly, at least until all the workable metal is straight. Because some fenders used wire in the rolled bead, it is nearly impossible to get each tiny dent out so some filler must be used.

Irregularities in fender edges are sometimes difficult to see. Draw a straight reference line on the floor and run a straightedge along the fender bead while holding a piece of chalk. The line on the floor indicates the fender waves.

Another very common problem with old fenders is that they are prone to rust and deterioration where the fenders join the running boards. This damage is usually out of sight, but it should be stopped before the cancer spreads up to visible areas. The common way to repair such damage is to cut out the damaged section and weld in a replacement section.

With the high cost of beautiful fenders, many restorers and street rodders are resorting to making a good fender out of two bad ones. A typical way of making two otherwise useless fenders into one good one is to take a fender that was "bobbed" (an old customizing trick consisting of cutting several inches off the rear end of a fender for a "sportier" look) and mate it to the good rear section of a fender that was hit very hard in front. Conservation projects like this can save lots of vintage tin.

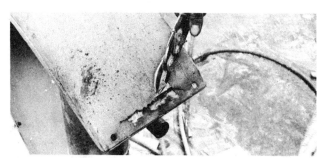

The bottom of the rear fenders, where they meet the running boards are prone to rust. The damaged area should be cut out and replaced with a patch panel.

Filling with Lead

One of the most common catch phrases concerning bodywork on old cars is "it was all done in lead." There is sort of a snob appeal to saying that there is no plastic filler in your old car. Leading was the accepted way of filling holes and other imperfections before plastic fillers achieved their current state. Modern plastic body fillers are quality products that are easy to use and quite durable. Still, the connotation of lead work is one of old time craftsmanship and quality.

With the current interest in high quality restora-

If a commercially made patch panel isn't available, one can be made from the same gauge sheetmetal as that used on the original fender. Clamp the metal in place, trace it, and cut it out with metal snips.

Vintage Bodywork

Clamp the patch panel in place and spot weld it. Use hammer welding to complete the seam. Hammer welding is necessary to control warpage.

Ditzler Alum-A-Lead is preferred by many bodymen because it is harder and less prone to shrinkage than plastic fillers. Alum-A-Lead is applied like ordinary fillers with a plastic spreader.

Gray primer should be sprayed over the fender and sanded. Then lightly spray a guide coat of darker primer or black paint.

Block sand the guide coat and low spots will still be darker than the gray primer.

tions there has been a renewed interest in working with lead. There are even companies that sell all the supplies necessary for lead work. These firms usually advertise in the old car publications like *Hemmings Motor News*.

The advantage of lead is that when it is correctly alloyed, it is especially well suited for auto body repairs. Lead can be heated and easily shaped. It bonds perfectly and permanently to sheetmetal. It is easy to finish, and it will accept paint like sheetmetal.

Lead will bond to metals because it will tin the surface with its own properties. Although tinning is often accomplished with a secondary compound, the lead itself can be used. Tinning is made possible by heating the sheetmetal to the melting point of lead, using some kind of flux to clean the metal and applying a thin coat of lead. If the metal is the right temperature and has been cleaned well, the lead will flow across the metal surface like water.

Lead that is alloyed for body and fender repair has its own peculiar melting characteristic, in that it does not melt from a solid to a liquid immediately. Most body leads start to soften about 360 degrees F. and become softer as the temperature is raised. The point at which a particular lead compound will melt is determined by the percentage of tin in the mixture. Furthermore, the body lead alloy will melt below the melting point of pure lead, 620 degrees F., and it may be below the melting point of tin at 455 degrees F. The higher the amount of tin in a compound, the lower the melting point. This should be considered when buying lead.

For all-around shop use, the 70-30 alloy is best (70 percent lead and 30 percent tin). This alloy melts just under 500 degrees F., which gives a wide latitude or plasticity for working in prolonged areas. Lead is available in a wide range of percentages, but anything other than 70-30 or 80-20 is not easy to use.

The basic steps in lead work include cleaning, tinning, filling, shaping, and finishing. An area larger than that which is to be leaded must be cleaned before leading can be done. This is because the lead

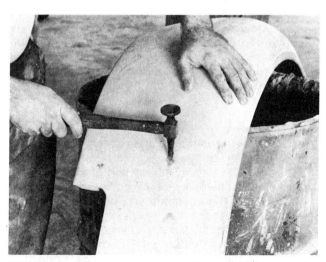

The high and low spots should be worked with a hammer and dolly until the fender is perfect. Then apply another coat of primer, finish sand, and apply the color coat.

The newly painted fender is beautifully finished inside and out, making it almost better than new.

The high cost of good fenders means that many bodymen are taking two damaged fenders and mating them to form one good fender. Such was the case with this '36 Ford that had bobbed fenders. A fender that was badly crunched in front was used to supply the missing rear section of the bobbed fender.

The patch piece was cut off the scrap fender with a saber saw. The saber saw leaves a clean edge with no metal distortion.

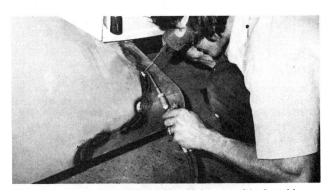

The patch piece was installed with widely spaced tack welds to prevent great concentrations of heat which can lead to metal warpage.

After the seam was hammer welded, a grinder was used to lightly grind scale off the seam. Standard metal finishing techniques were employed to prepare the fender for painting.

must blend perfectly into the surrounding area.

After a thorough cleaning, tinning is necessary. The tinning flux is a chemical cleaner for steel. Tinning flux comes in a variety of types, but the kind normally associated with other forms of soldering is not acceptable in bodywork. Tinning flux is usually wiped on with a rag or brushed on the surface. Steel wool dipped in the flux can also be used to apply the product to the work surface.

When a liquid flux is used, the area to be tinned is first lightly heated then the flux is brushed on. After the area is brushed with tinning liquid, the metal should be heated with brief passes of the torch until it is hot enough to melt the lead pressed against the surface. When pressing the lead bar, just a small mound will melt; then as the metal becomes too cold, the car crumbles. A slight twisting motion of the bar will help get the correct amount. Repeat this brief heat and solder treatment to about one-third the area to be covered with lead.

To spread the lead over the surface and thereby gain the full tinning advantage, heat an area around a lead mound or two. As the lead changes appearance from the solid, grainy look to a shiny look, wipe it across the panel with a wadded clean rag. Make all the wipes in the same direction, and make sure the entire area is tinned. There will be a series of overlapping wipe strokes, and when slightly cooled, the tinned area will appear dull in contrast with the freshly sanded steel. While the lead is being wiped over the surface to get a good tin, the flux residue is being wiped away. Tinning is an alternate heat-and-wipe situation.

Be careful when using heat and the rag on a tinned area. If too much pressure is applied to the rag, the tinning film can be completely wiped away. If too much heat is used over a tinned surface, the film can burn away. If a surface will not take a complete tinning, that is, if there are some small spots of bare metal that continue to show, it means the metal is not completely clean. Don't leave small, uncleaned, and untinned spots and hope to bridge over with lead, such as craters in a welded seam. Get the metal as clean as possible.

Controlled heat is important in leading. Only a soft flame, one that is spread over a wide area, is

Vintage Bodywork

The hammer welding was done so expertly that no filler was needed. Several heavy coats of primer/surfacer were applied and ample time was allotted for shrinkage of the primer before the final color coats.

The quality and working ease of modern plastic body fillers (right) is outstanding, but many old car fanatics insist on having all filling done in lead. A lot more equipment, time, and skill is required for leading.

required. Generally a medium-size tip is selected, one that might be used for welding slightly heavier steel gauge than sheetmetal. The acetylene is turned on as with welding and the torch is lit. Next the oxygen valve is opened slightly. The idea is to get a long fuzzy flame, which is usually made up of a long, irregular blue cone with touches of yellow at the extreme tip.

When applying this flame to the metal, keep the tip well back and use just the end of the flame. Let it "lick" at the work. Use the flame on the lead as it is used with brazing; flick the flame tip onto the metal, pass it across the lead; then flick it away. Repeat this process until the desired results are achieved.

It is important to learn good torch control before the application of lead can even be considered, since merely keeping the unfinished lead on the panel will seem almost impossible at first. The secret is in keeping the lead at that particular temperature between first softening and melting.

The beginner is advised to work on horizontal flat panels at first, until some experience has been gained in learning to recognize when lead is beginning to soften and how to control the torch flame. The beginner trying to lead a vertical panel will find most of the material on the floor.

Lead can be applied in two methods: from the bar or from a mush pot. The former is the most common for smaller areas, the latter is better for large areas or for beginners who have trouble keeping the bar at the right application temperature. The lead is scooped out of the mush pot with a wooden paddle and applied to the surface like stucco on a wall.

The key to successful leading is in the cooking. When the bar begins to get shiny on one of the exposed edges, the temperature is about right for the plastic state. If the torch flame is kept on the lead, the shiny appearance will spread throughout the bar which usually means the temperature is too high. When this happens, the lead will suddenly be-

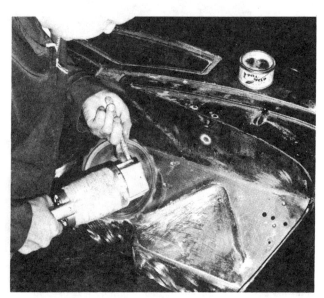

The area where leading is to be done must be completely clean and ground down to bare metal.

A lead alloy comprised of 70 percent lead and 30 percent tin is best for car bodywork. The lead is heated then spread like butter with a wooden paddle, but beeswax or oil should be on the paddle surface to keep the lead from sticking.

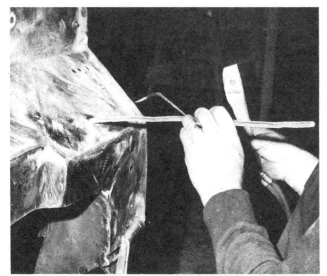

The lead stick is melted on to the firewall. The tip of the torch flame is allowed to lick over the end of the lead stick until it softens and begins to crumble.

The lead stick is pushed onto the metal until a low pile of lead is deposited. All this time the torch is kept in such a position as to keep the lead pliable.

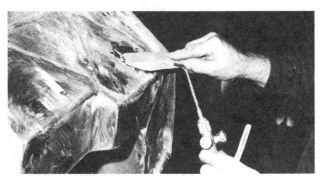

While the lead remains in a near-molten state, the wooden paddle is used to push the lead around. The flame must be applied repeatedly to keep the lead soft.

come liquid and run off the panel. Paddling lead across a metal surface is like buttering bread. If the butter is too warm, it flows too thin; if the butter is too cold, it doesn't spread at all.

The beginner will find that not having enough lead to work will be a major problem once the paddling technique is mastered. It is difficult to go back and add lead, since the temperature must be brought up carefully. The new lead must be applied and worked without overheating the already paddled lead film, and the two areas of lead must be heated enough to flow together at the mating point. If there is too much lead for a particular spot, it can be removed with the paddle while it is still in its plastic state. Ideally the lead surface should be reasonably smooth and only slightly higher than the surrounding metal.

Lead will grind away faster than the surrounding area so care must be taken not to cut the lead too much or make gouges and scratches in the lead's surface. Use a file rather than a disc sander for final finish work because it will cut slower and the long surface of the file will level the lead with the area of the surrounding metal.

When the area is finished with the file, all the edges should blend smoothly into the metal. If there is a tiny, low spot at the edge that does not smooth out, it may be picked up slightly or filled with putty later. A large, unfilled area indicates the lead was not run into the surrounding metal far enough, or the metal has distorted. Additional lead is the usual remedy if the panel cannot be picked up with a pick hammer.

After the initial filing, the area should be block-sanded with #80-grit paper. This paper is coarse enough to cut the file marks from the lead without loading up. It is only intended to finish off the lead and not to shape it.

Lead is an invaluable aid to the bodyman and restorer, but it must be used properly. Never use lead where the spot can better be repaired or shaped; only use lead for the final finishing.

Horizontal surfaces are easier to do than vertical ones since the lead tends to melt and fall away. The lead should be allowed to build up higher than the surrounding area since a second coat is not advisable.

A fine-toothed body file should be used to bring the leaded areas down to the height of the adjoining metal. If low spots show up from filing, more lead cannot be added because it will ruin previous work. The solution is to leave the necessary filing to heavy priming and lots of block sanding.

Customizing Tricks

Customizing isn't a fad that died with the Fifties. It is still with us and going strong. The lead sleds of yesteryear aren't as common as they once were, although there has been a noticeable resurgence of interest. Many old customs that were thought to be part of a new Toyota are finding their way out of dusty old garages. Other enthusiasts unable to find a vintage custom are making new versions of those once popular cars. Since the cost of radical bodywork like chopping, sectioning, and channeling has risen so dramatically, the current trend seems to lean toward the mild custom look.

Many of the mild customizing tricks that are so vital to a custom cruiser also work well on other types of vehicles. Almost any vehicle will look better with some of the excess trim removed and the holes filled. Many of these customizing tricks are subtle, but that is what makes them so universal.

To learn how to perform some of the most popular customizing tricks we contacted expert customizer, Eddie Paul, who operates Customs by Eddie Paul, 124 Nevada Street, El Segundo, CA 90245. Follow along as some easy customizing tricks are explained.

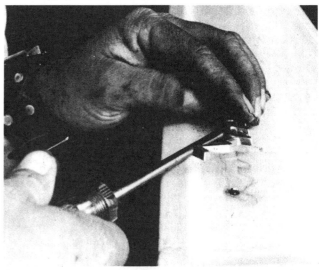

1. Filling the small holes left after emblem and trim removal is a basic customizing trick. Some emblems are fastened from the back side, but most are snap-in affairs. Use care when removing emblems so as not to make a depression with the screwdriver.

Filling Small Holes by Welding

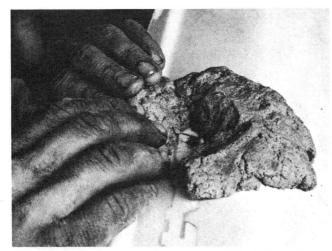

2. To prevent warping, pack the area around the holes with lots of Moist Bastos which is available at welding supply stores.

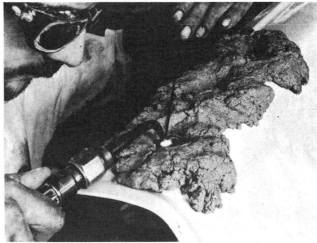

3. Fill the holes by using a 1/16-inch welding rod and an oxyacetylene torch.

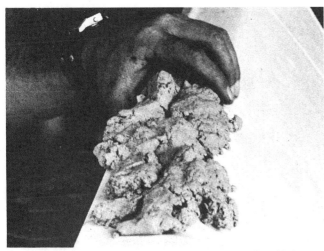

4. As soon as a hole is welded, push the surrounding Moist Bastos over the weld to help cool the area. Wet rags can also be used in the cooling procedure.

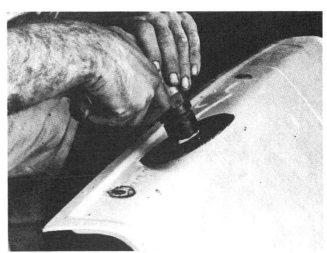

5. Grind down the welds with a disc sander.

6. Fill any low spots or grinding,scratches with body filler and spot putty.

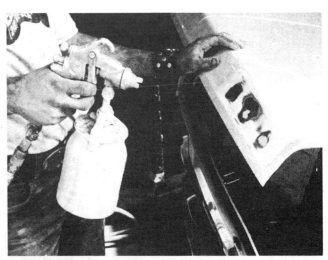

7. Block sand the area until it is perfectly smooth. Cover the area with a couple of coats of primer, and it will be ready for final painting.

Filling Small Holes with Body Filler

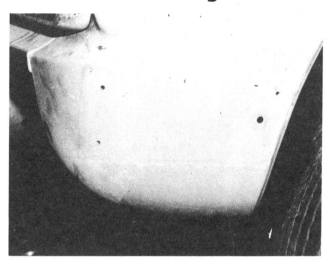

1. Little holes like these can be filled without welding, although welding is still the preferred method.

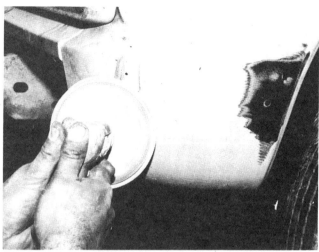

2. Plastic filler needs a clean, semi-rough surface for best adhesion. Remove old paint with coarse sandpaper. A disc sander will make the job quicker and easier.

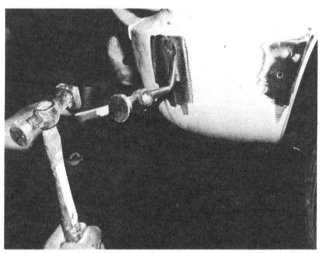

3. A slight crater will give the filler something to adhere to while bridging the hole. This recess can be made by placing the pointed end of a body hammer in the hole and hitting the flat end with another hammer.

4. Cover the area around the hole with a liberal application of body filler.

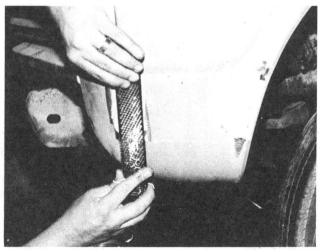

5. After the filler has dried enough so that it is no longer soft, yet is still pliable, shape the area with a cheesegrater file. The filler should come off in long strings.

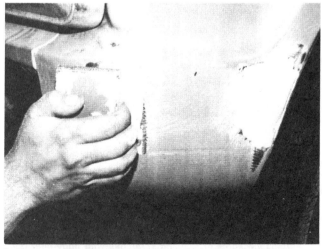

6. Use a sanding block with progressively finer sheets of sandpaper to smooth the body filler.

7. When the sanding is finished, cover the area with primer.

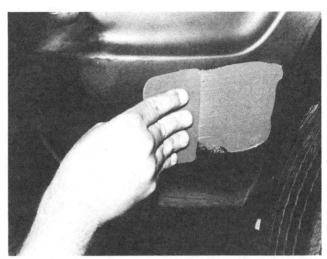

8. After the primer dries, use spot putty to fill any pinholes left by the filler.

9. After the spot putty is completely dry, wet sand the area with a sanding block using 400-grit or finer sandpaper.

10. Apply a final coat of primer, and the filled area is ready for paint.

Filling Large Holes

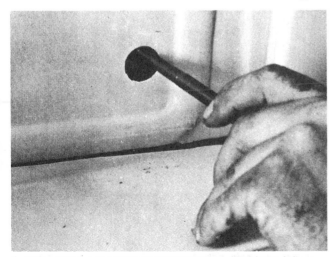

1. Holes that are too large to fill by brazing, like those left when door handles are removed, must be filled with the same gauge sheetmetal as the surrounding area. Hold a piece of sheetmetal behind the hole and mark the size of the patch.

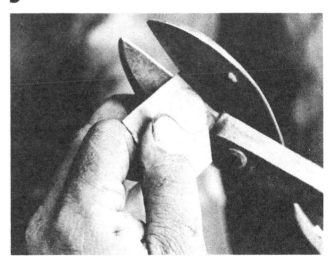

2. Trim the patch with a pair of tin snips.

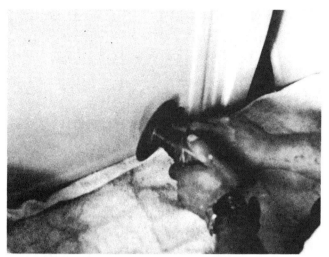

3. Grind away the paint surrounding the hole.

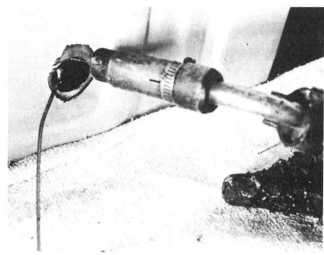

4. To hold the plug piece in place while welding it, tack on a piece of welding rod to act as a handle. Arc weld the patch in place. When the patch is secure, cut off the welding rod handle.

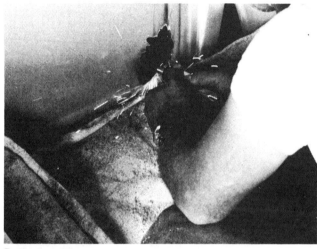

5. Finish the job by grinding down the welding slag.

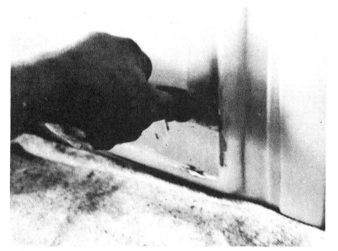

6. Make the area smooth with filler, if necessary; sand, prime, and paint.

Recessing an Antenna

1. A sunken or recessed antenna has always been a popular customizing trick. To sink the antenna, some kind of tube is needed. This tube can be made from tubular stock or an old shock absorber. The part to use is the outside collar. Cut off the mounting bracket.

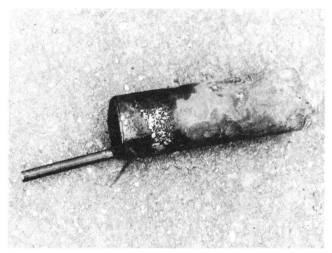

2. Drill a small hole in the bottom of the shock and weld on a small piece of tubing to act as a water drain. A rubber hose can be attached to direct the water to a convenient outlet.

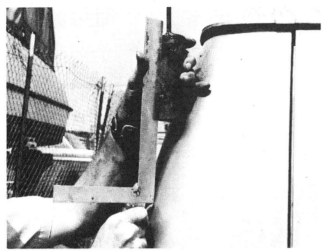

3. If the antenna is sunk into a flat surface, only a hole the size of the tube needs to be cut. If the area is sloped, as it is on this van, it is necessary to use a square to figure out where the top and bottom of the opening will be. The opening will be oval shaped, but the same width as the shock tube.

4. A starting point is needed to make a hole in a sloped area. A screwdriver hit with a hammer will do the trick.

5. Use metal snips to cut the opening. Cut slightly inside your marks and trim for an exact fit around the shock tube.

6. The shock absorber tube must be trimmed to match the slope of the body. Hold the tube in place and mark it.

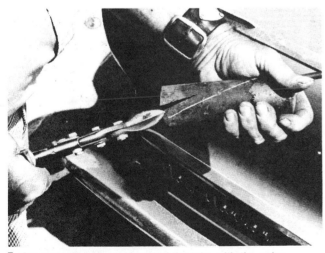

7. Cut away the unwanted part of the tube with the snips.

8. Use Vise Grip pliers to hold the tube in place and tack weld the tube to the body.

9. Finish welding the tube to the body.

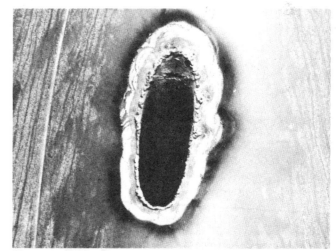

10. The sunken antenna recess is now in place, and all that remains is the finishing bodywork and the wiring of the antenna.

Truck Tailgate Filling

1. Most pickup trucks have either recessed or raised letters on the tailgates. The recessed letters can be filled rather easily. The tailgate can be ground with a disc grinder, but a sandblaster is probably quicker and easier.

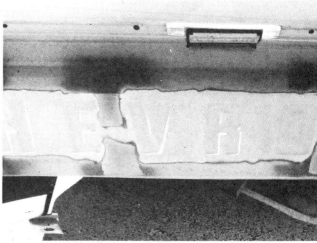

2. The letters and the area immediately surrounding them should be free of paint.

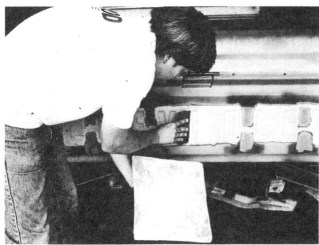

3. Body filler is spread over the recessed areas. If the recesses are deep, apply several thin coats of filler rather than one thick one.

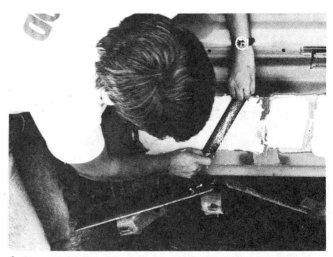

4. Shape the area with a cheesegrater file. Keep adding new filler as long as any low spots remain.

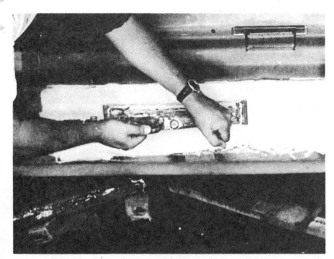

5. A big flat area like a tailgate is best sanded with a long sanding board. An air-powered sanding board can save a lot of time and energy.

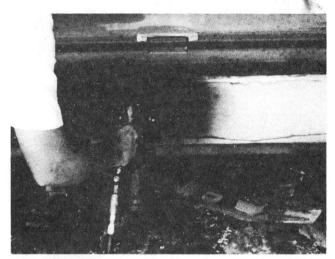

6. Cover the filled area with primer. Sand the primer when it is dry.

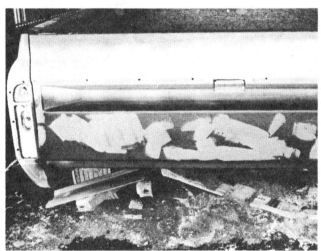

7. Spot putty should be used wherever there are any imperfections in either the filler or primer.

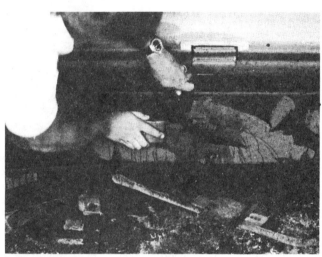

8. Block sand the area with a rubber sanding block and lots of water. Use 400-grit or finer paper.

9. Apply a final coat of primer and let it dry. The longer the primer dries before final painting, the better, because primer has the tendency to shrink slightly.

10. Here is the tailgate after it was painted and reassembled.

113

Working with Aluminum

LONG A FAVORITE "SKIN" FOR SPECIALTY MACHINES, ALUMINUM OFFERS SOME UNIQUE CHALLENGES—WITH ADVANTAGES TO MATCH—FOR THE BODYWORK CRAFTSMAN.

If there is a magic metal, it must surely be aluminum — that exotic alloy which few people really understand and fewer still honestly appreciate. Aluminum can be many things: a cooking pot, a jet airplane, a fancy table, a sleek automobile. In general, aluminum can be classed as one of the most easily worked alloys now in existence.

Aluminum is one of the most readily weldable of all metals. But it has individual characteristics which must be thoroughly understood. These are the low melting point, presence of an oxide film, low strength at high temperatures, and no color even at temperatures up to the melting point. Pure aluminum melts at 1220.4° F., while various alloy constituents will melt as low as 900° F. Since iron melts at 2700° F., it is obvious that aluminum requires more care when welding.

The oxide film melts at temperatures considerably above the melting point of the base metal. Before a good weld can be made, this oxide must be removed either chemically, electrically or mechanically and it must be kept from reforming.

Since aluminum strength falls rapidly with increasing temperature, adequate support is required to prevent distortion or collapse. Aluminum's high thermal conductivity also means that heat applied at one point quickly spreads throughout the entire piece.

Aluminum can be brazed, strangely enough, but this will not ordinarily concern the body man. Several satisfactory solders and fluxes have been developed for joining aluminum, but soldering is not recommended where strength is a factor. This, of course, would rule it out as a method of joining automobile body sections.

While the body man may not get deeply involved in the properties of various aluminum alloys, it will become increasingly important for the specialty builder to know everything he can

about the subject, particularly about sheet products.

For general auto body use, series 1100 H-14 aluminum sheet .063-inch thick is just about right. This material is softer than half-hard, but work hardens as it is being worked until the finished product has all the attributes desirable for an aluminum auto body.

Sheets are available in several sizes, but the 4 x 10-foot lengths seem just about right for shop use, as they can be readily stored. Aluminum is not inexpensive; a 4 x 10 sheet will cost nearly $40, and the average car body will require about three sheets. Since the metal is not stocked in most communities, it will take a little while to get just a single sheet; therefore it is important to be close on the original estimate of how much will be required to do the job.

To estimate the need, figure the square footage of the plan view, both

end views, and both side views, then add 20%. Obviously there will be some waste, but by careful placement of each pattern on the panel, most of the sheet will be utilized. Keep in mind that there will be some waste along the edges of each and every panel, due to trimming, buckling, etc. This is to be expected, whether the work is done by an amateur or a professional. The 20% overage margin is not out of line, therefore.

Before any kind of body is created out of so costly a material, it is obvious that some kind of formal plan should be involved. This may not hold true for the real aluminum body masters, but it is practically imperative for the amateur. It is not uncommon for a famous European body designer to sketch out a new body design on scrap pieces of paper, and give the body shop nothing more for a guide. The shop then works with the most rudimentary approach to de-

1

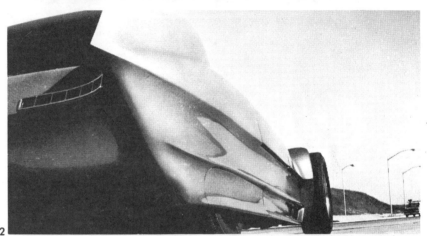

2

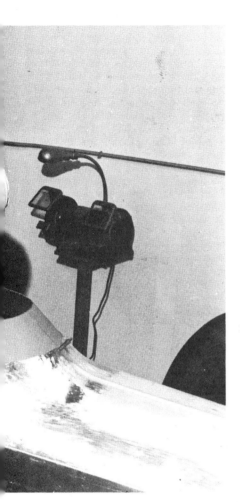

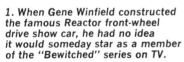

3

4

5

1. When Gene Winfield constructed the famous Reactor front-wheel drive show car, he had no idea it would someday star as a member of the "Bewitched" series on TV.

2. This low-angle view of the Reactor accentuates horizontal styling ridges. Because aluminum is a soft metal, it can be formed in complicated shapes with ease.

3. Reactor started life as a derelict French Citroen chassis stripped of all body panels. Engine was removed in preference to a Corvair which would give the car a lower front-end silhouette.

4. All phases of body buck construction should include constant check and recheck of measurements from a fixed point. Metal tubes over wooden buck will support body.

5. When a station is not exactly true, it must be marked and trimmed until "flow" from one station to another is smooth, uninterrupted.

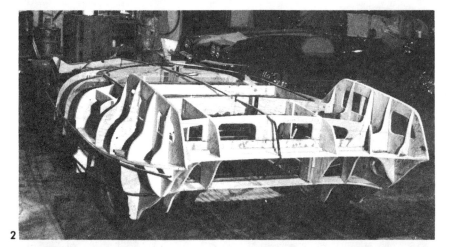

Working with Aluminum

velop the idea, since such cars are usually of the one-only type.

A note here about the so-called fantastic European "dream cars." While the chassis and mechanical components of these very expensive cars are truly outstanding, the bodies are strictly second rate. Not all of them, for production vehicles from Germany are very good indeed, but as a rule, anything made on the Continent from aluminum is not of the quality expected. Ask any body man or painter who has worked with these bodies and he will confirm the fact that most bodies are not metal finished to a perfect state. Instead, the shape is brought to what can best be described as a finished-rough, then coats of filler and putty are applied to get a smooth appearance. American special car builders have long marveled at how such a body could command high prices. That doesn't mean the same construction method is not used on American cars; indeed, some race cars seem to be more putty and paint than aluminum ("Don't matter whut it looks like, long's it goes!"). But by and large, the American craftsmen produce outstanding aluminum bodies, with no filler necessary. All it requires is plenty of patience.

From the design sketch, a full-size set of plans are ideal for the beginner. These can easily be scaled up from the drawing or scale model, and may be worked out on large sheets of butcher's paper taped to the garage wall. Ideally, such drawings should include all the basic views: plan, side, front and rear. This will allow close measurements for the forming buck and often indicate where a particular difficult shape is likely to be encountered.

When making up the buck, which is a former either directly on the chassis or a substitute support, everything must be done from a central measuring point. That means the chassis should be dead level, and there should be a framework on the floor that is also perfectly level. The type of buck made may depend upon the individual, but unless

5

6

7

8

1. Chassis is set on large wooden planks which have been leveled; chassis is then leveled taking into account sag that will result from loaded, finished condition.

2. This is how a finished buck looks, with windows cut in wood for interior sighting, lightness. The buck should be made as strong as possible to eliminate distortion when vehicle is moved.

3. Some kind of support must be provided for the aluminum body; tubing is perhaps the most useful. Framework for doors, hood, deck lid is made operational before the aluminum skin is installed.

4. Winfield unlimbered his dream car when rear panels were formed. Buck for front panels was not needed since all panels were mostly long with minimal crown.

5. English roller is aluminum shaper's best friend. This panel is being given full-crown treatment with short reverses on either side; roller has been home-made.

6. Finish in very tight radius areas can be accommodated with plemishing hammer, which is an air-operated, rapid-action hammer.

7. It is sometimes necessary to shrink or stretch metal as it is being formed; this foot-operated spreader does the job quickly. Tools of this nature are often available in larger cities' used equipment sales outlets.

8. The three-legged sawhorse made from heavy wall pipe plays a big role in aluminum forming; here nose piece is having contour trued.

some previous experience can be called on, it is best to make up the wooden bulkhead type of buck.

The wire stringer bucks are for more advanced workmen and are nothing more than skeletal frames to give a general idea of the body shape. When a wire buck is made up, the general outline of the body is shaped and wires are added at significant points where body contour changes, such as at the fender top crown, the grille opening, etc.

Wooden bucks are easier to make, and look a great deal like the framework for a wood boat hull. To start such a frame, cut a full-sized "keel" from cardboard or inexpensive plywood (wood is better) which will represent the side view. If the vehicle chassis is being used, mount this keel board with brackets and double check all the measurements from the leveling plane, which will be the perfectly level floor or a leveled wooden framework around the chassis.

Next add bulkheads, which are fashioned much the same as bulkheads in the boat hull, or a model airplane fuselage. These bulkheads are called stations, and should be about 12 inches apart from one end of the keel to the

other. If there are areas where the shape will be very intricate, the stations should be closer together. It is possible to make these station members perfect by trimming each station until it flows with all the others. If a station is too large, the contour line will bulge; if it is too small the line will sink.

It is vital that measurements be taken from like points on all stations, which will eliminate the chance of having a twist or other deformity in the finished body. When a station is placed on the keel, select like points on either side and measure to the level base. Detroit stylists use a "bridge," which is a large framework that moves — like an automatic car wash. From it all measurements are made to hold each area constant. Be sure to check and double check all measurements.

After all the stations have been secured to the keel, it is wise to add plan view stringers, or a keel on either side of the body as seen from above. These extra pieces of board will give the total buck extreme rigidity and keep each station from misaligning.

To check station alignment, droop a piece of long (6 to 12 feet) flexible flat iron over the buck. This is a piece of

cold rolled steel about 1/2-inch wide and 1/8-inch thick. When it is held to the stations, it should touch the neighboring stations. In essence, this is what the body outline should be, as viewed from any particular point. Check the entire buck this way — top, sides, fenders, everything. If a buck is too high, trim it; if too low, add a piece of aluminum nailed to the station to raise it.

It is necessary to use this type of check since measurements can be off ever so slightly and cause considerable distortion over a long length. At the same time, just sighting down the stations will not reveal slight variations in contour.

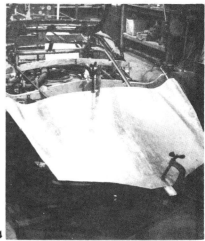

It is possible to save some plywood by making these original stations from cardboard, then transferring the patterns to wood. In any case, there must be centerline measurements drawn on the wood stations, both vertical and horizontal. Many measurements will be taken during actual panel construction, and it is handy to have a true reference point. Also label each station for reference, particularly if the buck must be dismantled before the actual body is built. Stations and keel should be made from 1/2 or 5/8-inch plywood. If there is any chance the wood may get wet, use marine plywood, as the standard wood can swell and distort when damp.

After the final stations are cut from wood, cut large holes in each station, again like a model airplane bulkhead. This is necessary in order to reach behind the panel being formed, and to look inside to see if it is touching the

6

7

8

station. It has an added advantage of making the overall buck considerably lighter.

When the buck is being assembled, it is wise to use metal angles throughout. These are screwed in place to hold all the pieces rigid, and glue may be added if the buck is not to be taken apart again. Because the buck can be torn down and when disassembled takes up very little space, it is advisable to save the parts, suitably marked.

Once the buck has been sanded and all the contours have been carefully checked, the body may be started. Make rough patterns of a particular piece from thin cardboard. Always leave three to four inches of margin around a pattern for waste. As the metal `is shaped to fit the buck, this margin will seem to shrink, and there will be considerable careful trimming necessary. On pieces that are formed with rather severe curves, the metal near the edges will buckle; trim this off.

Figure what will be the easiest panels to make in a single piece, such as a deck lid, or hood, or cowl, or door panel. Generally speaking, the more

complex the curves, or crown, the smaller the pieces must be. Always keep in mind that aluminum is a *tender* material, so change the shape slowly. Aluminum is much easier to stretch than sheet metal, so constantly check each piece against the buck during forming.

When the cardboard patterns are being transferred to the aluminum sheets, work from one end toward the other, placing each pattern as closely as possible to the next. Women do this when sewing, in order to save waste material. A major caution: do not lay the aluminum sheet directly on the floor. Dirt and grime will easily imbed in the soft metal surface. Don't walk on the metal, as this will scuff it. In all cases, keep aluminum protected with the cardboard it is shipped between.

Cut the metal out with right-and-left-hand aviation snips. For long cuts, resort to deep shears or a Beverly shear (older sheet metal shops will likely have the latter). Electric shears (nibblers) are handy and may be available through a body shop or a sheet metal supply. Remember that it is easier to

weld aluminum in open flat spots, since the metal is easy to work afterward. Trying to work peaks will be much harder.

Once the various pieces have been cut out, then you are ready for forming. Aluminum may be formed in many different ways, but the auto body builder is usually restricted to an English roller, a plemishing hammer, or the hand-held hammer. The English roller is a rather unique device that has different size rollers to form the sheet. It is usually a very deep throated rig, like a large C-clamp. At the open end are two rollers, one larger in diameter than the other and with a different crown. As the

Working with Aluminum

aluminum is pulled between the rollers, pressure is applied to the rollers, causing the metal to roll up (or down) around the smaller roller. The sheet is pulled back and forth through the rollers until the right crown is obtained. By changing rollers, it is possible to get several shapes in a single sheet. English rollers are expensive, but anyone contemplating extensive aluminum work can make duplicates for very little. There is no power involved.

The plemishing hammer is different, in that it is air operated and works very much like an automatic hammer. instead of the body man getting a tired arm, the hammer does all the work. Like the English roller, the plemishing hammer can be fitted with various heads depending upon the type of curve needed. It is possible to make up this tool from an old air hammer. Many body shops will have one of these tools, but they are seldom used anymore.

There was once a rolling device made that looked like an air hammer (large C-shaped piece of pipe framework, about three feet square). This unit had rollers at the open end and was pulled manually over a creased fender to iron out the wrinkles. It works beautifully on aluminum surfaces.

And finally there is the hammer. Rather, hammers. Several different hammers will be necessary, including wooden mallets with flat and domed heads, rubber mallet, and ordinary body dinging hammers with slight and domed heads. It is advisable to polish the dinging hammer faces before using.

To get an idea how metal can be displaced when working, take any piece of sheet metal and start hammering on it against a good flat surface. As the ham-

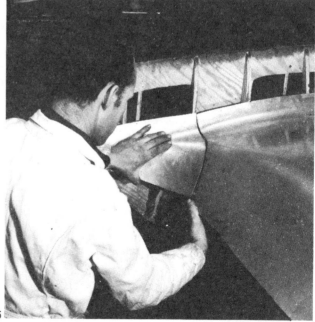

mer blows mount up, the metal will begin to curve upwards around the hammer — so for working aluminum a good flat anvil should be available. Such an anvil can be made up from a piece of steel, about 3 inches thick, 8 to 10 inches wide, and 2 feet long. The surface should be smooth, with no nicks or gouges.

A sawhorse anvil can be made for creating curves, usually constructed of four-inch diameter heavy wall pipe. This sawhorse has only three legs, one leg being vertical to allow for more room. This is also a homegrown tool that will eventually find use in many body projects, whether of aluminum or steel.

The sand bag is essential to aluminum work; it is a universal tool for metal formers. The best bag is made from heavy cowhide. It is round, about 24 inches in diameter by 6 inches thick, and filled with sand. Any shoe repair shop can stitch up such a bag, with the seam open to the outside. Fill the bag almost full of sand, leaving only slight room for displacement.

Other tools that will be handy may be located at the sheet metal shop. They include the standard two- and three-element rollers (the long rollers are the best, for large panels that need a slight crown), the sheet metal break, the crimper, and perhaps the bead

roller. Of all these items, the customizer would perhaps want the crimper and bead roller most, with the other tools available on call.

There are practically no straight lines on an automobile, but the reason is not generally known. Although a door panel may look perfectly flat from front to rear, it is actually curved outward ever so slightly so that the panel is really a compound curve. Bumper splash panels and panels beneath the bumper, both seldom seen, are usually the only flat panels on a car. The reason is one of illusion. Designers have long since found that a flat panel will tend to "read" hollow — that is, it looks as if it is bowing inward.

When the English roller is being used to get a very gentle curvature, keep the panel at eye level so the curve can be "read" easily. If the contour must be

increased, increase the amount of tension (pressure) on the rollers. This will cause more metal to be displaced, and the curve will tighten. When a reverse crown must be made, do it first, then work in the more gentle curves.

If a very gentle shape is required, this is easy to acquire with the hammer and steel anvil, working with very light hammer blows to the inside of the curve. Working aluminum with a hammer requires more of a slap than a hard blow. If severe shapes are necessary, the metal can be driven into the sand bag. Pound a hollow in the bag and then work the aluminum into it, working with the domed and high crown hammers. Final shaping is again done with the dinging hammer and steel anvil.

Once a panel has been brought to a very close shape, it may be secured to the buck or reinforcing framework.

1. The completed front section is one, long, flowing mass of body, with no sharp ridges anywhere. Since this is a show car, there is no provision for bumpers.

2. After the fender panels have been formed, lips are rolled and styling pieces added. In this case it means the fins are mounted on the sub-frame behind front wheels.

3. The lowest rear panels are rolled out first, with special templates used to make each side symmetrical. This is a vital point to special car building, whether using aluminum, 'glass or steel.

4. Next the large deck panel is shaped and secured to the wooden buck. This makes adding the smaller panels easier, gives contour check.

5. Small panel at corner of fin must be shaped from another piece, and trimmed exactly to mate with big panel. The more severe the shape to be made, the smaller a panel.

6. Lower panel is made from six separate pieces of aluminum, although general shape does not seem severe or overcomplicated.

7. Outer fin panels are formed in one piece since they include two simple rolls with a connecting reverse crown. Trimming of peaked areas must be virtually perfect to keep finished line straight.

8. Each panel is held in place and the edges trimmed until all joints mate with minimum overlap or gap. Do all trimming with aviation snips.

6

7

8

Working with Aluminum

Metal screws work well, but the aircraft industry makes use of quick release fasteners that are even better. After the very first panel has been set in place, all the others may be added, each trimmed very carefully to get a perfect edge fit.

Welding aluminum is an art unto itself, but something that the beginner will pick up faster than the professional who already knows how to weld. It is possible to lay a perfect aluminum bead with pratically no filler rod required. This would be ideal for bodywork, since it would reduce the work required around a welded seam.

For welding aluminum, set the torch with slightly carbonizing flame — that is, the inner cone should be slightly fuzzy, almost as though soldering were in store. The heat can't be as intense, and good torch control is a must.

All aluminum surfaces to be welded must be absolutely clean! This cannot be overemphasized. Some chemical cleaners are available, but most aluminum body men rely on new wire brushes, and they brush both sides adjacent to the proposed weld. Sandpaper may work, but there are chances of leaving bits of sand imbedded in the metal.

Exchange the ordinary welding goggle lenses for blue lenses. If this isn't done, the flame will appear very yellow — and it is quite difficult to see the metal under the flame. With a blue lens, everything will be clear.

While there are several aluminum filler rods available already fluxed, they will normally contain too much flux. Instead, heat the rod and paint it with a paste flux (Airco white powder flux can be mixed with water to form a paste). Preheat the surface to be welded and flux it on both sides. This is important.

Now comes the tricky part. Since aluminum does not change color, welding it will be more like soldering. Heat the surface to be welded until the flux flows. This will happen rapidly, and the flux will flow much like water. Keep the torch tip moving in a tight circle to distribute the heat, otherwise a spot will get too hot and suddenly there is a hole.

Heat the pieces being welded and the rod at the same time, trying to keep the working temperature as constant on all three parts as possible. If relatively flat pieces are being welded, do not make tacks down the opening. Instead, work with a partner who can raise or lower each piece to keep the

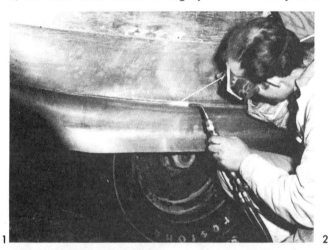

1. Tack weld high-crown joints, then complete the weld as with sheet metal. For low-crown panels, which are easier to weld, make the bead all at one time (see text).

2. The body begins to take on visible form with completion of the deck section; many, many hours of labor were involved to this point.

3. Side pieces with the three strong styling ridges are made from several smaller pieces; bottom panel rolls around metal support.

4. Intricate problems should be worked from small panels, such as gas filler opening. Shaping here is done on the sand bag.

5. Since a wraparound Plexiglass windshield was involved, the buck was made from aluminum then covered with felt and Plexiglass formed by heat lay-up. It is possible to shape car around stock shield.

6. The completed rear section has very sharp fins and horizontal belt line; paint is then applied to accent these very unusual lines.

7. Note how the side ridges, gas filler indentation stand out in stark relief. This is a good styling point for a car with long, flowing body shape.

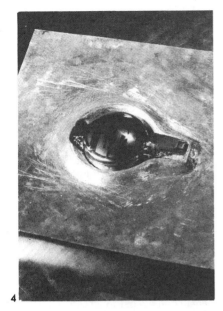

4

5

edges aligned. Tight crown may be tacked since they will not distort as readily.

Lay the torch tip at a flatter angle than when welding sheet metal. This will tend to direct more flame down the joint, pre-heating it as the bead is made and not concentrating heat on a specific spot. The rod is also laid flatter than when one is working with steel.

When a weld is started, complete the entire piece while it is still hot, making as small a bead as possible. The bead may be worked down with hammer and dolly later, but the less such working required the better.

While the panels are still warm, work with a hammer and dolly or slapping file

as the metal works better when warm. This is really just a roughing operation and should not be intended to result in a perfectly smooth finish. Don't hammer on the weld too much until it has been cleaned with a wire brush and water. This is to flush away leftover flux which will cause corrosion later. In all cases, the bead should be cleaned before the final shaping, both inside and out.

Final metal finishing may be started before the entire body is formed. A slapping file is imperative to good aluminum work, since it takes care of such a large area at once. A slapping file is nothing more than a mill file with a kink in the middle. Either offset end can be

used as a handle, and the teeth will make light marks in the aluminum to tell where the high and low spots are.

When working a section, use a loose dolly (the dolly does not rebound as with sheet metal) when the surface must be flatter. To raise the surface, hold the dolly firmly against the underside. Aluminum will tend to pull readily into a higher crown when this method is used.

It makes things easier to work with a light shining directly on the panel being worked. Change this light to different angles as work progresses and sight along the crown to discover low and high waves. When a low spot is being worked with the slapping file, the edges

6

7

123

Working with Aluminum

will show with file teeth marks and the low spot will be vacant. Slap away with light strokes and the low spot will raise quickly. At the same time, the metal begins to work harden, which is highly desirable.

After all the panels have been finished, spray on a thin coat of primer (zinc chromate is the most common, unless the car is to receive epoxy finishes — for those special "race" paints, a different primer works better). Use the file to locate high and low spots as with sheet metal, and continue to use the slapping file and dolly to smooth the surface. The weld beads

may be filed down, but don't file too much metal away at any particular place.

Fender openings require a special technique. The panels will have been cut with a couple of inches of extra material. Mark off the opening radius, and then use a flat dolly and high crown dinging hammer to make the rolled edge. Hold the dolly at the desired line and bend the flange over, or use a pair of flange pliers. After the flange has been broken to about the 45-degree point, direct the hammer blows on the flange edge. This will cause the metal to roll. The edge is not shaped around a contour dolly. Continue to work the roll around the full wheel opening.

It is possible to shape the wheel opening with pliers specially made for the purpose. These would be of wide-mouth design, with a male and female tip of the exact radius the lip should be. If several bodies are to be made, such pliers would be worth consideration.

After the roll has been accomplished, the area immediately adjacent must be finished with the hammer or slapping file and dolly. Such a roll should be of 180 degrees duration, with the inside edge trimmed and filed smooth.

Wire is sometimes used to strengthen wheel openings. For this select 3/16-inch galvanized wire (it won't rust and discolor later on). Start the roll as before, but at the 45-degree point insert the curved wire on the inside. Hold it in place with clamps, and roll the aluminum completely around until the panel edge almost touches itself. Here is where some careful measuring is required. With a piece of waste aluminum, decide how much metal is required to roll around the wire, then trim the opening to this margin before starting.

Leave a piece of wire at both ends of the roll for added strength. This wire will normally tuck inside the body (about two inches) and will keep the roll in tension. It may be welded at the ends.

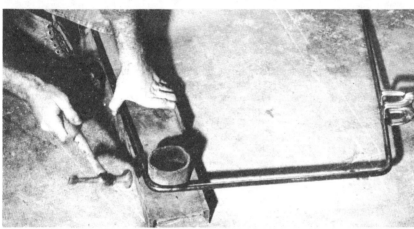

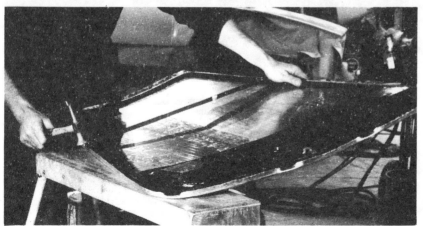

1. Hood must be attached to a framework, in this instance made from steel tubing. The framework is built to work in opening first.

2. Hood will have almost no crown, ridge down middle. After it is formed, edges are flanged over and panel is sighted for high/low spots.

3. If panel is very close to final shape the edges are hemmed over steel framework. Large, flat anvil table is ideal for backup.

4. The finished panel works on small sports car hinges, sits tightly against rubber laid on support ledge. Note how compartment inner panels are louvered, strengthened by bead-rolled ridges.

5. With headlights extended and doors opened, Reactor looks like it's ready for a shot at the moon. Note how straight ridge down the front of the panel and hood is.

6. Smaller items provide excellent practice point for beginners in aluminum. Reactor's headlight was made from four pieces of metal, tack welded and trimmed before final welding was attempted.

7. Smaller pieces are easier to weld without help for alignment, but aluminum must be attached with pessimism to be successful. Use blue goggle lens, clean metal.

8. Finished, the square headlamps would do justice to any rod. These headlights were constructed during early part of project.

Openings for the hood and deck lid normally require a squared lip. Some kind of substructure must be built for these openings, with 1/2-and 1/4-inch angle the most popular. The aluminum is then formed over this angle and usually flush riveted at the bottom.

Opening structures must be made with reinforcements, which may be of any material but are usually tubing, either square or round. The outer aluminum panels are then crimped as with sheet metal. If the substructure frame is round tubing, then an angle or a piece of heavy-gauge sheet metal is used for a flange support. Roll the exterior aluminum over the flange and finish the outside. Where the metal must curve, as at the corner of a hood, cut the lip to be rolled under slightly closer to the flange. This will reduce the tendency of the metal to pucker and buckle.

Finally, before the body is ready to mount on the chassis, it should be carefully checked with templates to insure that all panels are the same. This is not difficult, but will consume the better part of a day. Symmetry is necessary unless the car is deliberately made asymmetrical.

The car body will be mounted at all openings, as around the cockpit, deck lid and hood, as well as along the bottom edges. Where aluminum, metal or wooden bulkheads are to be used as part of the chassis, they should be isolated from the body by ordinary door sealing rubber. For thin material, such as metal, rubber hose may be split and slipped over the edge. Glue all sealants with yellow 3M cement.

All inner panels, like those used in the engine and trunk compartments, should be stiffened with the bead roller to reduce any tendency toward oil-canning and drumming. The body underside may be sprayed with underseal to reduce noise transmission if so desired.

Aluminum bodies are not the easiest to make, but they display a definite craftsmanship not apparent on most specialty vehicles. While aluminum may be magic, it needs a magician to bring out its best qualities. The really accomplished body and fender man will thoroughly enjoy creating with this jet age material. ∎

Rear Fender Flaring

A sensible bodyworking beginner's project to make those fat tires legal.

There's no doubt that "mag" wheels and wide tires have become trademarks of the street machine movement. They're so popular that today you find new car dealers selling them as options, and on the road you can find them on old cars, new cars, tiny import cars, big luxury cars, and even on pickups, vans and semis. Everybody likes them, but they do have their drawbacks. The drawback we're concerned with here is the tire-to-fender clearance problem. Although in recent years the Detroit manufacturers have taken this into consideration in the styling and design of a few models, installation of wheels and tires that are wider than stock, especially on the rear, still creates a clearance problem on most street machines. Oh sure, you may be able to bolt them on the car, but what about when you hit a bump at speed, even low speed? Scraaape goes the fender on your nice new tire that you paid top dollar for!

In some cases, where the clearance problem is a small one, the solution can be as easy as simply notching the *inner* lip of the fender edge with a hacksaw cut every inch or so, and then bending the lip up inside the wheelwell to gain maybe a ½-in. of clearance between this lip and the sidewall of the tire. We tried that on a '66 Mustang with limited success; it would only scrape the tires on big bumps.

The best solution to the problem, in fact the *only* solution in cases of extreme interference, is to re-radius the wheelwell opening. On a lot of cars you might want to do this even if there isn't a clearance problem, just to make the car *look* better. Flared wheelwells generally look sharp, but the style is up to you as long as it suits your purposes. Depending on the tire and wheel size, the flare can be mild or wild, 1 in. or several, and the shape can be rearranged to suit you also, from square to round or vice-versa. This is customizing, so use your own imagination.

We wanted just a simple flare job at the rear to save wear and tear on tires and make the car distinctive. Customizer Carl Green has performed dozens of these transformations and agreed to do it for our camera. Carl has done paint and body work in three of the top custom shops in the nation, Darryl Starbird's in Wichita, Kans., Dean Jeffries' here in Hollywood, and Dave Puhl's House of Customs in Chicago, so he's eminently qualified to show you how this job can be done.

You start by buying some e.m.t. tubing, otherwise known as electrical-mechanical tubing or simply conduit. It's light and inexpensive; we bought a 10-ft. length of ½-in. tubing for $1.29, and that's generally enough to do two wheelwells. There's no real "trick" to the procedure, just go carefully, think, and don't rush it. Basically, you hammer and dolly the fender from flat to an outward flare or curve around the opening, braze the tubing to the edge all around the opening to form a smooth, new lip, grind it down and follow normal filler and sanding procedures to smooth it out. You can make the flare large or small, depending on where you braze the tubing•onto the fender. You can dolly the fender until it flares out several inches, or even add new metal if you need to. The conduit also strengthens the fender greatly, and you can make the opening larger in *diameter* if you want, just by bending a larger radius in the conduit before you start. For a simple, same-diameter opening, just shape the tubing around the tire you plan to use. How you make it meet the body at the front and rear of the opening is up to you also. On ours, the body was cut so the tubing could fit in it ahead of the wheel, and blend gradually outward as it went around the opening, while at the rear it was bent into an extra outward flare at the bottom to form a small "splash guard." The use of this lightweight tubing allows a lot of creative freedom in this kind of customizing, and varied effects can be gained with different shapes, and even different diameter tubing. And when you've found the design you want, and you've done it, not only will the car be more individual but in states (like California) where you can't have the tire stick out of the wheelwell, it'll be legal, too. All this and custom wheelwells have the practical benefit of allowing those big tires to clear the body on bumps and drive-in ramps! ♨

Stock wheelwell on '66 Mustang is a good starting point, as it's round in stock form, but wide mag wheels brought tires out where fender lip scraped sidewalls.

1. The new "bead" for the reshaped opening will be made from light electrical tubing. It is easily shaped by bending it carefully over a tire or similar object.

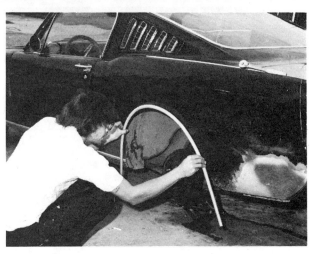

2. After bending, trial fitting, and even bending the tubing over other objects, the tubing can be curved into the shape and the radius size desired.

3. The fender's inner lip must be bent outward to form the flare. In the case illustrated, the lip had previously been notched and hammered flat on the inside.

4. Once the kinks are out, the inner and outer lips are separated with a pry bar, and the metal at the front of the wheel-well notched to receive end of the conduit.

5. Body man Carl Green deftly uses a body hammer and dolly to make the now-flat fender edge flare outward instead of in. He works slowly, carefully around radius.

6. Bird's eye view after fender metal has been brought out to new shape. If the job is done with proper care, as little distortion as possible will make finishing easier.

7. When amount of flare is determined, the conduit is clamped in place to show the excess metal to be trimmed. Tube would be brazed outside for larger lip.

8. With the outside edge trimmed to fit snugly against the conduit all the way around the new opening, Carl next trims back the metal edge of the inner panel.

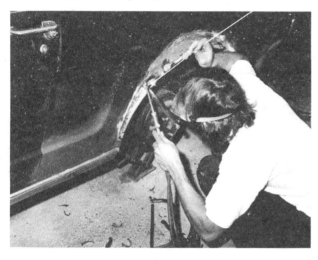

9. The conduit is carefully tack welded in place at widely spaced intervals to reduce heat buildup and resulting warpage. Inch-long tacks will suffice for now.

10. It's a good idea at this point to bounce the car as hard as you can to make certain that the fender and its new lip will clear the tires on a hard bump.

11. With the conduit fully brazed along the fender, the extreme back end of it is now heated and slowly bent to follow the contours of the fender at this point.

12. When conduit is cut and brazed, fender lip (arrow) sheet-metal at corner is pried out to form an extra bit of flare, making a small, built-in splash guard.

13. Most of the hard work is out of the way now. The last metalworking step is to beat the edge of the inner panel down to the conduit and braze the inside seam for strength.

14. With brazing completed, the whole fenderwell area is ground down and the old paint sanded off the body around the opening in preparation for the final bodywork.

15. A thin coat of body filler is spread over flare to smooth it into the fender. If work has been done right, little filler is needed, and much will be sanded off.

16. Before the filler has completely hardened, a special "cheese grater" hand file is used to carefully remove excess filler and form the basic blending contours.

17. A combination of sander, files, and hand-sanding gets everything smooth enough for paint. Another small batch of filler may have to be mixed to fill minor low spots.

18. Although light colored primer doesn't show off the amount of flare, you can see how it smoothly blends to body at front, and the splash guard width at rear.

The Technique of Hammer Welding

Often compromised in a large shop, that "certain feel" will never come from a blacksmith's bludgeon.

Late-night TV watchers have probably seen blacksmiths in old Western movies heat two pieces of iron in a forge, then join them by pounding them on an anvil. This is *not* hammer welding by today's bodyworking standards. Hammer welding as it's done in the bodyworking trade is ordinary gas welding followed by some tricky hammer and dolly work on the welded joint to provide as smooth and distortion-free a seam as possible.

Among the several facets of bodywork and painting that require a certain finesse and "feel," hammer welding is perhaps the most prominent. It isn't difficult, but because several basic tenets of metalworking are involved, very few metal men practice the art. While it may be easier for a quick repair to use a filler, the workman who strives for quality will take a moment longer and do the best job possible.

Customizers particularly find hammer welding advantageous, usually in situations calling for maximum strength and minimum filler. This might be a front end modification or a top chop, but the finished job is far superior to the use of lead or plastic. It also allows the metal man to gain better control over the panel, to shape and mold it the way he wants it with stress in the right place.

Hammer welding is normally involved in only three bodywork situations: repair of a tear, replacement of a panel and modification of a panel. In all three, the emphasis is upon quality and metal control, not economy. A commercial body shop cannot expect to include hammer welding on a large scale, simply because every minute spent in labor reduces its profit margin. Where quality is stressed, as in a custom or restoration operation, the customer demands premium work and is willing to bear the extra cost.

Consider a metal tear in a quarter panel. It is easy to rough the panel into shape and then weld the tear quickly. The bead is then ground off and beaten down so filler will cover the depression. Most modern body shops rely solely on plastics for this repair job. Obviously, there is some unusual stress buildup around the welded area, which may cause problems elsewhere in the panel.

It is also possible to rough the panel back into shape until the torn metal edges can be aligned carefully, then hammer weld the rip closed. With such a situation, the area adjacent to the tear will probably be stretched, but when the metal is welded and hammered, a natural shrinking force is introduced that tends to pull the stretch out. After the initial hammer welding, the area may be treated as a gouge—keep on shrinking and working the panel until it assumes its original shape.

It is in panel replacement and modification (especially by the customizer) that hammer welding takes on such importance. Unless the panel is preshaped to the new contour it is entering (with seams hammer welded), there will be a need for an excessive amount of filler material. In some radical cases, the entire panel will end up with a filler coat to varying degrees. It was from a situation like this that early custom cars earned the nickname "Lead Sleds." Anyone can sling lead and plastic, but it takes a craftsman to work metal. That's what counts.

This is not to say that every seam should be hammer welded; far from it. When a panel can be replaced and the joint made by spot welding, riveting or even ordinary fusion welding—and the joint will not show—fine. But if the seam is in the open and affects the panel's strength, hammer welding must be considered.

Take the situation where the bottom edge of an exterior panel has rusted away. Only about 2 ins. of the metal is really cancerous, but the replacement strip will be from 3 to 4 ins. wide. This strip will usually have very little (or no) crown and will gen-

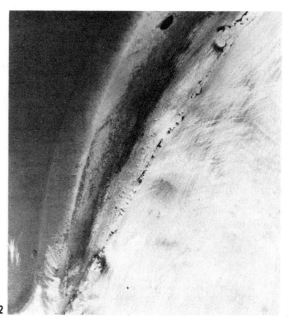

erally include a folded lip of 90° or more. Whether the panel is on a door, cowl or quarter area, it does not matter. The metal man will be working directly in the middle of a nearly flat surface with heat. That means a high distortion possibility, which requires torch control.

AN IMPERATIVE

It is absolutely imperative that all hammer welding include the smallest possible weld bead. To accomplish this, the panels to be mated must fit as closely as they can. The replacement panel should be shaped and trimmed first, then held over the area to be replaced and well marked. It is wise to cut away the bad metal with as little distortion as possible, so this rules out the "hot wrench" immediately. A manual or air-operated chisel can be used, but there is a rather rough edge left which must be worked. Better yet, use a saber saw or nibbler.

After the initial rough cut, try the replacement panel on for size. It will generally be off just a whisker, because there is usually too much metal

3

1. Hammer welding is a time-consuming technique not often seen in regular bodywork, but necessary for show-quality work when butting two pieces of sheetmetal together. One of the prime tools needed is a (homemade) torch rest like this one, which has a shield to keep the lighted torch from scorching the floor; a tray for tips, and tubes to hold welding rod.

2. Here's a typical butt-joint of two pieces of sheetmetal which has been hammer welded. A few passes of the grinder and this undistorted seam is almost ready for primer and a few dabs of glaze. Normal overlap seam would have been quicker, but would have required lots of filler.

3. Here's a typical problem (for the early car restorer/rodder) that took good hammer welding to solve. A '32 Ford roadster had badly damaged rear corners, so this coupe rear section was purchased for needed parts.

4. Unfortunately, our sources were wrong when they said a coupe section was the same as a roadster; so this would be no cut-and-weld easy task. The bead lines didn't line up.

5. Bodyman Carl Green saved as much of the original metal as possible, cutting off the part to be replaced.

6. With the coupe section held up in place, the fit looks good except for the outside two bead lines.

7. Carl carefully made a sectioning cut through the middle of the body's depressed area, using masking tape as a guide. If the cut had not been made through the middle, the bottom raised areas would not match up.

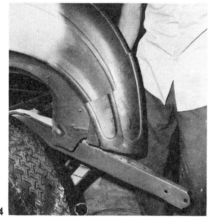

4

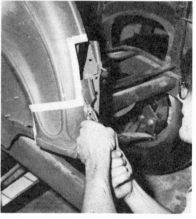

5

6

7

Hammer Welding

remaining on the parent panel. This thin strip may be trimmed off with a good pair of aviation tin snips, although such snips have a tendency to roll the tiny edge rather than make a clean cut, while the body grinder will make the ultimate fitting easier. The two panel edges should fit flush along the full length, with no more than 1/16-in. gap at any part. If the edges touch, all the better. A gap requires too much filler rod, resulting in a larger bead, and as the bead size gets larger, the hammer weld becomes increasingly poorer.

Clamp the pieces together and tack weld the edges. Use very little or no filler rod and make the tack tiny. Speed is important here, as well as a very small flame. Often too large a tip will be used, resulting in too much heat immediately adjacent to the edge. This causes the metal to crawl excessively and makes a perfect fusion weld almost impossible. A correct hammer weld cannot be made if the metal edges lap.

Make sure the edges are level during and after the tack weld. If not, heat the tack in a restricted area and use the hammer and dolly to level the edges. This means a few light taps, not heavy blows, as the metal is hot.

After the panels are tacked, start at one end with the hammer welding process. Be prepared to travel rapidly, not so much with the torch as with the hammer and dolly. The railroad dolly is well suited to hammer welding, since it has a number of convenient crowns and is easy to hold. The hammer face should be nearly flat.

Hammer welding calls for an alternate use of torch and hammer/dolly, so some sort of torch stand is required. This will allow the torch to be hung out of the way and remain lit, yet close at hand. A bucket of water will be useful if an extensive weld is involved, as the dolly will become hot after awhile and can be cooled by dipping it into the water. It is also wise to wear a glove on the dolly hand, to protect against a burn from either the dolly or slag falling from the welded surface's underside. Remember, every tool must be close at hand to ensure speed.

There are two ways to make a hammer weld. The simplest method is to weld the entire seam at once, then follow with spot heat and the hammer/dolly. A better way is to weld a short 2-in. section, then use the hammer, then weld again. This way the area is still hot from welding and does not need reheating, allowing better control of the metal.

Lay the torch tip flatter to the plane of travel than with normal fusion

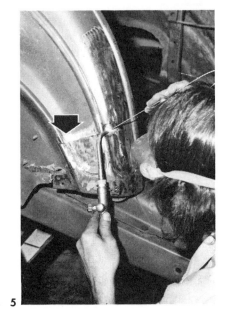

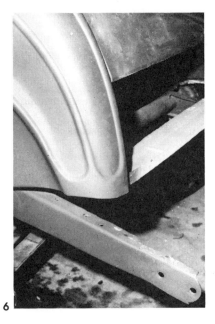

1. With the body and the new piece cleaned of paint along the cut edges, Carl clamped the pieces together with vise-grips. Arrow shows portion that was rotted out originally.

2. Carl places short tack-welds at about three-inch intervals, applying as little heat as possible.

3. Now the hammer welding starts! With the tacks completed, but with the visegrips still in place, Carl starts the full weld. After each length of about two inches of bead, he quickly stops welding; lays torch in his rack, and starts with hammer and dolly. Since welded panel usually shrinks along weld, he uses the dolly from behind to slap up the low area, then hammers bead flat.

4. Where the beads meet body, Carl creases the hammer weld with the wedge end of a finishing hammer. His shop (Carl Green Enterprises, 7749 Densmore #7, Van Nuys, Calif.) does a lot of antique and custom car work, so hammer welding is an everyday job.

5. A thin strip was trimmed from the left-corner piece so that the center bead would line up on the body, and this was hammer-welded in place. Fit of the fenderwell bead (arrow) was accomplished by using again the wedge end of the finishing hammer. Corner finally takes shape.

6. After grinding down the seams, a little primer and putty brings this part of our roadster project that much closer to completion. No one will ever know (except you) what went into these stock-looking corners.

7. Another typical problem that is best solved with hammer welding is replacing a lower, rusted-out area on an early car's cowl or quarter. Here the rusted section is cut off and the trim line ground straight. Flush fit of the panels to be welded is critical to a good hammer weld.

8. Vise-grips will keep the panel in place during tack welding; mating surfaces should be hammered up or down to flush exactly during tacking.

9. Anytime a butt weld is being made it can distort nearby low-crown panels. The torch should have a very small flame; the tip may be laid flatter to direct flame at area just welded.

10. Hammer each tack immediately, as this will tend to shrink the area and eliminate any distortion caused by the heat. It also keeps the edges flush. Don't worry about distortion in larger panel at this time.

11. This is how a good fusion weld will look, with little bead buildup. Such a weld is possible as panels grow together when heated edges melt and form bond without filler rod drops.

12. Continue the alternate welding, hammering schedule until the entire joint is closed. Keep the dolly firmly against underside of panel to reduce rebound; use hammer smartly.

7

8

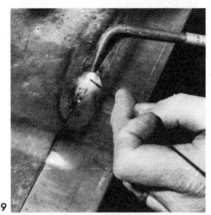

9

10

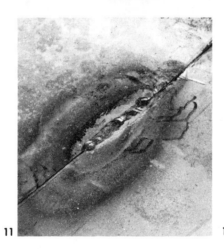

11

12

welding, thus reducing the heat to the metal. The filler rod can also be held at an opposite low angle to shield the edges. Although the two metal pieces touch, they will tend to grow toward each other even more when the heat is applied, allowing the edges to melt and flow together without the necessity of the filler rod. Such flowing may be difficult at first, but can be accomplished easily as experience is gained. An occasional hole will develop which must be filled by a drop from the rod, but the idea is to make the weld rapidly and with as little heat and rod as possible. At the same time, the edges should be kept level.

Immediately upon setting the torch

aside, place the dolly against the underside and hold it firmly to the weld. Slap the bead rapidly with the dinging hammer—working back and forth from one end of the seam to the other. This will cause the bead to flatten out and have a shrinking effect on the panel, which has tried to grow with the heat. If one panel has not stayed level, that area must be reheated and hammered until it is level across the bead. The objective here is to flatten the mating joint so as to minimize follow-up work.

Continue across the entire joint in this way, alternating between torch and hammer/dolly. It is possible to feel the area with a palm, but remember that the metal stays hot. Wipe the

Hammer Welding

hand quickly across the surface to detect stretched spots and to determine how the panel contour is being affected.

STRETCH MARKS

After the seam has been hammer welded, check for a stretched area. Wherever one is found, shrink the panel as necessary. The welded seam should look almost flush with the surrounding panel, or even be in a very slight valley. If the bead has been too big, it will have been flattened on top and bottom by the hammer and dolly, but will still stick up from the surface slightly.

Grind the weld with a disc sander, using a flexible disc pad which will allow the disc to follow the contour rather than cut into it. This grinding should cut down the bead ridges and will show up the low spots along the bead that must be picked up. Use a picking hammer from the bottom and a picking dolly on top (an ordinary dolly will substitute) and raise only those low craters that remain. At this stage, hammer welding is very similar to crease repair and requires a good deal of patience, particularly from the beginner.

Resort to the file and grinder often during this picking operation, as no filler will be used since the two panels have become one. As the small craters are raised—and the high spots taken down with normal hammer/dolly technique—keep running the hand across the entire panel. Look across the panel from several different angles, trying to find a break in the contour. For the most part, the problems will be confined to the immediate seam area.

After as many of the craters and tiny low spots have been removed as practical, wash the surface thoroughly with a good metal prep, using a wire brush to clean out the minute depressions that remain. Finish off the surface with the smoother grinder discs, followed by a "jitterbug" oscillating air sander. Prime the bare metal and allow the primer to set completely before going over the seam with a thin coat of glazing compound. This glaze will get down into the small pockmarks that remain, resulting in a perfectly smooth job.

There is no substitute for hammer welding on a panel that's being repaired or patched, if *both* sides of the panel will be visible. Though this is not common in ordinary bodyworking, it's becoming more prevalent on restored cars slated for display, where onlookers or show judges may inspect the underside of a fender as closely as the top side. An example

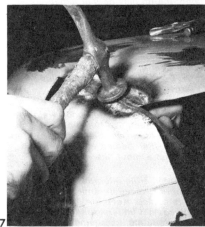

of this, with step-by-step photos, is included in another chapter.

For a number of years now, it has been common for the more experienced automotive enthusiasts to extol the virtues of this or that custom job by claiming hammer welding. There are a number of customizers famous for this type of work, and their products show the quality. Obviously, any car that has been modified will stand a better chance of lasting indefinitely (the sheetmetal, that is) if it has been hammer welded. This kind of technique requires practice, no doubt about it, but the results are immediately apparent. Fortunately, the student need make only a few short hammer welds to get the idea. From there on it's a matter of using his new-found secret.

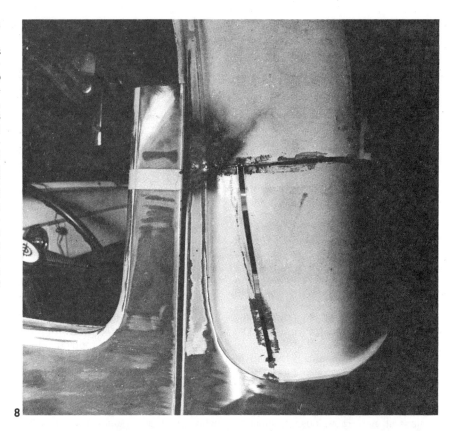

8

1. Pick hammer is used to raise the low spots, but dolly is kept on top to keep from raising spots too high. This is where experience with the hammer will begin to pay off.

2. After the new section is hammer welded, the surrounding panel may be worked as necessary since "growth" through heat of welding may cause distortion. In this case, original part of weld needed several shrinks to remove "oil-canning."

3. Although it usually isn't to be found in the average body man's kit of tools, the shrinking dolly is a handy item. It is grooved to "grip" metal and is used in conjuction with an aluminum hammer.

4. This is the panel as it appears in nearly finished condition. Some tiny low areas remain to be picked up and filed, then panel will be primed. Remaining imperfections are glazed.

5. Then there are the more ambitious hammer welding jobs, such as this top chop on a 1954 Ford pickup truck. Long section of metal was roughed into shape, then hammer welded.

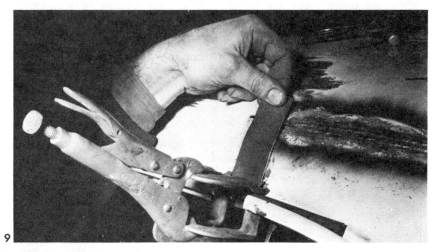

9

6. Because so very much hammer welding was necessary, convenient hook was made from handy sheetmetal for torch. Forming metal in this fashion may be time consuming, but it means excellent result.

7. With most top chops, strips of metal must be added. These should be formed before tack welding to top, but edges should mate as closely as on panel previously discussed.

8. This gap is much too big for a hammer weld bead, although it can be filled with large rod. Such cuts are necessary in many customizing jobs to get proper contour relationship.

9. For such gaps, insert small strips of metal, weld short beads on either side and hammer weld away!

10. Norm Grabowski's finished '54 Ford pickup is so well executed, that few people realize extent of work done. Thanks to hammer welding, Norm's pickup is a real winner.

10

Louvering

How to make an apple-pie example of Americana— Louvers for a "Nostalgia Rod."

One of the more colorful trends in the street rodding world to surface in the last few years has been the "nostalgia rod." Dozens of old customs and early rods are being rebuilt and brought back to their former glory by rodders who remember fondly the era of "American Graffiti" and before. Not only that, but new rods and customs are being built from scratch to look just like they were built in the '50's. People are actually once again combing the swap meets for flathead Ford V-8 speed equipment, fender skirts, Carson top frames, Appleton spotlights and "flipper" hubcaps. The Good Old Days are being relived today by some automotive enthusiasts. One fad of the early rods that has never really died out but is now enjoying a revival of sorts is louvering. Back in the early days, a *car* was simply not a *machine* unless it had racy louvers punched into every panel that could be removed from the car and would fit into the local customizer's louver press. The most common application was of course on hood panels, where louvers served some practical purpose in letting hot air out of the engine compartment where a ⅜ by ⅜ flathead was always running just short of overheating. But many other panels were also punched out, such as deck lids, fenders and even skirts felt the

bite of the louver press.

The early drag racing cars made extensive use of louvers. Ostensibly the louvers were to make a car faster by letting the trapped wind escape, but they also held a psychological advantage in that the car with the most louvers and lightening holes just *looked* faster. Hot rodders always tend to emulate race cars with their street machines; and louvers became even more popular on the street than at the drags. There , the racers eventually found out that louvering the turret top of a '40 Ford coupe was expensive, but not necessarily effective in producing better performance. Since most of the hot rodding trends, especially in the early days, were started in Southern California, it's no surprise that louvering was started there, too. It's said by old-time rodders that the first guy they ever saw who had louvers on his hot rod had actually cut a panel out of a gymnasium locker and had welded this louvered panel into his hood! Luckily for the schools back then, customizers saw the popularity of louvers and built or bought the presses to turn out thousands of air slots for hot rodders and custom car owners. If your car had a hood, then it became de rigueur to "louver everything but the handle."

Now that the nostalgia-rod builders

are bringing back louvers to their former prominence, we thought you might like to see how this is done. Louvers are still a valid customizing technique for sheet metal, and still serve the practical purpose of letting out hot, underhood air. In that respect, they may even do something to improve your gas mileage, what with the high underhood temperatures cars are currently running; laboring as they do under a maze of plumbing and smog contraptions.

We took the top hood panels from our own '32 highboy roadster project car to Kent Fuller Manufacturing (19019 Parthenia, Northridge, Calif.) for the venting process, so we could show you what's involved. Kent explained to us that the actual punching of louvers is very simple, and that most of the work is in the layout and measurement of where you want the louvers to go. On our '32 hood, the panels are narrower at the front than at the rear, so the problem was how to install straight rows of louvers that seemed to match both the straight line of the hood centerstrip, and the *angle* of the panel's outer edge.

Kent Fuller has been around hot rodding since the very early days, and besides his wealth of knowledge in chassis building and aluminum-forming, he also has two louver presses together with the expertise in

using them. After a few minutes, studying and measuring our hood panels, Kent decided to stagger the rows of louvers (there would be two rows of louvers on each top panel) such that they were neither parallel to the hood centerline or to the outside edge. By splitting the difference between the two angles, the louvers "cheat the eye" and appear to be "right" with both edges of the hood.

Once you've settled on the width of the louvers and have decided where on the hood the rows will go, next comes the time-consuming setup of the press. The press has an adjustable guide along which the sheetmetal slides as it is fed through the press, and this must be adjusted to maintain the louvers at the desired angle and position on your panel. When the angle gets tricky, and you have to have more of an angle at one

end of the panel than at the other, you may have to clamp a piece of metal to one edge of the hood as a spacer from the guide. This is what Kent did with our hood panels.

After checking the alignment of the male/female louver dies by louvering a scrap piece of aluminum, Kent and an assistant punched out our louvers—72 of them—in about five minutes. The dies have an edge that makes the spacing between the louvers an automatic proposition: You punch a louver and then butt the edge of this louver up against the die's outside edge before punching the next one. This keeps all the louvers spaced exactly the same distance.

If you live near a big city, you may be able to find someone in your area who is punching louvers, such as a locker company. By contacting the local street rod club, you may learn

some additional clues beyond the yellow pages; or you could even mail your part to Kent Fuller. Expect to pay about 50¢ a louver at most places, and you may also have to pay $5 or more for a setup charge. We're not suggesting that you louver the hood of your 1975 car, but we do feel they are a legitimate customizing trick for which you may find many applications on specialty vehicles.

The one caution that we might give you is to have your panel completely stripped of paint and all bodywork done before you have it louvered. Naturally the hood must be flat and without waves or the louvers won't all be straight. Also, there should be no paint in the areas where the louvers will go, because after they are punched, the job of sanding the hood prior to finish-paint is made much more difficult. 🐛

1. Louvering has been an effective custom trick for many, many years, and is now seeing a resurgence of popularity among street rodders, like Kent Fuller. Kent's nifty, original Volksrod features a louvered hood and even louvers in the fiberglass bed! This is accomplished by glassing a louvered metal panel into the bed.

2. Kent Fuller carefully scribes the guide lines on our '32 hood panel. By "splitting the difference" of the side and center angles, the rows of louvers cheat the eye and appear as parallel to the hood edges.

3. The most important part of the louvering process is setting the guide bar properly, so that the rows of louvers are straight, and are at the desired angle to the hood's edges.

4. After adjusting the guide bar, Kent checks the alignment of the male and female dies with a piece of scrap aluminum, before doing hood.

5. Usually some assistance is needed to keep the workpiece snug against the guide bar as the panel is fed through, one louver at a time.

6. To get the spacing and angles you desire, you may have to clamp some strap metal to the panel edge to space it from the guide bar.

What Price Impact?

What happens to your car (and purse) when a 5-mph bumper gets a 6-mph (or off-center) tweak.

BY KALTON C. LAHUE

Until a few years ago, the federal government kept itself occupied running the business of the nation and that of several foreign countries, but somewhere along the way Washington bureaucrats suddenly became instant experts in the field of automotive safety, and so the Federal Motor Vehicle Safety Standards came into existence. Despite admonishments from many recognized traffic safety authorities that the answer to the mounting highway slaughter really rested in more and better driver education, and more stringent licensing of those who use the roads, Washington eventually decided that Detroit will build a crash-proof vehicle, even if it has to bring it into being piece-by-piece.

And that's just about what the 1973 Safety Standards are doing. New from the drawing boards are the impact bumpers that can withstand a 5-mph front impact, and a 2½-mph rear impact into a fixed vertical barrier without damaging safety-related systems such as those dealing with fuel, exhaust, cooling, lighting, latching, etc. Actually, much of the credit for this legislation coming to life belongs to the nation's insurance lobby, which now extends a 10% to 15% discount to all who drive vehicles so equipped. Many people are still wondering why—in the past, damage resulting from such impacts was often not even filed with the companies, and that which *was* fell under the owner's deductible clause, in which case the greatest share of the financial burden fell upon the claimant, anyway. But for whatever reason, we now have the bumpers, and body shops across the country are rubbing their hands in glee, for as we'll see, things didn't turn out quite as our near-sighted bureaucrats planned.

After studying the requirements, the Big Three took their usual divergent paths to meet the regulations for the 1973 model year, and so we have three different bumper systems currently in use, ranging from a rather elementary, nonrecoverable design to the quite complex, which do return to their original position after impact. Chrysler Corporation must have seen the fallacy of the whole thing from the start, for it went to the least amount of trouble to meet the new safety standards.

Essentially, Chrysler's new system

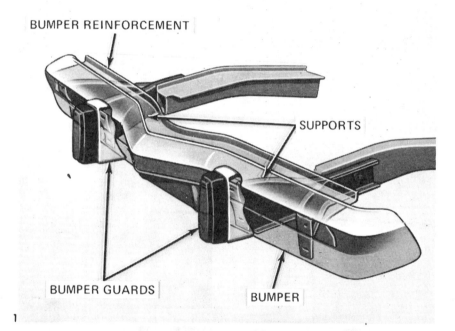

BUMPER REINFORCEMENT

SUPPORTS

BUMPER GUARDS

BUMPER

1

2

STUDENT DRIVER

3

138

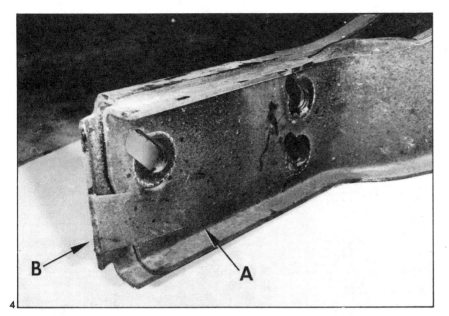

is the 1972 bumper design beefed up to the impact-absorbing task by adding two large rubber-faced guards to the bumper, a reinforcement plate behind it and a support to the bumper attachment arm. These arms are attached to the front of the frame with three slotted bolt holes that allow the bumper to move backward upon impact, where it stays until you visit your friendly body shop to have it repositioned. Neat, clean and simple . . . and sure to cause frame damage in many frontal impact situations.

Considerably more complex, Ford's front impact bumper uses a heavier steel than in 1972 and a full-width steel (or aluminum) reinforcement behind the bumper. Larger mounting brackets and two impact-absorbing devices are fastened to the frame or underbody structure, depending upon the particular car design. These devices consist of a steel I-beam section or ram that rides inside a steel outer casing. A rectangular rubber block on either side of this ram connects it to the outer case. These rubber blocks are permanently bonded to both the ram and casing with a special thermo-setting adhesive. The ram is attached to the bumper reinforcement and the casing is bolted to the frame. A contoured wedge plate welded inside the casing top applies a preload to the ram to prevent minor movement and bumper vibration under rough road conditions.

1. Chrysler Corp.'s approach to the "impact" bumper was fairly straight-forward, and appears on all their cars as in this Dodge example. Idea is simple; mounting bolt holes are slotted and allow the bumper to ride back the depth of the slots—and it takes a body man to move it forward again.

2. A Plymouth bumper is pulled from a driver education car for repair. Majority of frontal impact situations are off-center, occuring at an angle instead of directly head-on.

3. Three bolts in slotted holes secure the bumper support and its attachment arm to the frame attachment box. Slots are long enough to absorb rearward movement of bumper under a 5-mph impact.

4. Undamaged side of bumper shows support (A) fastened about 3/4-inch shorter than attachment arm (B). Slotted holes line up perfectly.

5. Frame attachment box on undamaged side is intact and attachment/support arms can be refastened without work.

6. On damaged side, support has moved backward about half-way, throwing it out of line with the attachment arm. Unit will be discarded and replaced with new one.

7. Top view of undamaged (right) and damaged (left) arms show how support slides backward in attachment arm channel under impact.

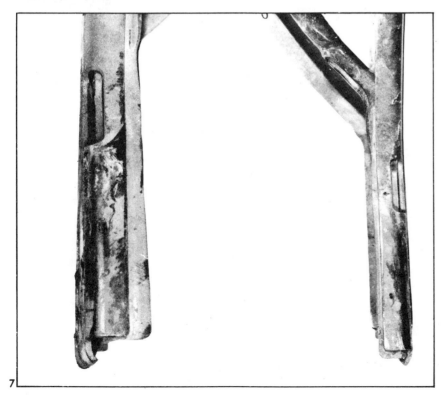

What Price Impact?

When you impact with a Ford Motor Company product, the ram is driven backward up to 3½ inches, stretching the rubber blocks which temporarily absorb up to 70% of the impact force. The remainder is absorbed by the car, or more specifically, the frame rail. As the rubber blocks resume their normal shape after impact, the bumper returns to its original position.

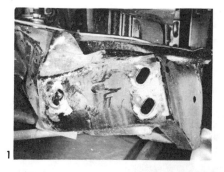

To provide a minimum of ½-inch clearance between bumper and sheetmetal during a 5-mph impact, all Ford-designed bumpers are located 3 to 4 inches ahead of the front-end sheetmetal. Stone deflectors that were previously stationary between bumper and body are now flexible to move with the bumper. The frame or underbody used in 1972 had to be redesigned to accept the impact-absorbing devices, and they were strengthened to transmit the impact. And in many cases, depending upon the particular car in question, changes had to be made to both the body and the engine mounts to accomodate the installation of the impact bumper system.

General Motors went all out in designing its elaborate hydraulic bumper system, a variation of which is also used by American Motors. The front bumper is attached to the frame with a pair of hydraulic cylinders that act quite similar to shock absorbers. Upon impact, a needle valve controls the rate at which the hydraulic fluid enters the gas chamber. Once the stress has been relieved, the bumper returns to its original position as the gas pressure forces the fluid back out, or so the thinking goes.

But like much of the other thinking done on the banks of the Potomac, it has little bearing to the reality of the situation. Any body shop will tell you that 90% of all frontal impact situations occur at an angle, instead of directly head-on. In the case of Chrysler, it makes little difference since the front bumper is nonrecoverable, but whenever impact is not spread equally across the surface of those that are supposed to return to their original position, the system breaks down. The Ford I-beam moves into the casing at an angle and refuses to come back; the GM hydraulic piston also retracts off-center and jams. And since there's no repair possible or practical with the I-beam or hydraulic units, dealership body shops are replacing the bumper attachment devices as a complete unit. In the case of less-than-ethical shops, you'll get two even if you only need one. The sad part of the whole thing is that impact bumper systems were

specified to work under what a body man would consider ideal conditions, and in the case of an ideal impact, they're fine. But whether it's stop-and-go traffic or just a failure to judge distances in a parking lot, only a small percentage of front-end collisions take place under ideal conditions. And to a driving public accustomed for years to bumpers that were designed almost as an integral part of the front end, the protruding Ford

bumpers are proving quite frustrating in backing out of parking spots. More than one is caught on the side of the garage or another person's car and turned inside out, necessitating a new bumper between angry words. Where will it all lead? Who knows? But in the meantime, impact bumpers are here, and we might as well live with them. How can we convince those who told us we needed them that they goofed again?

5

6

1. The frame attachment box must be cut off, the frame must be straightened and the new box welded in place. According to this body shop foreman, his repair estimates are running 40% to 50% higher than for comparable damage to 1972 cars.

2. Ford's '73 bumper system is a bit more complex, shown here on a model without sheetmetal. Channel-like bumper attaching arm can be "rammed" back into receiver, both of which are bonded via rubber. Theoretically, the rubber will resume its normal shape after impact and return bumper to original position.

3. Ford impact-absorbing device is steel casing/inner I-beam that connects to bumper reinforcement plate.

4. Rear view shows rubber biscuits that are bonded to the I-beam and casing wall. Rubber absorbs 70% of impact and returns I-beam to original position in under-5-mph collisions. Casing bolts to frame on this Ford LTD.

5. Top view of casing and I-beam ram shows redesign of frame rail (A) and contoured wedge plate (B) which applies preload to prevent vibration and movement on rough roads.

6. Stone deflectors on 1972 Fords were metal painted to match body color; on 1973 cars they're a plastic-type material designed to flex under impact and colored to match body color.

7. The GM bumper system is the most exotic of all; shock absorbers take the brunt of the blow, then return bumper to normal position—provided impact is head-on and only up to the required, by law, 5 mph. Hit harder than this, the system still works, but impact is transferred to frame member which will bend.

8. GM attachment bracket, here on an Olds Cutlass, is welded to beefed up frame horns. It's very difficult to straighten if bent, and usual procedure is to replace it completely, but since it requires welding, it's expensive, especially since surrounding sheetmetal components have to be removed for access.

9. Body men of the future may run across one of these and wonder what it is, since the "impact" bumper came along in '73. Well, this is one of the intermediate steps taken for the '72 model year, a "sort-of impact" bracket that Pontiac used. It's a telescoping unit, filled with fluted urethane cushions that are already under partial tension when assembled.

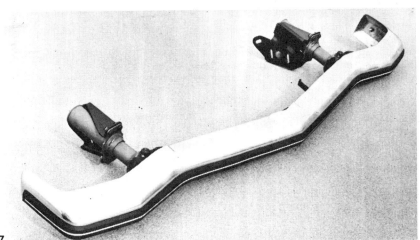

7

8

9

Late-Model Windshield Replacement

The job isn't all that formidable—if you know how to go about it.

Installing a windshield or backglass on a late-model car is relatively easy for an experienced glazier, but for an amateur it could turn out to be more than he bargained for. If you do not know how to go about this work, you can easily get into trouble even before you have removed the chrome molding.

Generally speaking, on all late-model cars the windshields and backglasses are installed in much the same manner. There is a rubber-set installation and a glue-in type of installation.

Variations of the rubber-set have been around for quite some time, but the glue-ins are relatively new; they showed up for the first time in 1964 on some of the Chevy models. Now the glue-ins are used almost exclusively throughout the industry with the exception of compact cars that have mostly stayed with the rubber-set style.

On the late-model rubber-set style, the rubber gasket remains attached to the body and the glass is set into the recessed groove on the rubber. The rubber is flexible enough to allow the top side to be pulled back allowing the glass to be easily set into place and worked back around the glass. This installation requires more supplies to do the job. You need a spray can of rubber lubricant, a windshield sealer, and a black caulking compound.

With the glue-ins the only sealant needed is PTI Liqui-tape or a Butyl tape sealer. This is the only type that can be used on Ford products, but it can be used on all other makes as well. This glass set does require a few more tools to do the job properly. A must for glue-in replacements is a windshield knife and a molding tool for removing the chrome molding.

For the amateur with no experience in this type of glass work, we suggest studying the step-by-step photographs very carefully before deciding whether or not to do the job. A few pointers are hereby offered for the avid do-it-yourselfers. Do not cut or tear the rubber gasket on the rubber-set units, because the entire gasket will then have to be replaced. The critical step on the glue-ins is cutting the old glass away from the lower glued surface. If the lower surface is torn up, then the entire lower area must be completely cleaned of all glue. Then it requires starting over with a new base being layed in using a Butyl tape. Yes, it is much easier and faster in the long run to take pains to save the lower surface.

For those who are new to this field, the tools may be hard to come by. The only place you will be able to get them and the sealants is from a glass shop or from one of the companies that supply these products to the auto glass industry. One such large company is C.R. Lawrence Co., 720 So. Mateo St., Los Angeles, Calif. 90021. They have branches in San Jose, Calif.; Dallas, Tex.; Chicago, Ill.; and Atlanta, Ga. Another is Somaca Co. with general offices at 5501 W. Ogden Ave., Chicago, Ill. 60650. They also have branches in Atlanta, Ga. and Santa Clara, Calif.

When you start replacing your own windshield, you had better realize in advance that you are working with an expensive piece of glass. Correcting your mistakes could cost you double.

HOW-TO

1. *Place cloth on the hood to protect the finish and provide place for tools. Begin the procedure by removing both of the windshield wipers and setting them aside.*

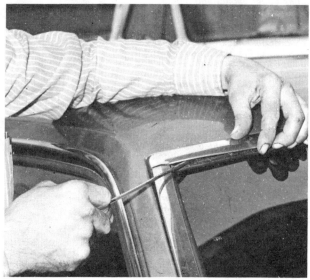

2. *Use care when removing chrome molding. It is thin and kinks easily. Slide a long, thin screwdriver under molding to find each of the hold-down clips. Pry them away.*

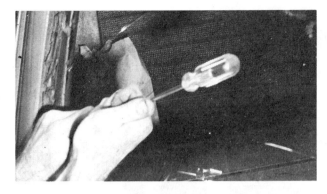

3. After trim is removed, work screwdriver around edges of the windshield between rubber and glass to cut sealant. Leave the lower-edge molding in place.

4. After outer lip of rubber is loose, Bob Isbell presses outward against windshield. If glass sticks, carefully work screwdriver around glass until it is loose.

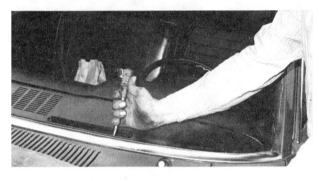

5. Two men make the job easier. John's Auto Glass, 1423 E. Rosecrans, Compton, Calif. removed the broken windshield from a MoPar. Be careful of cuts.

6. After glass is out, use screwdriver to remove all old sealant and any glass chips. Slot must be thoroughly cleaned to prevent water leaks later on.

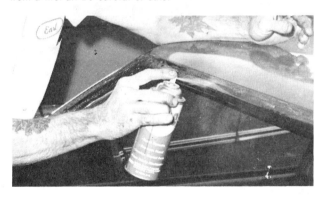

7. Earl Ramsey sprays WD-40 into slot in rubber before new glass is installed. This makes it easier to get rubber around edge of the new windshield glass.

8. When installing new glass, set the lower edge in the rubber first. Here, extra hands come in handy, but a real professional glass-man can do it alone.

9. Place screwdriver into slot and work lower edge into rubber. Be careful not to force screwdriver against the glass edge or it may crack or chip the glass.

10. Pull down on top edge of glass so lower edge is completely seated in rubber at bottom. Here, rocking and wiggling will help if rubber is well lubed.

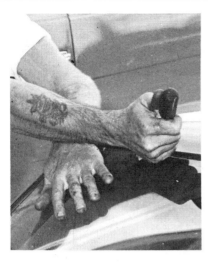

11. Use screwdriver to pull outer lip of rubber around edge of glass. Start at sides and work up. Then do top edge. Use care with screwdriver.

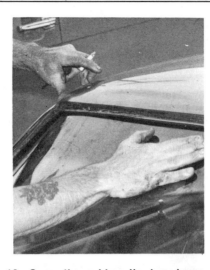

12. Once the rubber lip has been worked around edge of glass, gently shove glass inward to seat it completely within the rubber insulation.

13. Now, double-check the rubber to make sure that the glass is in all the way. If not, then work with hands and screwdriver to seat it further.

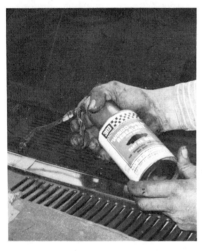

14. Use Windshield Resealer, placing nozzle of applicator well into slot. Use plenty. Flow on even amount all around edge of windshield.

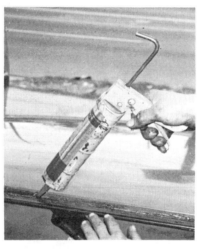

15. Between rubber and body, black caulking compound is used. Again, use plenty as it's easier to clean off excess now and prevent water leaks.

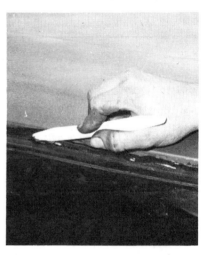

16. Use a windshield setting tool to spread the black caulking compound evenly around the joint between the rubber and the body sheetmetal.

17. Here, Bob locates the chrome molding clips, bending them away from the rubber to insure a tight grip on the chrome trim pieces.

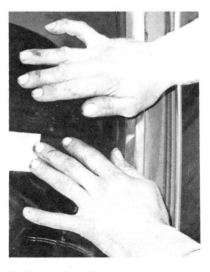

18. When reinstalling the chrome molding, press down with the palm of the hand to avoid bending it. A firm, even pressure will seat it on clips.

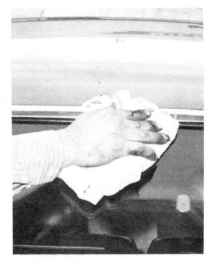

19. Now cleanup begins. Use solvent to remove excess caulking. Also check that chrome trim is properly seated all the way around the glass.

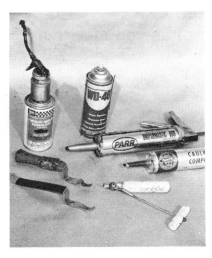

20. These tools are needed to install most any late windshield or backglass. Three in foreground are for removal of glass that is glued in.

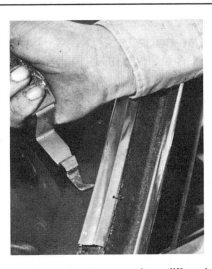

21. Glued-in glass requires different procedure. Molding tool is worked under edge of molding, as shown, and pulled upward to cut the glue loose.

22. Now take knife and place hooked blade under glass edge. Push top handle forward, pull cable toward you. Do not cut lower mounting material.

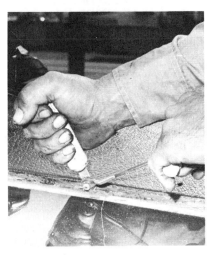

23. Cut mounting material loose along top edge in same manner, starting in center and working out to sides. Use a firm, steady pressure on the tool.

24. Clean all of the old cement out of the area around the clips. Bend clips out a little to insure holding the chrome molding tightly on glass.

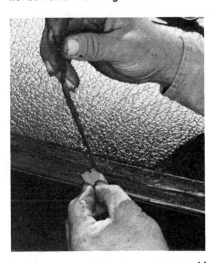

25. Use a razor blade to remove any old glue in the groove. Debris will make it difficult to properly seal the new windshield. Don't cut rubber.

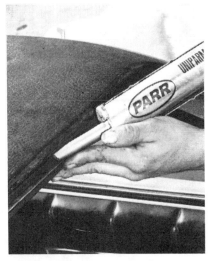

26. Parr's Uniparmastic 600 is applied to lower surface of Chrysler product. For a Ford, use PTI Liqui-tape sealant or other butyl-type sealers.

27. Set windshield in place and spread sealant to insure good bond with glass. Before sealant hardens, work molding into position. Press with palms.

28. Work chrome molding onto clips, starting at sides and working up. A minimum of cleaning should be required to remove excess sealant.

Side Glass Replacement

Installing new door or vent-pane glass is not as hard as you may think. These tips will help see you through.

Many novice body men learning the skills "on the job" as helper-outers, rather than as students in a school auto shop or professional trade school, will have a yen to do repair work on damaged cars but are not yet proficient enough to tackle the rigors of actual metal straightening. As such, they may be given simpler but nontheless important chores to do. One such job that may seem hard or especially tricky is the replacement of glass. But it isn't all that formidable, and after a pro has been watched while he in-

stalls a new door glass or windshield, the manufacturing methods used to retain glass in its channels or moldings become obvious, and the novice should be ready to tackle a similar job himself. Luckily, most of today's automotive glass is molded to curved shapes, so new pieces are obtained from an agency ready to install. Some older cars that the body man may encounter will have flat glass, especially on windwings, but these can be cut from sheet stock by the glass dealer and, again, simply installed by the body man.

While replacing a windshield is a tricky job which requires two people to lift and position the glass, door and vent windows and quarter glass installation are operations you can do by yourself. The major requirements are patience and care. Never try to force the glass in or out of position; a bit of jiggling and juggling will work miracles that brute force can't perform. Besides pocketing the installation fee yourself, there's a certain pride in telling friends, "I did it myself." The accompanying photos show how it's done.

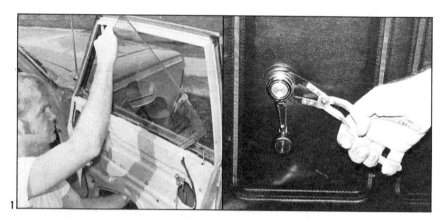

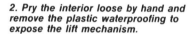

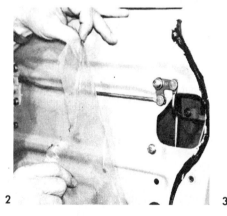

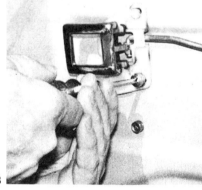

1. Remove all fixtures from the door interior and place on the car's floorwell for safekeeping. The spring-loaded window handle comes off by sliding a handle remover in place and pulling toward you. A stiff putty knife or large flathead screwdriver can be used to pop the spring, but it can slip and damage the interior if you're not careful.

2. Pry the interior loose by hand and remove the plastic waterproofing to expose the lift mechanism.

3. Unscrew the door release mechanism and let it swing down out of the way.

4. Set the window handle back on its milled shaft and turn slowly until the lift mechanism is positioned for easy access through the door cutout.

5. Reach inside the panel and locate the right channel guide with your fingers. This two-piece guide is hinged and held in place by a hex bolt which must be removed with a socket wrench. Swing the channel guide away from the glass.

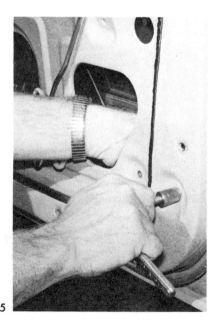

6. Three hex screws hold the glass securely to the lift mechanism. Take out the center one last, holding the glass in place with left hand. Grip the glass at the bottom and top, lift up and out at an angle. The window fastener is removed and replaced on the new glass by tapping with a rubber mallet. Then reinstall the new glass at the same angle.

7. Center the glass in its fastener by sliding the lift arm back and forth until the holes line up. Replace the center hex screw first and tighten.

8. Set the hinged channel guide in position, replace the hex bolt and tighten by hand.

9. Operate the window carefully to make certain it works properly in the channel, then tighten the hex bolt securely and replace the other two hex screws in the lift mechanism.

10. After reinstalling the door release mechanism, waterproofing plastic and door interior, replace the window handle. Be sure to insert the small U-clip as shown before snapping the handle into place by hand.

11. Power windows present no greater problem. If necessary, locate the power contact button on the door latch and tape in place so the window can be operated with the door open. The interior of this wagon gate has been removed and the waterproofing plastic peeled off.

6

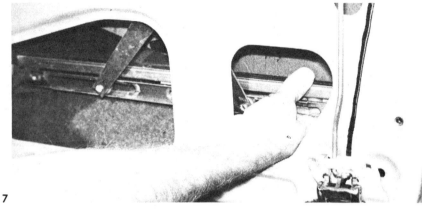

7

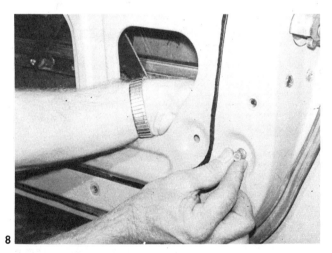

8

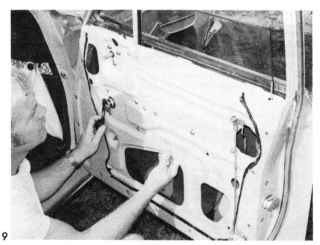

9

10

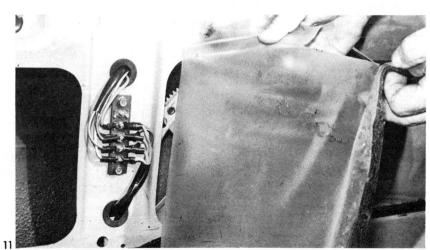

11

147

Side Glass Replacement

1. A hex bolt at the top and one at the bottom of the door hold the left channel guide in place. Remove both.

2. Work the channel guide free, move forward and out of the way. The lift mechanism is a scissor arrangement and must be positioned at the mid-point where each arm is close to the end of the lift channel.

3. Remove the four hex bolts holding the power unit in place.

4. Slide the power unit and lift mechanism to one side, slipping the guide wheel out of the lift channel. Now slide the other lift arm guide wheel from the opposite side of the channel. Set the unit down gently and push the glass up by hand.

5. Angle the glass and its fastener out of the door as shown. This will require more patience than effort. Tap the fastener from the old glass with a rubber mallet and install it on the next window. Slide the glass back into the door at this same angle.

6. Lower the glass to the power unit and slide its arms back into the fastener channel. Lift the power unit into place and fasten securely. This step also takes patience, as holding the unit with one hand after lining up the holes puts a momentary stress on the left arm until one hex bolt is replaced.

7. Raise the window up until you can slip the left channel guide back around the glass. Replace the top hex bolt and lower the window slowly to position the channel guide correctly at the bottom, then replace that hex bolt. Reinstall the waterproofing plastic and door interior.

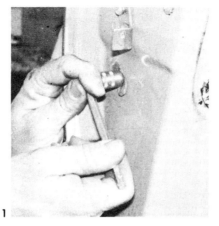

1

2

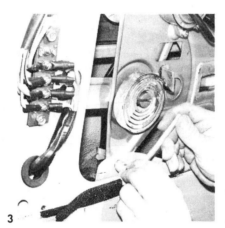

3

4

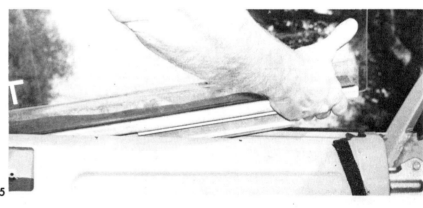

5

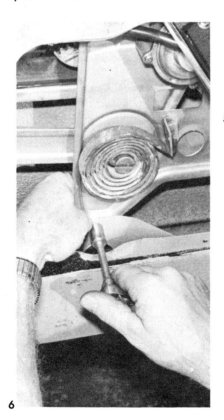

6

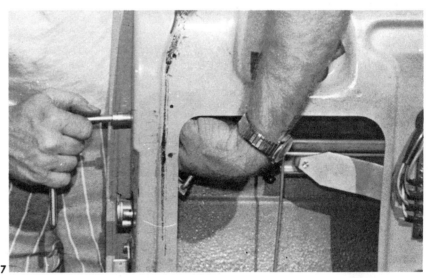

7

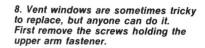

8. Vent windows are sometimes tricky to replace, but anyone can do it. First remove the screws holding the upper arm fastener.

9. This slips off, freeing the vent window at the top.

10. Use a socket wrench and short extensions to remove the nut on the window's lower shaft. A coil spring and several washers on the shaft should be removed carefully, and their original position to each other noted.

11. Angle the vent window as you lift it up and out of place.

12. Carefully pry the window frame from the old glass as shown, and install it on the new glass by tapping with a rubber mallet.

13. Replace the new vent window at the same angle it was removed, taking care to insert the two washers as shown. Oval-shaped with one flat end, these limit the angle at which the vent window can be opened and should be fitted into place carefully.

14. Install the bottom washers, spring and nut by hand, check the vent window for operation and then tighten the nut into place.

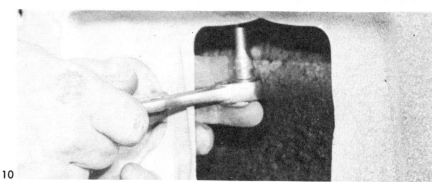

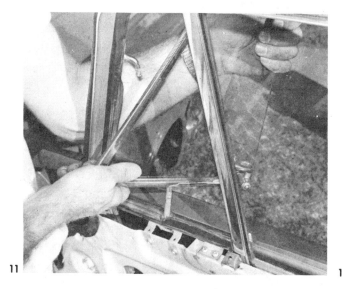

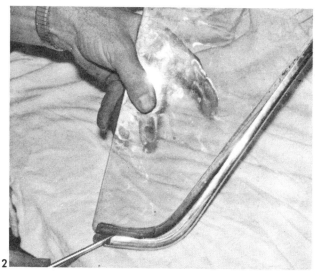

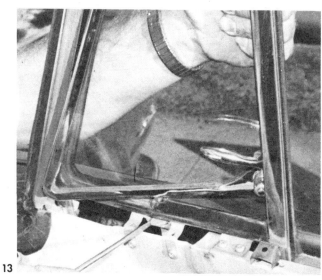

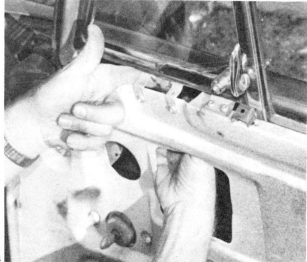

Now, for the Inside...

Bodywork and paint do wonders for a car's exterior, but there's still the interior to spruce up.

Bodywork and a new paint job can give an older car an entire new lease on life. It can even make you think twice about swapping for the latest chariot with its lower powered, emission system laden powerplant, provided that yours is in good mechanical shape to begin with. But once you've spruced up the metal work and dressed it in a new coat of enamel, the interior will take on a completely different appearance—in a word, the inside of your car is likely to suddenly seem shabby. So if you're going to redo the outside, you might as well give the interior its due at the same time. Here's a few handy hints on how to brighten things up inside.

As a first step, there are several things you can do that simply come under the heading of ordinary housekeeping—cleaning carpets, polishing metal areas, replacing floor mats, etc. But this can be done for you by any car wash and after all, the end result is just a temporary improvement. Detailing like this won't

renew the interior and the dirt will shortly return. What we have in mind is providing a whole new face-lift for that interior; a fresh personality to match the recently pounded out dings and dents on the outside.

If your car is over 3 years old, it's very likely that the upholstery can use a redo. Pulling out the old to install the new can be costly and, unless you've ripped and torn it badly, isn't really necessary. You can refinish upholstery at home with just a spray can, and in the process, remove those unsightly stains, ground-in dirt and grease, and even change its color. Of course, if you've got a black interior to begin with, you won't be able to change colors easily, but lighter colored vinyl has a habit of fading or discoloring with age, losing its sheen as well as showing any water spots or stains. The best thing here is a complete color change.

If your interior falls in this category, pick up a few cans of vinyl spray. This can be obtained from nearly any auto supply store like Pep Boys,

Western Auto, etc. While several manufacturers package vinyl spray in aerosol cans, we've had good results with that put out by Ideal Aerosol Inc. of North Hollywood, Calif. and Westley's Vinyl Color, a product made in Cleveland. Vinyl spray is available in 18 different colors and will give you the fastest, most durable refinish short of replacing the vinyl upholstery entirely. As the spray is actually vinyl, it permeates the upholstery instead of just lying on its top surface, thus the new finish won't crack or chip off and doesn't hide the original texture.

You'll need to use a good vinyl cleaner as a first step to remove as much as possible of the imbedded dirt, grease and wax (yes, some people do wax their upholstery thinking that it keeps the vinyl supple longer). We'd suggest that you go over all vinyl upholstery areas (including headliner and door trim panels) with the cleaner at least twice just to make sure you've got it all thoroughly clean, then mask. Mask? That's right, you'll need to mask off certain areas

1

2

3

4

5

6

when applying vinyl spray, so pick up a roll of masking tape where you buy the spray and save your newspapers for a few days. If you take pains in masking trim panels on the doors, it won't be necessary to remove them. If your dash is part metal, part vinyl, you'll also want to use care in masking that.

You'll find that best results come from holding the spray can 12 to 14 inches from the vinyl, moving it back and forth rapidly as you spray and misting the spray on with several light coats instead of trying to cover the old finish with a single coat. It's easy to apply the spray too thickly, and just like paint, you'll have a run that's difficult to remove—you can't sand vinyl. Misting the spray on with about three light coats should do it nicely and provide a good, uniform surface that'll surprise you with its fresh newness and covering quality.

Don't try to do the whole job in one day. There are at least two very good reasons for spreading the renovation task over several weekends. One is the very sore index finger

you'll have after spraying two or three cans; the other is one of drying. While vinyl spray will dry to touch in 30 minutes, any area where friction is to be applied (meaning sitting on it or leaning split-back seats forward to climb in the rear seat) should set for 24 hours. If you plan on remasking to do a second color or in the case of spraying a new metal finish on the dash where masking the vinyl is necessary, let it stand for about a week. After this length of time, you can also touch up areas like those underneath the seat back on a split-back bench seat. There's no problem of color match or blending to worry about.

If your upholstery was a fairly dark shade to start, you'll find that red or black are the best choices for a color change, as they work best in terms of covering. But all can be used with lighter upholstery and will cover well in three coats. And if you're spraying essentially the same shade as the original instead of attempting a color change, you may even be able to get away with only two. But for the die-hard who presently has black uphols-

tery and wants to change it to a lighter color, it can be done; he'll just need several extra cans before the job is done.

Which brings us to what you'll probably regard as a very important point—how many cans should you buy and what'll the stuff cost you? About 9 or 10 spray cans should do the average interior, bringing your total cost for this colorful renovation project to about $16. This will let you do all seats, door panel trim, dash and headliner, giving you a completely new looking interior. Now the metallic trim areas on dash and doors will look shabby by comparison.

Once the spray has set for a few weeks, you can mask off the vinyl areas where necessary and spray the metal. Paint for such comes in a wide variety of colors and types, including such exotics as Metalflake and Wrinkle paint. If you're not too adept with aerosol can spraying, we'd advise practicing on a piece of scrap metal before you start work on the actual car. This may cost you a bit of money in terms of an extra can of paint, but the money spent this way is well worth it; if you lose control of what you're doing when working on the car, you'll end up with paint running down the dash or door and straightening out such a mistake can lead to a real mess.

But we can guarantee that once you've redone the interior as suggested here, you'll not only be very pleased with the fresh new atmosphere inside your car, you'll also be an expert aerosol spray man, and you can prove it by that numb index finger that pulsates all by itself. ❧

1. Upholstery in this 1966 Valiant 100 is in good shape but faded and discolored; a color change is in order to renew it completely.

2. We'll start by masking off the door trim panel with newspapers and tape as shown. If you have regular masking paper...use it.

3. Aerosol can should be held 12-14 inches from work to mist vinyl spray on in the proper manner.

4. Voila! The finished trim panel! Highlights from camera flash make it appear uneven but the panel is really very even in color.

5. A couple of weeks after the vinyl spray has been applied, you can mask off the metal trim and renew that with a variety of paints. Again, spray light coats to avoid paint drips and runs.

6. Vinyl trim on dash is masked off and trim sprayed. Depending upon your particular car, masking can be a very time-consuming job.

7. Seat back has a patterned insert. If you want it all one color, simply spray. This one's masked to allow application of a contrasting color on the insert panel.

8. Spray the entire seat—front, sides and back—at one time.

9. The finished seat seen from the front. Patterned insert can be done about 15 days later, giving the vinyl spray ample time to dry thoroughly.

10. Don't forget this part of the seat if yours is a split-back bench. This comes under "touch-up at a later date" category.

11. The finished dash, door panel and seat with patterned insert gives our Valiant interior a fresh new look —and at a very minimal cost.

7

8

9

10

11

buying USED

THE BEST ROUTE TO LOW-BUDGET BODY BUILDING

By Brian Kennedy

1.

Repairing and straightening the sheetmetal on a car involves many talents, tools, and decisions.

Whether you are a full-time bodyman, or someone trying to do his or her repairs at home, the question will always arise: "Should I try to straighten that damaged body panel, or should I replace it?"

Unless the damage is minor, or the part is from some rare and exotic car with an equally rare and exotic price, it may be wiser to replace the damaged part with one that is fresh and undamaged, or at least one that can be more easily repaired.

Most body parts for newer cars can be purchased from your local new car dealer, but in some cases new parts may have to be ordered, taking additional time to complete the repair, or the cost of a new part may be higher than the job warrants.

What about used parts? Most auto dismantling yards (not junkyards, they don't sell junk!) offer a complete line of good, usable body parts (old and new) for most makes and models, at bargain prices.

To help our readers better understand how to locate and purchase used body parts, we stopped by Ferrill's Auto Wrecking, Inc. (18306 Hwy. 99, Lynnwood, WA, 206-778-3147) for a tour.

After pulling up in the lot at Ferrill's, our first reaction was, wow! No mud bog to park in, no plywood shack for an office, check the sign again Brian, yep this is the place. Once inside, our next question was, where's the potbellied stove? Or the poker game in the back? Gee! This place doesn't even have a greasy old dog sleepin' in the corner. Instead we found a first-class operation, with first-rate parts counter personnel.

Bruce Thomson, manager of Ferrill's, was happy to show us the entire setup, starting with the counter operation, to the dismantling area and parts storage.

2.

We were told that when a customer comes in looking for a certain body part, the process starts with the counter person establishing the year, make and model of the car being worked on. Once this has been done, the counterman will then go to the interchange book to find out how many different models the part in question will fit. This interchange book is the auto wreckers Bible, giving him information otherwise impossible to remember or recall. Each part is given an interchange number that is then cross-referenced to establish whether the part is common to other models or years.

With the number in hand, the counterman can now check a vast inventory listing all parts on hand. All of this takes just a minute or so. If he has the part on hand, he will then quote a price for that particular part. Prices for parts are generally half of new in most cases, but some wreckers may be willing to deal on a larger purchase.

A trip out into the yard put us in the middle of a vast array of front ends, all placed in large racks to keep them from possible damage. Doors, hoods and other parts are also stored in the same manner.

3.

PHOTOGRAPHY: BRIAN KENNEDY

Before any sheetmetal is stored, each piece is carefully checked for damage or rust. This is done by examining the outside of the part with a magnet for signs of body filler, then checking the inside for signs of previous damage. Prices for damaged parts are then adjusted accordingly.

If a major body part such as a quarter-panel or rear clip is needed, the customer can visually inspect the part, and then show the salesman where it will need to be cut.

While listening to the various personnel, we noticed that they have their own language pertaining to the various body parts that they deal with every day. This jargon seems to be

parts

4.

5.

6.

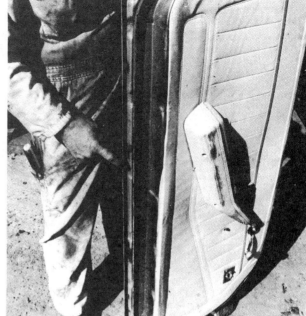

7.

1. We stopped by Ferrill's Auto Parts to learn what to look for when shopping for used automotive sheetmetal.

2. The counter personnel are experienced in all facets of the auto parts business. Bruce was happy to show us some of the inner workings of a modern, up-to-date wrecking yard.

3. The auto wrecker's Bible, the interchange book helps the counterman make certain that the body part that you have purchased will fit your car just like the original.

4. All front end assemblies are stored in racks to ensure against damage or yard rash.

5. This late-model Camaro door is a good example of the quality of the body parts available to the bodyman and hobbyist alike.

6. A magnet is used to detect the presence of any body filler in the door.

7. The bottom of the door is also checked for signs of rust or other damage.

universal among all wrecking yards.

Terms such as rear clip, cowl out and tower cut are all specific areas of a car's structure that the auto wrecker deals with during the course of a usual business day.

The auto dismantler also uses a special telephone hot line to help the customer locate that hard-to-find fender or other auto component. This hot line reaches other auto wreckers who are tied in to the system. When an auto wrecker calls on the hot line looking for a specific part, he may get a response from yards hundreds of miles away that will have the part the customer is looking for. Once the part is ordered, it is then shipped to the wrecking yard within a couple of days.

After our visit to Ferrill's we were convinced that the age-old junkyard we remembered from our high school days with its less-than-professional atmosphere is surely a thing of the past. Today's auto dismantler is sophisticated and ready to meet any need.

If that body repair job requires a replacement panel, we suggest that you give your local wrecking yard a try. They are in business to supply you with good usable auto parts, at a fraction of the cost of new parts.

8.

11.

9.

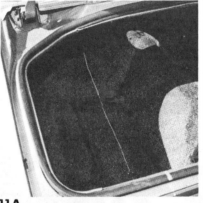

11A.

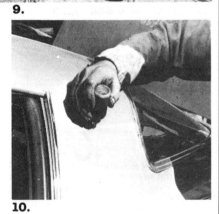

10.

8. As with the doors, the fenders are also closely inspected for any signs of damage.

9. No matter how well a repair has been executed, the inside surface of the damaged panel will still show signs of the repair.

10. The quarter-panel on this Camaro is being marked before removal. A special paint bottle is used to mark the area to be cut. This ensures that the customer will get enough surface area to make a proper repair.

11. A normal quarter-cut will be made so that the customer will get a portion of the trunk and rear body panel . . .

11A. and a portion of the trunk floor.

12. This is a body saw that is used to cut quarter sections from a car. All glass and other body parts attached to the quarter-panel will be removed before the actual cut is made.

12.

13. This is a cowl-cut nose assembly. The floor stringers are left intact, which will make for a much better repair if the floor has been buckled on the car that's being repaired.

14. Moisture has rusted this quarter-panel area, but the outside of the panel was unmarked and looked to be in good shape. There's no substitute for close inspection to ensure that you get a usable part.

15. After the body and paint work have been completed, how about a set of special wheels to finish it off? Most auto wreckers have a vast supply of custom wheels in all sizes and styles.

14.

15.

GLOSSARY OF WRECKING YARD TERMS

BODY SAW: A special saw either gas or electric, equipped with an abrasive blade, that is used to cut floor sections, quarter-panels, frames.

COWL CUT: A nose or front end that is cut behind the cowl or firewall. A cut such as this will include the area that the door hinge bolts to. Any dash parts such as instruments or dash pad are sold at extra cost.

FACE BAR: A bare bumper with no hardware.

FENDER COMPLETE: A fender with all attached parts, such as headlight inner fender panel and trim.

FENDER SKIN: A bare fender.

FILLER PANEL: A panel between the body and the bumper.

GAS AXE: A wrecker's term for a cutting torch.

HEADER PANEL: The panel that ties both front fenders together, just ahead of the hood on some cars.

JUNK YARD DOG: The animal that you will encounter if you climb over an auto dismantler's fence after closing, generally speaking the type that will eat out of your hand . . . and your leg.

NOSE: The front body section ahead of the doors. This includes fenders, hood with hinges, grille, bumper with brackets, radiator and radiator support.

T.P. OR TELEPHONE POLE NOSE: Same as a nose, but without the fenders.

TOWER CUT NOSE: Same as a nose, but also includes a portion of the inner structure known as the shock tower or strut tower. This type of cut will ensure that the suspension will be mounted squarely when the repair has been finished.

QUARTER CUT: Think of a quarter as a rear fender that is welded on. The quarter cut will also include a portion of the floor and trunk area.

REAR CLIP: The entire rear portion of the car, with part of the roof attached. The roof can be included if desired.

TRICK
BODY WORK

This section on bodywork deals primarily with attaching the hood scoop and front spoiler. The Camaro used for the project was selected for its excellent sheetmetal, among other reasons, and didn't require serious rework or rot repairs.

Through the years, hundreds of articles have been written about attaching fiberglass components to your car's sheetmetal. Although most of them stress cleanliness, they often miss an important point about ensuring integrity of the new

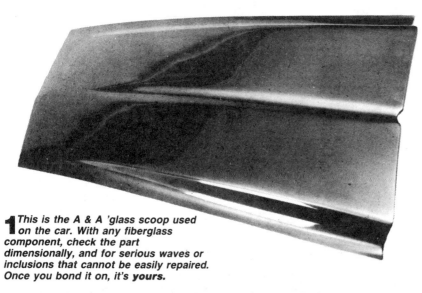

1 This is the A & A 'glass scoop used on the car. With any fiberglass component, check the part dimensionally, and for serious waves or inclusions that cannot be easily repaired. Once you bond it on, it's **yours.**

2 Begin by locating the scoop exactly where you want it, and marking the location with chalk. Leave lines along the sides for positioning the scoop later.

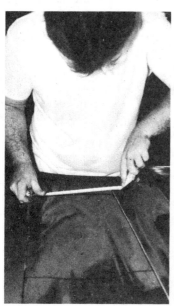

3 Since the scoop was supplied with extra material at the front so you can position it anywhere on the hood, Rick Leonard here marks the amount to be trimmed, and then whacks it off with a disc. Wear a particle mask and eye protection whenever grinding or cutting 'glass.

bond; you must grind both the fiberglass and the metal in the bonding area to get a good bond. If paint remains on the metal, or gelcoat on the fiberglass, it increases the potential for cracks or even the complete separation of the two materials.

The following procedure for attaching the hood scoop can be applied to fender flares, rear deck spoilers, or any fiberglass component. Position the 'glass piece where it will be bonded, mark the location, grind the mating surfaces, drill the holes for the drill-headed screws used to clamp the components (which will be removed prior to the finish bodywork), apply the bonding agent, clamp the whole mess together, let it dry, remove the screws, fill the holes, and finish with a little plastic filler. If you work carefully, observing the temperature recommendations on the fiberglass and plastic filler cans, the finished joint should be crack-free, even on a hood, where conditions are the worst. The scoop used for the Aero Camaro is a product of A & A Fiberglass, and resembles the cowl induction hoods GM used on the Chevelles and Corvette. Duraglass, bonding and finish resins, and plastic filler can all be found at suppliers for bodyshops. If you can't locate a good one, talk to your local bodyshop owner and find out where he buys his materials.

5 *Because of the scoop's wide, unsupported span across the hood, a wood brace was made for the center.*

6 *Notice the measurements chalked on the hood; when you grind off the paint, you lose the lines you made earlier, and with the measurements, you can reposition the scoop exactly where it was.*

4 *To ensure an excellent bond between the fiberglass and the hood's steel, grind every contact point between the two.*

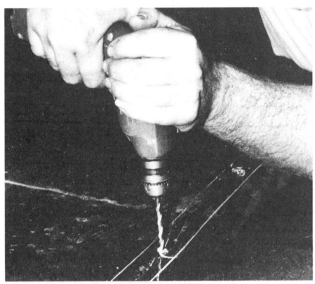

7 *The brace will be secured in place by bonding to the scoop and screws from below through the hood. Rick here drills holes for the screws.*

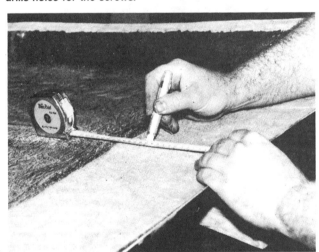

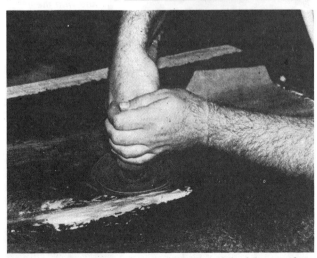

8 *Mark the location of the brace, and grind the 'glass surface for good bonding.*

9 *Rick used Duraglass, which is a fiberglass-reinforced plastic filler, to bond the brace as well as the scoop/hood interface.*

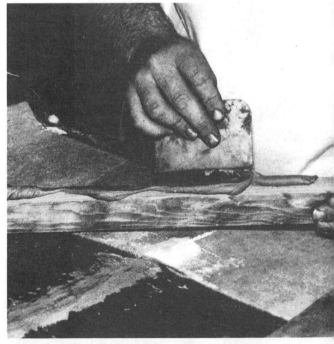

10 *Duraglass is similar to normal filler, but tends to set up quicker because of the increased volume of solids (and subsequently reduced resin volume).*

11 *Because the underside of the scoop may be visible at certain angles from within the car, the bonded brace and lower surface are sprayed with black lacquer.*

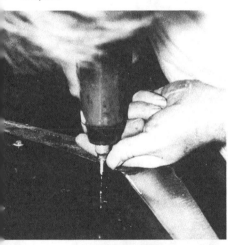

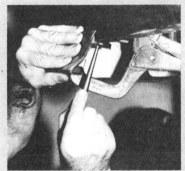

MOUNTING A FRONT SPOILER

GM still sells the OEM spoiler assemblies for late-Seventies Z/28s. The Mr. Gasket Aero Camaro is equipped with both front (which was added) and rear (which came on the car) spoilers. With the spoiler kit come relatively basic instructions, but we wanted to show you the sequence followed on this car.

The side flares have a molded-in stud that will go through to the inner face of the fender. Position the entire spoiler assembly carefully using clamps to secure the lower panel and sides in place. You may find the side pieces require a little tune up to fit the body perfectly. If so, take material off where you need to using a DA sander. Ready? Mark the holes you need and drill through the fenders.

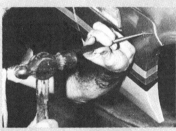

12 *Using drill point screws, the scoop is positioned once again prior to bonding. Because the scoop will "squirm around" as the screws are tightened, work from the front and alternate from side to side as you progress rearward.*

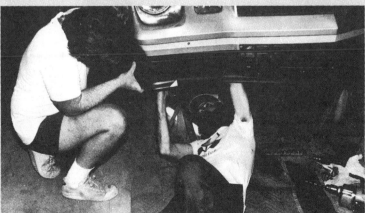

The lower panel bolts to existing locations in the front end and supporting braces. When everything fits, bolt it up.

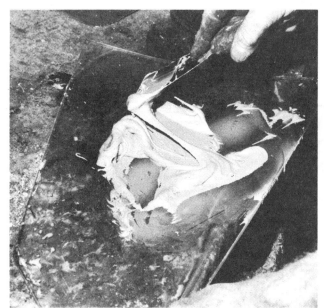

13 *As you can see from this photo, the bonding agent is considerably thicker than common body filler. In addition, the catalyst is clear, so measurement is important.*

14 *Working as quickly as possible, glob the bonding agent along the entire mating surface of the scoop, and then (also as quickly as possible, because the stuff is thinking about going off) place the scoop in position.*

15 *Are you hurrying? Reinstall the screws to compress the bonded joint. It really helps to do all this indoors, to keep the temperature under control. Heat accelerates the process.*

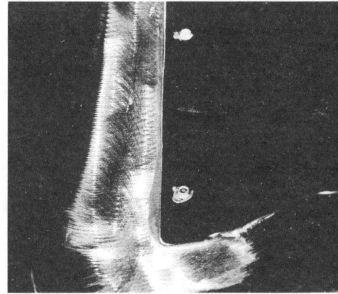

16 *If you applied the correct amount of bonding agent, it should have squeezed from between the joined surfaces around the entire perimeter of the scoop.*

17 *Take a break as the material sets up like a rock, which will happen **soon**. The screws stay in place until the next step.*

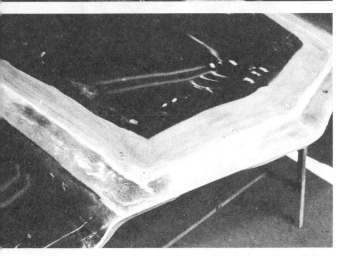

18 *After removing the screws, grind the top surface of the bonded scoop to blend it in to the hood contour. Working back about three to four inches should be sufficient; be careful not to make the 'glass too thin in an attempt at overblending. Fiberglass mat and body filler will make the finished shape.*

19 *Contour should look like this at this point.*

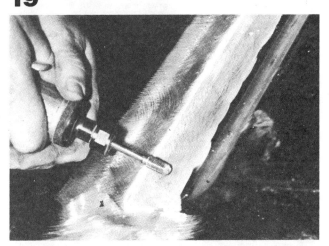

20 *Grind out the holes where the screws were to form a pocket for plastic filler. Giving the filler extra area to adhere to prevents it from dropping down through the holes.*

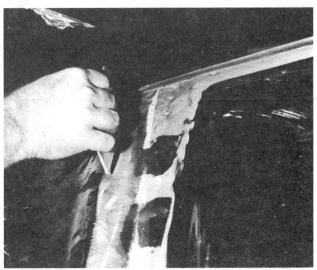

21 *Fill the holes, using a minimum of filler. This step also seals the holes off, preventing anything from getting into the joint from below.*

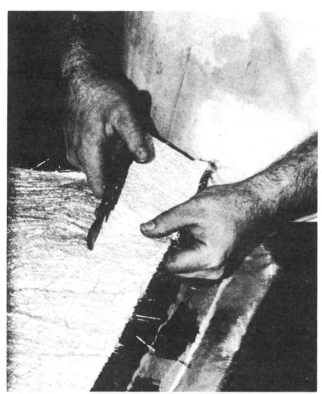

22 *Fiberglass mat is cut in two to three-inch widths and sections about 10 to 12-inches long, making them a convenient size for soaking in the resin.*

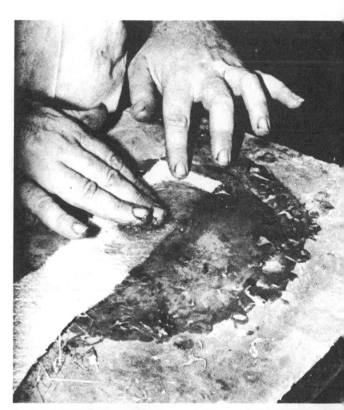

23 *The fiberglass resin is catalyzed, turning from clear to an aqua color as it reacts. Three common resins are available; **bonding** resin is best for this job, but **finish** resin will work.*

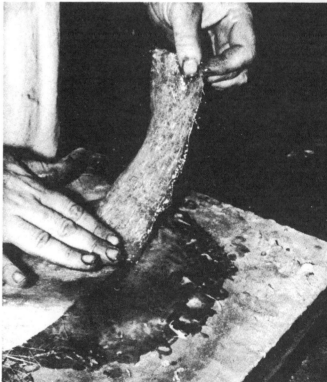

24 *After cutting all the strips, lay them in the resin, making sure the cloth is completely saturated. Make only enough resin to deal with two to three strips at a time. The resin is soluble in lacquer thinner, making it easy to remove from your fingers; otherwise, your Spiderman impersonation would improve dramatically.*

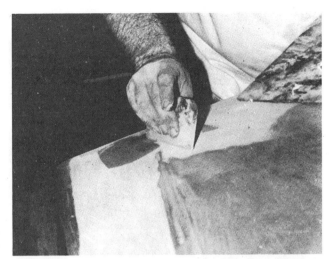

26 *After the 'glass cures (overnight), grind off any rough areas and establish a more finished contour. Fill any small imperfections with plastic filler.*

25 *Place the soaked mats in position and work out all visible air bubbles with a roller (available at large hardware and auto repair supply houses). Keep the roller in a coffee can with a couple inches of lacquer thinner to keep it from accumulating resin.*

27 *Using plastic filler, tune up the remaining surface on the scoop. Filler was also used to finish the contouring around the scoop/hood bonded area.*

28 When you get the contours finished, blast on a coat of your favorite primer and let it dry.

29 In Carter's paint shop, Mitch blocks out the assembled hood in final preparation for paint. Check out the color elsewhere in this book for the results.